The Culture
Solution

Praise for *The Culture Solution*

The Culture Solution has it all: a deep command of the key intercultural concepts, scores of spot-on, real world examples, pages of immensely practical and instantly applicable advice—all in language immediately accessible to the non-specialist reader. This is a book to read and savour, to be sure, but most of all it is a book to be ***used***.

> —*Craig Storti, intercultural trainer and consultant, author of The Art of Doing Business across Cultures: 10 Countries, 50 Mistakes, and 5 Steps to Cultural Competence*

Dr. Mendez's new approach provides useful and practical tools based on real-word situations. I highly recommend this book to anyone considering an assignment overseas.

> —*Terry B. Kahler, Vice President, Dell, Inc.*

The Culture Solution is useful for the novice and expert alike, providing a comprehensive, yet easy-to-use system for diagnosing cultural patterns and using this knowledge to be more effective at creating successful international business partnerships and relationships. I will use it as a key resource in my own work with students, managers and executives.

> —*Andy Molinsky, PhD, author of Global Dexterity: How to Adapt Your Behavior Without Losing Yourself in the Process*

Dr. Mendez postulates that it's important to learn and use the skills of cultural and team dynamic analysis to size up situations and locations effectively. From my own business experience, this is the way it really happens. Do enough intentional business and you will find yourself someplace you know little about, trying to achieve something under circumstances where you could really use a "map." Dr. Mendez's new book, *The Culture Solution*, provides just such a map. In addition to the utility of the approach, this is a fun read, enlightening and even self-illuminating.

> —*Raymond J. Brimble, CEO Lynxs Group*

As a practitioner, I appreciate the fact that *The Culture Solution* is based on analysis of people's actual behavior of and not on aggregated country profiles. The result is specific and tailored coaching—much more useful to clients than generalizations associated with national norms. The book provides links to practical exercises and tools as well!

—*Betsy Neidel, Managing Director, Blue Heron Holdings, LLC*

I recommend *The Culture Solution* to anyone who leads international teams. Having spent a good part of my career creating and managing international organizations for software development, I know that the topics discussed in this book are a must-read for anybody who needs to accomplish an international mission. This book takes you quickly from understanding to strategy.

—*Karl Wimmer, PhD, Director, Design Enablement, GlobalFoundries*

The Culture Solution is a crucial guide for those looking to develop an understanding of modern challenges in the global workplace. With her international business acumen and meticulous analysis of eight cultural dimensions, Deirdre Mendez opens the door to success for those navigating the waters of cross-cultural ventures. As a seasoned international consultant who has seen countless collaborations fall apart due to ignorance of cultural protocol, I thoroughly recommend Dr. Mendez's book as a resource for anyone who wishes to execute tactful, culturally-appropriate communication that fosters strong business connections.

—*Sharon Schweitzer, JD, author of Access to Asia: Your Multicultural Guide to Building Trust, Inspiring Respect, and Creating Long-Lasting Business Relationships*

The Culture Solution

How to Achieve Cultural Synergy and Get Results in the Global Workplace

Deirdre B. Mendez, PhD

NICHOLAS BREALEY
PUBLISHING

BOSTON • LONDON

First published in the USA in 2017 by Nicholas Brealey Publishing
Second format published in 2020

An Hachette company

25 24 23 22 21 20 1 2 3 4 5 6 7 8

Library of Congress Cataloging-in-Publication Data

Names: Mendez, Deirdre Brown, 1959– author.
Title: The culture solution : how to achieve cultural synergy and get results in the
    global workplace / Deirdre B. Mendez, PhD.
Description: Boston, MA : Intercultural Press, Inc., 2017.
Identifiers: LCCN 2016034440 (print) | LCCN 2016045160 (ebook) | ISBN
    9781857886580 (pbk.) | ISBN 9781941176184 (ebook)
Subjects: LCSH: Management--Cross-cultural studies. | International business
    enterprises. | Corporate culture--Cross-cultural studies. | Intercultural
    communication. | Cultural competence. | Diversity in the workplace.
Classification: LCC HD62.4 .M463 2017 (print) | LCC HD62.4 (ebook) | DDC
    658.008—dc23
LC record available at https://lccn.loc.gov/2016034440

ISBN 978-1-52935-913-8
U.S. eBook ISBN 978-1-94117-618-4
U.K. eBook ISBN 978-1-47364-418-2

Printed in the United States of America

Nicholas Brealey Publishing policy is to use papers that are natural, renewable
and recyclable products and made from wood grown in sustainable forests. The
logging and manufacturing processes are expected to conform to the environmental
regulations of the country of origin.

Nicholas Brealey Publishing
Carmelite House
50 Victoria Embankment
London EC4Y 0DZ
Tel: 020 7122 6000

Nicholas Brealey Publishing
Hachette Book Group
Market Place Center, 53 State Street
Boston, MA 02109, USA
Tel: (617) 523 3801

www.nbuspublishing.com

To my parents

Contents

Introduction

Welcome to the International Marketplace

As his employer's top performer for the U.S. market two years in a row, Peter Chenault was confident that his skills and drive would make him successful anywhere. But six months after the company promoted him to its new international management team, he's less certain. The sales, negotiation, and management techniques he's perfected over the past decade seem not to work overseas.

Peter was delighted when his manager announced that his first assignment would be in São Paulo, Brazil. The companies he visited there greeted him warmly, but after a series of facility tours and excellent meals, he couldn't seem to move his hosts toward serious business discussions. Peter came home feeling guilty about spending so much time and money with so little to show for it. His trip to Berlin shortly afterward was no better. Peter arrived with presentations on the innovative features of his company's new product, which the German customers all but ignored. They seemed more interested in service agreements than in the product itself, and two of his contacts requested annual reports from his employer, expressing skepticism that they'd still be in business three years down the road.

And now it looks like his trip to Seoul has accomplished nothing, despite a promising beginning. When he presented a new marketing strategy for a struggling subsidiary product group, the members of the Korean marketing team reacted favorably, and he went home feeling optimistic. But although they agreed to send him a revised marketing plan, there has been no follow-through, and his attempts to move things forward since his return have met with polite evasiveness. As the leader of the team, he's insulted by this apparent insubordination, but he also has a feeling that there was something he missed.

His problem in each of the three countries is different, and Peter can't discern a pattern that makes any sense. Although all his contacts seem to understand him, he feels that he hasn't really gotten his message across. He suspects that his problems have something to do with cultural differences, but he can't figure out what's going on.

Thinking back, Peter reflects that his preparatory efforts didn't help much. The books he read on doing business in each target market were generally helpful but had little information on negotiation. He gave up on memorizing the etiquette tips, and various online articles on the "Dos and Don'ts in Country X" only addressed a limited set of situations. Meanwhile, the book he picked up on general cultural awareness was long, theoretical, and mostly irrelevant. Although he gained some understanding of the cultural tendencies of his target countries, his research failed to result in a coherent strategy for each environment. He feels he misread the signals delivered by his international contacts, which prevented him from adapting his approach to their expectations. And he doesn't understand how his experience in each market relates to what happened in the others.

Sorting It Out

Peter is not alone. Many people today are expected to manage intercultural teams, serve culturally diverse customers and communities, and support partnerships with international companies and governments. Diplomatic negotiations, traditionally conducted by seasoned and carefully mentored experts, are increasingly practiced by people who lack this careful training. Those working for organizations with international connections are likely to have at least one intercultural assignment in the course of their careers. If you are one of them, this book is designed for you. It will help you discern the cultural orientation of international contacts, no matter where they—or you—are from, and understand behavior and expectations in any environment you encounter. It will guide you in creating strategies for managing cultural differences and learning from the approaches of new counterparts. *The Culture Solution* is a practical system that applies straightforward principles to real-life situations.

You don't need to be involved in an intercultural project to begin using the system; you can practice with any person, group, or location—be it that strange new guy in accounting, the off-the-wall community group you meet with each week, or your husband's odd hometown. It applies anywhere you find behavior that is different from what you're used to. And you can create a preliminary profile for regions you haven't had a chance to visit by using the ARC method to analyze descriptions from other sources.

Although cultural differences are often identified as a source of conflict and dysfunction, integrating diversity has benefits that go far beyond solving problems and resolving conflict. Research shows that intercultural groups that successfully integrate their differences actually perform better than monocultural counterparts.[1] Achieving intercultural "synergy"[2] will help you leverage the strengths of diverse approaches and systems.

How to Use This Book

This book is designed to help you adapt to new cultural environments and deal with people from unfamiliar cultural backgrounds. You will develop the skills needed to anticipate challenges and promote your agenda in culturally appropriate ways.

The ARC system will help you create a Personal Profile for eight cultural dimensions that identifies your own cultural orientation. It will also show you how to make one for your "counterpart"—the person, group,

---

[1] N. Adler, *International Dimensions of Organizational Behavior* (Thomson Learning, Inc., 2008), 148.

[2] Nancy Adler defines cultural synergy as a process that enables organizations to "transcend the individual cultures of their members." (N. Adler, "Cultural Synergy: The Management of Cross-Cultural Organizations," in W. Burke and L. Goodstein, eds., *Trends and Issues in OD: Current Theory and Practice* (University Associates, 1980), 172).

or place you choose to analyze. By comparing the two profiles, you will identify cultural tendencies likely to become sources of confusion and frustration. Based on these specific differences, you can develop strategies for managing problems, explaining yourself effectively, and communicating persuasively. Finally, you'll learn ways to leverage the talents of culturally diverse people and capitalize on the benefits. The more you practice the approach, the faster you'll recognize cultural differences and the more skillfully you'll handle them.

If you don't have much time, don't worry. Once you've identified the differences between yourself and the person or place you're analyzing, you can focus on just those cultural dimensions in each chapter.

This book will take you through the following steps to develop your own intercultural skills and strategies:

- Learn how cultural variation affects business (Chapter 1).
- Create your Personal Profile (Chapter 2).
- Create a Counterpart Profile for the individual, organization, or location you want to study and compare it to your Personal Profile (Chapter 3).
- Identify the critical dimensions for your particular intercultural relationship (Chapters 4–6).
- Review differences between your Personal and Counterpart Profiles and identify potential areas of misunderstanding and conflict (Chapters 7 and 8).
- Predict and solve culture-based problems for your relationship (Chapter 9).
- Confirm your familiarity with cultural tendencies and practice managing intercultural problems (Chapter 10).
- Learn strategies for persuading people with each of the tendencies (Chapter 11).
- Apply cultural knowledge in specific business contexts, including hiring and management, sales, negotiation, team management, and leadership (Chapters 12–16).

- Develop strategies for managing intercultural conflict and achieving cultural synergies (Chapter 16).
- Increase your cultural intelligence (Chapter 17).
- Learn ways to use cultural analysis in intercultural training and consulting (Chapter 18).

The order of the chapters assumes that you're a busy person who needs to get to the bottom line as quickly as possible. If you have more time to read and digest the framework, consider studying the cultural dimensions in Chapters 4–6 before creating your Counterpart Profile in Chapter 3.

Cultural analysis can be helpful for any type of intercultural interaction—be it international business, travel, engineering projects, education, health care, aid programs, conflict resolution, or mediation, to name a few. I use it to help business clients understand their international partners and customers and improve intercultural communication and teamwork. In executive courses, I use it to teach skills in leadership, project management, decision making, and conflict resolution. In management courses, students use it to analyze group strengths and weaknesses, avoid and resolve conflict, and achieve intercultural synergies. International MBA students are using the system to adapt to US employer norms for communication and self-presentation. I hope it will help you manage intercultural difference to meet your goals, whatever they may be.

1

Coming to Grips with Culture

E ach of the cultural dimensions in this book identifies a particular facet of culture and the way it affects behavior. For our purposes, culture is *a system of shared values and practices learned through social interaction that shapes people's beliefs, attitudes, expectations, and actions.*[1] All of us participate in cultural groups that share values and practices. Cultural values shape our beliefs, attitudes, expectations, and actions as well as the systems and processes we create.

There are several important things to recognize about cultural variation:

We all operate according to "cultural scripts." We unconsciously replicate the social patterns we learn from exposure to people around us. These cultural scripts, or "recipes for behavior," help us interact smoothly and achieve our social goals. Here's an example from my daily life—getting a cup of coffee in Austin, Texas. When I get to the coffee shop, I park my car within the lines of an available space (probably not as carefully as I would if I were German, but more carefully than I would if I were Egyptian). Once I'm inside the store, I stand behind the last person in line even if

---

[1] The term "culture" is problematical on many levels, and the way it is used is evolving. Kevin Avruch's book *Context and Pretext in Conflict Resolution:Culture, Identity, Power and Practice* (Paradigm Publishers, 2012) offers a detailed discussion of the way it has been used in professional contexts.

I'm in a hurry (rather than in a group, as I would in Mozambique), and I don't cut in line (as I might in France). I exchange brief pleasantries with the server behind the counter (not taking as long as I would if I were Brazilian, but longer than I would if I were from Hong Kong). These actions are consistent with the expectations of people I encounter. They're easy to understand and respond to, and appropriate to the situation. My cultural scripts work well for me in my home environment.

Following cultural scripts helps make interaction smooth—*as long as our scripts are shared by the other people we deal with*. Imagine what would happen if I pulled into the coffee shop parking lot and straddled two spaces, walked in and cut in line, and then spent five minutes visiting with the server while the people behind me waited. These other customers would be annoyed, to say the least. Yet any of these behaviors would be acceptable, and even expected, in other places. All of us follow cultural scripts all the time, and differences in our scripts can lead to misunderstanding and conflict. While our behavior is appropriate in the environment each of us comes from, it may be inappropriate elsewhere.

We don't realize we're operating according to cultural scripts. Even when we know about them, we're apt to forget that our behavior is shaped by cultural scripts. We see ourselves as individuals with unique personalities and agendas who make our own decisions. We see our own behavior as innately human and "normal." In intercultural interactions, we perceive other people in terms of our own scripts, and they do the same to us.

We tend to misinterpret culturally based behavior as resulting from *personality*. We assume that someone's odd behavior is due to individual quirks or preferences, a tendency known as "attribution error."[2] One of my clients described a problem he was having with some Japanese colleagues by saying, "I know all about that cultural stuff. I majored in Asian studies! But I'm telling you, these people are irrational!" Although he was famil-

---

[2] L. Ross, "The intuitive psychologist and his shortcomings: Distortions in the attribution process," in *Advances in Experimental Social Psychology*, vol. 10, ed. L. Berkowitz (New York: Academic Press, 1977), 184.

iar with the *concept* of cultural difference, when his colleagues' real-life behavior didn't fit his own cultural script, he failed to look for a culture-based rationale for their behavior. He instead jumped to the conclusion that they were incapable of thinking straight.

"Incompetent," "irrational," "uncommitted," and "malicious" are labels people use when they mistake cultural scripts for individual traits. Knowing your own cultural tendencies and learning to recognize those of others will help you distinguish culturally based behavior from true incompetence, irrationality, lack of commitment, or malice—which you'll want to recognize if you should actually encounter them.

Being "nice" is not enough. It's natural to think that intercultural conflict should be limited to confrontations such as arms negotiations or contract disputes, while collaborative projects should go more smoothly. When people or groups come together with a common purpose, shouldn't cultural differences be easy to resolve as long as everyone is polite and fair? Unfortunately, what seems polite and fair to one cultural group may not be for another. Consider the example of two Japanese software designers sleeping at their desks during a presentation by U.S. colleagues who have traveled to Tokyo to provide important information to their Japanese counterparts. When I discuss this scenario with Americans, the word "disrespectful" quickly emerges. Sleeping while someone presents is rude in the United States, and Americans agree that it would be more appropriate for these two to stay at home and skip the presentation altogether.

We then discuss the fact that these Japanese team members, exhausted from working around the clock to meet a deadline, got up early in the morning, dressed in business suits, and rode commuter trains a long distance, probably standing up, to attend the presentation. They assuredly would rather have slept late at home. So why did they come at all? To show respect. In Japan, it's disrespectful to skip important group activities, so people come to work and sleep at their desks instead. But Americans interpret this show of respect as just the opposite—an insult. When cultural scripts aren't shared, goodwill is just not enough. We need a way to identify and manage the differences.

How Cultural Variation Affects Professional Contexts

The fact that similar terminology is used throughout the world in business and diplomatic contexts masks the fact that the same term can be understood very differently in different places. Consider the following descriptions of a *business meeting*, a forum for discussion, problem solving, and decision making in organizations everywhere:

1. Meetings are planned to begin and end at specified times. They start as scheduled, with everyone arriving before or at the start time. Meetings proceed according to a detailed agenda whose topics are addressed in order. When the end time is reached, if there are topics that haven't been covered, another meeting is scheduled to handle them. When problems are discussed, any participant may suggest a solution, and the pros and cons of each suggestion are debated until a final solution is reached.

2. Meetings may start well after the time specified, with people joining in at any point, and may last as long as it takes to conclude business, sometimes causing later meetings to be postponed. A general agenda will be provided, but topics may be considered in any order, with digressions to a broad range of other issues. To avoid confrontation during the meeting, solutions to important problems will have been discussed and agreed to by the major players beforehand. Discussion during a meeting will be limited to reviewing the preferred solution and agreeing to proceed.

It's easy to imagine the confusion that could result when people from these two traditions attempt to solve a problem together in a "meeting." The same is true of nearly any business term or procedure. No matter where they originated, how they were originally designed, or how widely they are used, terms are understood and applied in different ways in different places.

Play the Right Game

1

When talking about intercultural interaction, I find it helpful to think of cultural systems as being like athletic games with similar goals but different equipment and rules. For example, baseball and basketball have certain similarities. In both, teams of people compete to earn points by delivering a ball to a specified target, and the team that scores the most points wins the game. But the balls and their targets are different, the rules of play and the number of players are different, and so on. You wouldn't take a baseball bat to a basketball game, and if you did, you wouldn't get far insisting that other players use it. People would be surprised and confused if you swung a bat at a basketball, and if you did, they would be unenthusiastic about having you on their team. As ridiculous as it sounds, this scenario illustrates what happens to people on international assignment when their cultural scripts are at odds with local expectations.

Intercultural interaction often involves people trying to reach their goals using incompatible tools and methods—like two teams showing up for a game, one expecting to play baseball and the other basketball. But there's an important difference between cultural systems and athletics. It would be easy to sort out a baseball/basketball misunderstanding because players of either game probably know something about the other, and differences in gear and uniforms would be easy to spot. But people are usually only vaguely aware of cultural systems and often don't recognize signs of difference. And even when they do, they may be unable to identify one another's cultural scripts. Unlike the rules of athletic games, cultural rules are rarely clear and explicit, even to the people who use them. This book makes these cultural rules explicit, outlines ways to detect cultural difference, and explains how to manage intercultural situations successfully. Using the ARC system is like learning the rules of new games and developing skill at playing them, while teaching your counterparts the pleasures of your preferred game.

Cultural Frameworks

The cultural analysis system used here has its roots in work from the 1950s by the anthropologist Edward T. Hall, who first developed the concept of time as a "cultural dimension" perceived differently in the U.S. and the Middle East.[3] Hall identified other dimensions as well, and later researchers have introduced new ones. Although derived from these, my framework has been modified to make it easier to use in practical analysis and problem solving.

The ARC system includes eight cultural dimensions. One of these is **Emotion**, how much feeling people show when they interact. The poles of this dimension are the cultural tendencies **Neutral** and **Expressive**.

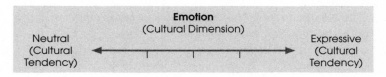

At one end of the continuum are Neutrals, who minimize emotion when they communicate. Their body language and facial expression are restrained, and they don't share their joys and sorrows openly. They talk about emotional matters in private settings, and do so quietly and undramatically. It's hard to tell how Neutrals feel during an interaction just by looking at them, and they offer little feedback during conversations and presentations. Sweden is an example of a country known for Neutral communication.

At the other end are Expressives. It's easy to tell what Expressives are feeling from their tone of voice and body language. They laugh out loud, frown, and use hand gestures to illustrate a point. They may raise their voices when they're angry. They celebrate enthusiastically and talk freely about their problems. Italians are well known for their Expressive tendencies.

---

[3] Hall, E. T. *The Silent Language*, (Doubleday, 1959).

There's nothing inherently good or bad about either of these cultural tendencies, and neither is better than the other. Each approach works in the environment it comes from, but when people from the two ends of the dimension come together, difficulties can arise. An Italian in Sweden might feel that Swedes are uncommunicative and unfriendly, and maybe that they're not very interesting. A Swede in Italy might find Italians loud and impolite, and possibly a bit out of control. Not everyone is as extreme as Swedes or Italians, of course. People in most countries fall closer to the middle of the dimension.

Although we're all familiar with the idea of cultural tendencies of particular countries, it's important to note that there's tremendous cultural variation *within* any single country due to differences in ethnicity, religion, socioeconomic status, and other factors. In fact, individuals can be said to have "personal cultures" based on how they've internalized their observations, experiences, and education. Learning the national patterns of Italy and Sweden wouldn't help you deal with an Expressive Swede or a Neutral Italian.

The ARC system will teach you to evaluate people, groups, and places based on their actual characteristics so you don't have to rely on country generalizations. To create a Personal Profile that identifies your own cultural tendencies, chart your answers to questions about your preferences and behaviors for each dimension. For a Counterpart Profile, record the tendencies that you observe in a person, group, or place. It would be awkward to ask people whether they're Expressive or Neutral, but you can answer this question for yourself by watching them interact, conduct meetings, and make presentations.

For the sake of conciseness, I use the term "counterpart" to refer to whatever entity you choose to analyze. You can use the system to understand the unspoken expectations of a new negotiating partner or the best way to motivate a new employee. You might want to assess the cultural orientation of a new work group you've been assigned to, a project team you'll be managing, or a customer you want to attract. Completing a profile of a city will help you work there effectively or negotiate successfully with a group there, and evaluating an acquired company will help you develop policies to integrate it with yours. Create a Counterpart Profile for any international person, group, entity, or location you would like to understand better.

The Neutral/Expressive distinction is the easiest one to understand and recognize in action. We can't identify most of the cultural tendencies just by watching to see whether people gesture and laugh out loud in conversation, so for each dimension, there's a list of things to look for in public places, homes, and, of course, professional settings and meetings. There are questions to ask a stranger, things to look for in restaurants, ways to interpret annual reports, and many things to observe during social functions, business meetings, negotiations, and institutional visits.

Some Clarifications on the Approach

If you're skeptical about the validity of reducing human variation to eight bipolar scales, you have a point. Any model that divides human behavior into categories is artificial and arbitrary to a degree, and no model captures all the complexities of cultural variation. But this one covers enough to provide useful insight without being too complex to manage.

There is disagreement in the field about the number of cultural dimensions and how they should be characterized. I've selected a group that accounts for most misunderstandings and conflicts in business dealings and diplomacy. It's based on the work of respected researchers in the field of anthropology and cross-cultural business, drawing most heavily on the Trompenaars/Hampden-Turner framework, adapted for hands-on application. An explanation of how it compares with other frameworks is provided in Chapter 19.

Although eight cultural dimensions may seem like a lot to learn, you probably won't work with all eight at once. Any two people or groups usually have at least some cultural tendencies in common, so you will probably focus on just a few at a time. Chapters 4–6 provide a detailed description of each and scenarios showing each pair of tendencies in action to make them easier to learn.

Given that no two people are alike, even within the same family, you might wonder where cultural tendencies end and individual personality begins. If there are Expressive Swedes and Neutral Italians, are they aberrations, and how do we evaluate their cultural tendencies? The answer is that each of us interprets cultural lessons in our own way, based on our unique personality and experience, so each person has a unique and personal cultural orientation. Cultural analysis will help you recognize and adapt to the way each person you meet acts out the teachings of their cultural environment.

The ARC System
Part I: Analyze

2

Know Yourself: Create Your Personal Profile

The first step in mastering any intercultural situation is to understand your own cultural tendencies. This chapter will guide you in creating your Personal Profile. Just answer the question(s) for each of the eight dimensions below. The key at the end will tell you which tendency each answer indicates. Mark each chart at the point that most closely corresponds to your answer. Don't worry too much about accuracy—you're indicating tendencies for which there is no exact value. Also, your self-perceptions will be influenced by the cultural groups you know best, and you may modify them as you work with new groups.

To get the best profile, think first about whom you represent in your international dealings. If you base your business decisions and actions on your personal preferences (say, if you're a corporate executive and have wide latitude in decision making), answer the questions according to your personal inclination. If you act according to your agency or company's policies, answer the questions according to your organization's approach.

If you really don't have any preference for a dimension, put your mark in the middle of the chart. This would apply if you've experienced both extremes and are comfortable with both or are just really flexible.

In some cases, there are multiple questions for a dimension. If your answers point to different tendencies (e.g., one indicates that you're extremely Process-oriented and the other that you're more Network-oriented), indicate *all* your responses for that dimension rather than averaging them.

Self-Analysis Questions

1. Clarity (Indirect/Direct)

QUESTION 1

A colleague at work makes a suggestion in a meeting. The idea is poorly thought out and would be impractical to implement. How do you respond?

1. If my colleague created an uncomfortable situation like this, I'd have to be tactful and say that it was a good idea. Everyone would note my facial expression and tone of voice and realize I didn't really think so, but at least I'd be polite.

2. To avoid embarrassing my colleague, I would begin by praising the suggestion, but hint at possible problems, and my facial expression and tone of voice would make it clear that it wasn't really a good idea.

3. Since proposing and discarding ideas is just part of the decision-making process, I'd thank my colleague for the suggestion while pointing out its flaws so we could move forward with the meeting.

4. I'd point out the errors and suggest that my colleague prepare more thoroughly in the future so we don't waste time in meetings. This is the best way to improve my colleague's effectiveness.

1—Strong Indirect orientation that emphasizes avoiding conflict and saving face

2—Indirect orientation that largely avoids conflict and preserves face

3—Direct orientation that views moderate frankness as constructive

4—Strong Direct orientation that views extreme frankness as constructive

QUESTION 2

You're preparing for a presentation to a group of people you work with. Which of the descriptions below is most characteristic of your approach?

1. I'll prepare a general presentation, laying out the basic items to be discussed. I'll focus largely on background information to give the full

context of the issues at hand. When questions come up, I'll take time to discuss them and see where they lead us. If I have a recommendation, I'll discuss it with some key participants beforehand. I'll ask one of them to mention it in the meeting, and we'll see where it goes.

2. I'll prepare a general presentation that provides plenty of background and contextual information. When questions come up, I'll take time to answer them to the audience's satisfaction. If I have a suggestion to propose, I'll mention it casually in the meeting. If there's any disapproval of the idea, I'll network with key players after the meeting to build support.

3. I'll prepare a clear presentation that includes the bottom line. When questions come up, I'll answer them thoroughly. If I have a recommendation, I'll present it for feedback in the meeting. If there are any objections to the idea, I'll find out what they are and come back to the issue later.

4. I'll prepare a clear and concise presentation that focuses on the bottom line. I'll answer any questions succinctly. If I have a suggestion to propose, I'll present it for feedback in the meeting. If there's any disapproval of the idea, we'll discuss the pros and cons during the meeting to reach agreement.

1—Strong Indirect orientation emphasizing context over content and managing possible controversy behind the scenes

2—Indirect orientation emphasizing context, introducing potential controversy cautiously and managing it behind the scenes

3—Direct orientation introducing source of potential controversy but avoiding open conflict

4—Strong Direct orientation viewing a meeting as an appropriate venue for decision making and conflict as a means of reaching decision

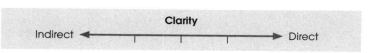

2. Emotion (Neutral/Expressive)

Consider the examples below of behavior in the workplace. Which is closest to your own attitude?

1. I'm a quiet person, and when I'm at work, I keep my feelings to myself. If I'm worried about something personal or have something to celebrate, I don't mention it because that would be unprofessional. By the same token, when I have a strong reaction to something a colleague says or does, I don't mention my emotional reaction—I wouldn't want to be seen as weak or childish.

2. I'm a fairly quiet person, and when I'm at work, I keep my feelings to myself in public. If I'm worried about something personal or have something to celebrate, I seek out a friend to share it with in private. When I have a strong reaction to something a colleague says or does, I don't mention my emotional reaction right then—I let them know later so we can work things out.

3. I'm a fairly demonstrative person, and when I'm at work, I tend to let people know what's going on with me. If I'm worried about something personal or have something to celebrate, I seek out friends to share it with. When I have a strong reaction to something a colleague says or does, I let them know how I feel because it's no good allowing bad feelings to build.

4. I'm a very demonstrative person, and when I'm at work, I always let people know how my life is going. If I'm worried about something personal or have something to celebrate, I talk about it with the people around me. Discussing things is a natural way of building rapport at work. When I have a strong reaction to something a colleague says or does, I let the person know how I feel so they won't make the mistake again.

1—Strong Neutral orientation with preference for maintaining order in the workplace

2—Primarily Neutral orientation acknowledging Expressive elements as an outlet

3—Expressive orientation that incorporates emotion sharing to manage relationships

4—Strong Expressive orientation that views emotion sharing as a tool for relieving stress and managing relationships

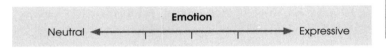

Emotion

Neutral ◄——————————————► Expressive

2

3. Status (Achievement/Endowment)

QUESTION 1

Consider the statements below about status. Which matches your own perspective most closely?

1. People should be judged based on their talent and initiative. A person who's born at the top may get by in spite of being lazy and unmotivated, but a person starting out with less will be skilled at persevering and overcoming obstacles. These traits, combined with natural ability, can make someone a leader with influence at an early age. Insular organizations tend to be out of touch with the times; it's vital to have new blood.

2. People with natural ability and initiative can come from any background, and their excellence should be recognized and developed through mentoring. Talented people will develop influence and leadership skills rapidly. Insular organizations may need help changing with the times, so it's helpful to have new blood.

3. People from a good background are likely to represent an organization well and contribute to society, although these attributes can be found in others as well. Talented people should be encouraged while developing their sphere of influence and a sense of graciousness. Hiring people with a shared background and values is helpful in creating a cohesive organizational culture.

4. People from a good background are the best equipped to represent an organization and contribute to society. People who start at the bottom

and fight their way to the top will focus on their own success, have less personal influence, and give less to society. Hiring people who share a common background and values is the way to create a cohesive organizational culture.

1—Strong Achievement orientation that prioritizes merit in promotion, values diversity, and equates insularity with obsolescence

2—Achievement orientation that rewards merit and values diversity

3—Endowment orientation that values inherent characteristics while recognizing merit as a basis for development

4—Strong Endowment orientation that prioritizes background as a source of character and influence

QUESTION 2

Which of the comments below best expresses your own perspective?

1. Exceptional people should be promoted quickly based on their skills and ability, and management should consist of top performers, regardless of their age. People can quickly become prominent based on their achievements as they rise to new challenges, and people who stop performing can quickly become "has-beens."

2. Exceptional people should be promoted faster than less talented peers. It's all right for outstanding young people to manage older employees as long as they're respectful to their elders. Learning by doing is an effective way to develop young people if they have adequate supervision. People can quickly become prominent based on their achievements, and a lack of continued performance can damage a reputation.

3. Promotions should factor in experience and seniority while acknowledging performance. Having managers who are younger than their subordinates would be awkward, and learning from mentors helps junior people avoid mistakes. Good reputations are based on what people have accomplished in their lifetimes, although someone who hasn't produced recently will have somewhat less prestige.

4. Excellence is developed through experience and sound guidance over time. Promotions should be based on experience and seniority. Having managers who are younger than their subordinates would be unnatural, and guidance by mentors is crucial in preventing junior members from making mistakes. Good reputations are based on what people have accomplished in their lifetimes, and once gained, a reputation is permanent.

1—Strong Achievement orientation rewarding merit and perception that reputation is based on recent success

2—Achievement orientation with respect for seniority and perception that reputation requires continued success

3—Endowment orientation emphasizing seniority with recognition of merit as a criterion and perception that reputation requires some continuity of success

4—Strong Endowment orientation basing promotion on seniority and perception that reputation does not require ongoing success

QUESTION 3

Which comment best expresses your own perspective?

1. I'm essentially an egalitarian, and I don't believe in social barriers. I think I should be able to approach just about anyone if I have something valuable to contribute. And I don't mind when people with less experience tell me their ideas. I remember when I was in their place, and since you never know who will be a future leader, it's a good idea to listen to everyone. I prefer an informal working atmosphere—it helps people exchange ideas more freely.

2. It's important for people to know their place and be respectful. When I'm talking to older or more senior people, I listen more and follow their lead. I don't say much about myself unless they ask, and I don't volunteer my own opinions. By the same token, I don't appreciate it when my juniors act too familiar. I've waited my turn to get where I

am, and I expect to be treated accordingly. I prefer some formality in the workplace, too—it keeps things professional.

1—Achievement orientation emphasizing equality and preferring a lack of formality

2—Endowment orientation emphasizing respect and preserving hierarchy

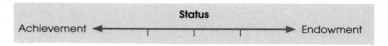

4. Involvement (Network/Process)

QUESTION 1

A boss and a subordinate run into each other at a sporting event and visit for a while. The boss knows relatively little about how the game is played, while the subordinate is an expert. Which scenario below seems most natural to you?

1. Upon learning that the subordinate is an expert on the game, the boss asks a question or two, and the employee answers them briefly. The boss does most of the talking, and the employee listens respectfully. The boss is the boss, after all, and it would be inappropriate for the subordinate to talk too much about her own expertise.

2. Upon learning that the employee is an expert on the game, the boss asks several questions about it, and the employee answers them in some detail. After that, the boss does most of the talking, and the employee contributes occasionally. The boss is the boss, after all, and it would be inappropriate for the subordinate to talk too much about her own expertise.

3. Upon learning that the employee is an expert on the game, the boss asks several questions about it, and the employee answers them enthusiastically. They engage in a pleasant exchange before the boss excuses

himself. Although the boss is the superior at work, in this context he recognizes the subordinate's expertise.

4. Upon learning that the employee is an expert on the game, the boss asks several questions about it, and the employee answers them enthusiastically. They engage in a lively exchange, with the employee doing most of the talking. Although the boss is the superior at work, in this context the subordinate's expertise makes her the most active participant in the conversation.

1—Strong network orientation viewing workplace hierarchy as a determining factor in how participants interact regardless of context

2—Network orientation viewing workplace hierarchy as being somewhat mitigated by context

3—Process orientation viewing context as a determining factor in how participants interact to a large degree in spite of workplace hierarchy

4—Strong process orientation viewing context as the principal factor in determining how participants interact in spite of workplace hierarchy

QUESTION 2

Your team is preparing for a first visit from a potential partner. Which of the statements below most closely matches your working style?

1. On a first visit, the most important thing is to get to know a potential partner. To be sure there's a good fit, we need to understand what kind of people we're dealing with and their philosophy of doing business. We'll prepare a number of social activities so we can get to know each other. If things feel right, we may talk business toward the end. We won't ask many explicit questions; we'll allow things to unfold gradually. A lasting partnership takes a long time to develop.

2. On a first visit, it's important to get to know a potential partner. We want to be sure they're reputable businesspeople and that their philosophy of doing business is a good fit with ours. We'll focus on social activities in

the beginning and move on to business discussions toward the end if things are going well. A solid partnership takes time to develop.

3. On a first visit, social preliminaries are mainly a courtesy. We don't need to get to know them that well personally—we'll have a contract to protect us. To save time, we'll initiate a business discussion as quickly as possible. Whether we extend the partnership past this initial deal depends on how well things go.

4. On a first visit, we'll be looking for a strong basis for business collaboration. We don't need to spend time on social preliminaries—we'll have a contract to protect us. We'll get right down to business. That way, if there isn't a good fit, we'll figure it out quickly and move on. Whether we extend the partnership past this initial deal depends on whether a compelling business case continues to exist.

1—Strong Network orientation with partnership viewed as the primary goal, requiring trust and a strong relationship

2—Network orientation toward relationship building with partnership viewed as an important goal while incorporating Process goal of time efficiency

3—Process orientation with partnership viewed primarily as a function of the business case while incorporating Network goal of relationship building

4—Strong Process orientation toward getting down to business, with partnership viewed as contractual and based solely on the business case

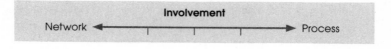

5. Collaboration (Independent/Group)

QUESTION 1

Consider the statements below about collaboration. Which best matches your perspective?

1. On our team, after dividing tasks up according to our expertise, we separate to do our work. Working apart helps us concentrate and make use of our special talents while avoiding "groupthink." We meet periodically to keep things integrated, and after we've all done our parts, we meet again to fit them together. We respect each other's work but aren't that close personally. We have our own friends and mostly just see other team members at work. Once our current project is over, we'll be assigned to new teams, taking our skills wherever they're needed for maximum effectiveness.

2. On our team, after dividing tasks up based on expertise, we work on them mostly separately, which is more efficient and avoids "groupthink," but we meet frequently to keep things integrated. We respect each other's work but aren't that close personally. We get together outside work on occasion, but we have other friends. Once our current project is over, we'll be assigned to new teams, but we'll let our managers know whom we work best with in case we work with them again.

3. On our team, we often work together because we like the camaraderie and it helps keep everything integrated. We take time for social activities, too, which helps us maintain a strong team dynamic. After a project ends, we may work together again, since our management understands the efficiency of grouping people with others they know.

4. On our team, we work on our assigned tasks together so no one feels isolated. It helps to have input from each other, and our work stays integrated that way. Our group members are very close, and we spend a lot of time together to keep the team dynamic strong. When this project is over, a new one will be assigned to our team. Keeping a top team together is the best way to deal with any project.

1—Strong Independent orientation to working separately, forming very loose internal relationships and assigning individuals to projects exclusively based on skills

2—Independent orientation to working separately, forming casual internal relationships and assigning individuals to projects primarily based on skills

3—Group orientation to working largely together, building strong internal relationships and valuing group preservation across projects

4—Strong Group orientation to close collaboration, building very strong internal relationships and prioritizing group preservation across projects

QUESTION 2

Which of the statements below best matches your perspective?

1. When our group collaborates with other teams, we try to integrate thoroughly with them to form one large group. It's natural to let our partners know what's going on with us internally, and talking about our problems is fine since our performance speaks for itself. It's more efficient that way, too, because each group is aware of problems that come up in the other, and there are no surprises. Good partnership means being as honest as possible, and we learn more from each other that way.

2. When our group collaborates with other teams, we integrate with them as much as is appropriate. It helps for our partners to know what's going on with us internally, as long as we don't make ourselves sound incompetent. It's more efficient when each group is aware of problems that come up in the other, and there are no surprises. Good partnership means being honest when appropriate, and we learn more from each other that way.

3. When our group collaborates with other teams, we try to be friendly with them, but we maintain a professional demeanor so they'll know they can rely on us. We try to solve internal problems ourselves unless they would affect our partner—we don't want to appear incompetent. Good partnership means having some professional distance and keeping our "dirty laundry" to ourselves.

4. When our group collaborates with other teams, we're careful to maintain a professional demeanor so they'll know we're reliable. We solve internal problems on our own and don't worry our partners unless something happens that we can't handle without their help. Good partnership means keeping a professional distance and preserving our team identity.

1—Strong Independent orientation that allows group boundaries to weaken in order to integrate groups and share and collaborate on problems

2—Independent orientation that allows some group integration, with some problem sharing and collaborating across groups and attention to group image

3—Group orientation that emphasizes maintaining group boundaries and keeping problems internal to maintain group image but allows for sharing internal problems as necessary

4—Strong Group orientation that prioritizes maintaining strong group boundaries and keeping problems internal to maintain group image

QUESTION 3

Which of the statements below best matches your perspective?

1. A good leader is someone who considers the priorities of relevant subordinates and decides which ones to emphasize. Although not everyone's preferences are accommodated, gaining the consensus of everyone at the table may be impossible. It's more efficient for one person to have responsibility for weighing alternatives and moving things forward.

2. A good leader is someone who considers the priorities of relevant subordinates and makes decisions that work for the majority. Although not everyone's preferences are accommodated, consensus building is slow and difficult to achieve, and it's more efficient for one person to decide which ones to prioritize.

3. A good leader is someone who seeks the recommendations of relevant subordinates and integrates them into a decision that works for all of them. Since their interests are factored into the decision, the stakeholders are committed to it, and the leader doesn't have inappropriate power. Working to meet the needs of everyone involved yields the best decisions.

4. A good leader is someone who can guide relevant subordinates through rounds of discussions to help them reach a joint decision that works for everyone at the table. Having participated in the decision, the

stakeholders are committed to it. No individual would be able to understand the interests of everyone involved, so consensus is the best way to make decisions.

1—Strong Independent orientation that gives full authority for decision making to an individual and prioritizes efficiency over consensus

2—Independent orientation that gives authority for decision-making to an individual, prioritizing efficiency while acknowledging the benefit of subordinates' engagement

3—Group orientation in which leader has an obligation to elicit and integrate subordinates' recommendations in decisions

4—Strong Group orientation that gives decision-making authority to the group and in which the leader is primarily a coordinator and facilitator of consensus building

QUESTION 4

A team has worked hard on a project with excellent results. The creativity and technical skills of one team member in particular moved the project forward. The company president is planning to give the team a financial award at the annual meeting for their excellent work and the success of their product. Should he mention and reward the team as a whole or should the top performer be singled out?

1. The top performer should receive special mention at the annual meeting and higher compensation than the rest of the team. She should be recognized through an article in the company newsletter. She deserves the recognition, and acknowledging and rewarding star performers motivates others to do their best.

2. The top performer should receive special mention at the annual meeting and in the company newsletter. Her supervisor should let her know that the company president is aware of her superior performance and is monitoring her progress. Knowing she is receiving special attention will keep her motivated, even without an immediate monetary reward.

3. The top performer should be acknowledged in private by her supervisor. She should not be compensated separately, since the outcome of the work was a team effort and other members deserve equal credit.

4. The top performer should not be acknowledged or financially compensated differently from other group members—the work was a team effort, and recognizing one person in particular would be insulting. Other team members might become resentful and less likely to perform well.

1—Strong Independent orientation to public recognition and compensation

2—Independent orientation acknowledging, but not compensating, individual contribution

3—Group orientation compensating the group effort over individual contribution, while privately acknowledging individual contribution

4—Strong Group orientation acknowledging and compensating only the group effort

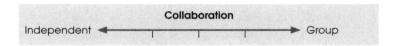

Collaboration

Independent ◄──────────────────► Group

6. Authority (Rule/Situation)

QUESTION 1

Consider the statements below regarding attitudes toward rules and authority. Which matches your own perspective most closely?

1. It's best for everyone to follow rules and obey laws—they're there for a reason. People should obey laws in traffic and at home and observe processes and procedures at work. Sometimes following rules is inconvenient or may even seem silly, but if everyone made individual decisions about how to behave, there would be anarchy.

2. It's generally best for everyone to follow rules and obey laws to keep things running smoothly. People should obey laws in traffic and at home for the most part and observe processes and procedures at work unless they really don't make sense. Following rules can be inconvenient or even a bit silly, but observing most rules is the best way to keep things stable.

3. It's normal for people to make their own decisions about following rules. In traffic and at home, most people obey laws and signs based on the situation, and it's natural to cut corners on processes and procedures at work if they don't make sense. There are reasons to ignore rules, and you must use good judgment to be effective and live comfortably.

4. People should live according to their own code rather than follow arbitrary rules. Laws can be unfair and inflexible and may not promote or protect our interests. In traffic, at home, and at work, people will make their own decisions about which rules to obey. Blindly following rules makes no sense—you have to make your own decisions to be effective and live comfortably.

1—Strong Rule orientation toward preserving structure and stability through compliance

2—Rule orientation with a relaxed attitude toward ignoring certain kinds of rules

3—Situation inclination with preference for context-based decision making

4—Strong Situation orientation with emphasis on context-based decision making and suspicion of rules

QUESTION 2

Consider the statements below regarding partnership, legal structures, and risk management. Which matches your own perspective most closely?

1. In any business deal, it's vital to have a detailed contract to make sure each partner's interests are protected. Risk is managed by factoring in likely scenarios and assigning rewards and penalties to projected outcomes. By signing a contract, each side knowingly assumes risk and

must be prepared to abide by its terms. In business, there are winners and losers—that's just how it is.

2. In any business deal, a well-written contract helps protect each partner's interests. Risk is partially managed by factoring in potential liabilities, although if one party suffers unduly from unexpected factors, accommodations should be considered. Once a contract is signed, it should be honored except in extraordinary cases. Businesspeople should accept that there are winners and losers.

3. Business deals are a basis for developing relationships that support each partner's interests, with legal structures as a safeguard. Since no contract can predict all eventualities, it's best to word them generally. Risk is managed through mutual accommodation. If changes cause one partner to suffer excessively after a contract is signed, the other should consider offsetting the loss in some way. A good partnership is one in which both parties benefit.

4. Business deals are a basis for developing relationships that support each partner's interests. Contracts are mainly a statement of intent, and since they can't predict all eventualities, they should be worded generally. Risk is managed through mutual accommodation. If changes cause one partner to suffer excessively after a contract is signed, the other partner should offset the loss in some way. A good partnership is one in which both parties benefit, and give-and-take is vital.

1—Strong Rule orientation emphasizing reliance on legal structure

2—Rule orientation emphasizing legal structure but allowing for flexibility

3—Situation orientation emphasizing relationship maintenance and minimizing reliance on legal enforcement

4—Strong Situation orientation emphasizing relationship maintenance to the exclusion of legal enforcement

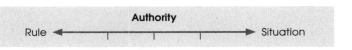

Authority

Rule ←   → Situation

7. Action (Opportunity/Thoroughness)

QUESTION 1

Several managers are discussing an inquiry from a potential partner. An overseas distributor sees an opportunity to introduce their product into a new, high-growth market, but they must move quickly before a competitor's product is released. If the initiative fails, the company could be perceived as hasty and unprepared. Which of the perspectives below matches your own most closely?

1. We should act now. The most important thing is to take advantage of the current opportunity. If it doesn't work out, we can always change direction.

2. We should act quickly. The most important thing is to take advantage of the current opportunity, but we should be cautious. Changing direction later due to a mistake would be embarrassing.

3. Our reputation is more important than current opportunity. To avoid having to change direction, we should move only when we're reasonably sure that this project will be consistent with our tradition and help maintain our reputation. Changing direction later due to a mistake could damage our reputation.

4. Our reputation is most important. We should not move on this project until we're sure it's in line with our tradition and will help maintain our reputation. Changing direction later due to a mistake would be very damaging to our reputation.

1—Strong Opportunity orientation emphasizing quick movement in response to potential benefit

2—Opportunity orientation incorporating concern for reputation

3—Thoroughness orientation emphasizing caution and reputation maintenance

4—Strong Thoroughness orientation emphasizing reputation maintenance even at the cost of loss of potential benefit

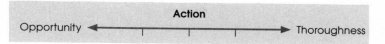

8. Organization (Schedule/Flow)

QUESTION 1

Which statement most closely matches your own perspective on time management and organization?

1. It's really important to keep projects and tasks organized. I plan my time carefully, scheduling tasks in the order of importance and priority. I get to work on time every day, and I like to focus intently on one task, getting to a stopping point before moving on to the next. If something unexpected comes up, I feel uncomfortable until my schedule is back on track. I really hate to miss deadlines. When I'm in charge of a meeting, I prepare a well-defined agenda, making sure we begin and end on time. Efficiency is a function of how much time things take, and my goal is to avoid wasting time wherever possible.

2. I'm pretty relaxed about the way projects and tasks are organized—unexpected problems inevitably come up, so there's no point in detailed plans. I organize projects loosely and work on multiple things at a time. I may not think about a project much at the beginning and do most of the work at the end. I don't mind interruptions, and when something comes up, I just move other things around to accommodate it. When I'm in charge of a meeting, we may start a bit late. We'll have a general agenda or maybe just brainstorm, and we'll finish when our business is concluded. Efficiency is a function of making sure all the angles are considered, and an excessively linear approach limits creativity.

1—Schedule orientation, with linear organization and attention to deadlines

2—Flow orientation, with loose organization, multitasking, and reordering of internal tasks

Your Personal Profile

For each cultural dimension, mark the chart below in the place corresponding to your answer to each of the self-assessment questions. Marking the chart will complete your Personal Profile, a snapshot of your cultural tendencies and preferences. Reviewing it will give you an idea of areas where you may encounter confusion and conflict with people who have different profiles.

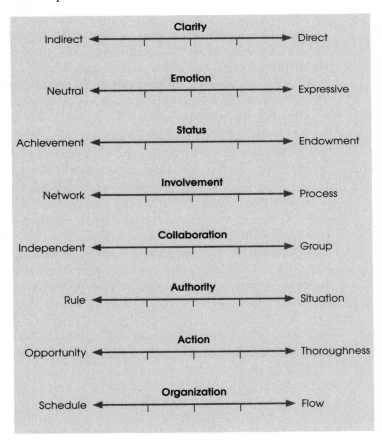

Clarity
Indirect ◄─────┼─────┼─────┼─────► Direct

Emotion
Neutral ◄─────┼─────┼─────┼─────► Expressive

Status
Achievement ◄─────┼─────┼─────┼─────► Endowment

Involvement
Network ◄─────┼─────┼─────┼─────► Process

Collaboration
Independent ◄─────┼─────┼─────┼─────► Group

Authority
Rule ◄─────┼─────┼─────┼─────► Situation

Action
Opportunity ◄─────┼─────┼─────┼─────► Thoroughness

Organization
Schedule ◄─────┼─────┼─────┼─────► Flow

Interpreting Your Profile

By answering the self-assessment questions, you've identified your preferences for each of the cultural dimensions.

YOUR STRONG TENDENCIES

2

Wherever a mark is close to either end of a continuum, you have a strong preference. Where you have strong tendencies, you also have less flexibility—you feel more strongly that your approach is "right," "fair," "efficient," etc., and will be less willing to compromise with the opposite approach. You're also more likely to react negatively to people with the opposite traits. Strong preferences are the ones that will most likely cause problems in intercultural interaction, so you should focus on them—especially if your counterparts have opposing tendencies.

It's also important to note that under stress, we exhibit strong tendencies *even more strongly*. A Direct person who doesn't get a clear answer from an Indirect counterpart will ask in even more concise terms, enunciate more clearly, and speak more loudly. Feeling pressured, the Indirect party is likely to be even more vague and evasive.

YOUR WEAK TENDENCIES

A mark placed near the middle of a continuum tells you that you have no strong preference for that dimension. You have more flexibility there and will adapt easily to either approach. These dimensions won't cause you much difficulty. You'll be good at working with people with either tendency.

Chapters 4–6 provide a detailed explanation of what each trait means. You may choose to skip ahead to learn about them and come back to Chapter 3 to complete your Counterpart Profile.

3

Who Are "*They*"?
Create a Counterpart
Profile

N ow that you've completed your Personal Profile, you can create
one for the person, group, or place whose cultural tendencies
you'd like to understand. If your counterpart is willing to complete a Personal Profile of his or her own, have them answer the questions
in Chapter 2 and move on to comparing your profiles (Chapter 7). Otherwise, use the assessment techniques described here.

If you want to practice creating a Counterpart Profile but don't have
a specific one in mind, you can profile any individual, group, or place
that seems significantly different from you or your home environment.

Preparing for Interaction:
Analyze Before You Go

The ARC system helps you analyze your counterpart through personal
observation. But you don't have to wait for a face-to-face encounter to
conduct an analysis. There are many sources of information on the way
people think and behave in other places. You can make good use of "Doing
Business in Country X" books and other publications by searching them
for cultural indicators. As an example, imagine that you are researching

a fictitious destination called Merubia. Suppose you read that traffic in Merubia defies all signs and signals, that friends and relatives of the police there are immune to ticketing, and that violations are often dismissed when the officer is presented with a small gift. These are signs of a strong Situation orientation. Identifying this tendency would give you an idea of what to look for in terms of the policies and attitudes of people living there.

From the attributes described in your resources, you could create a cultural profile of Merubia and predict Merubians' culturally based behaviors and attitudes. The same goes for lists of tips, etiquette books, and articles on Merubian "dos and don'ts." These are of limited value by themselves because they don't tell you what to do in situations other than the ones they describe. Combining them into a cultural profile, however, allows you to predict what you will find when you visit Merubia or work with Merubian people and companies. Current events articles and documentaries can be used in the same way, although these are often too general to give much insight into behavior. Novels written about a place by a native-born author can be a very rich source of information about the way people think, live, and interact, and films written and directed by natives and set in your target location can also be a good resource.

Design your strategy by using your preliminary profile to predict attitudes, expectations, and policies before your first visit to a new place. Just remember that outside resources mostly provide generalizations and are not always current. The profile they indicate may not apply to specific organizations or people, so you should begin asking questions and making observations to confirm and tighten your profile as soon as real evidence becomes available. In-person exposure is crucial to honing your preliminary profile. To use "nonprimary" resources to create a preliminary profile, review your resources for the indicators below. If you are in a hurry and need a ready-made resource, look for the *Quick Reference Profile* I have prepared for your target country on my website.[1]

---

[1] www.deirdremendez.com/quick-reference-profiles

Gathering Information

There are four ways to gather information about cultural tendencies:

Personal Observation

You can learn a lot by simply looking at what people do in public places. In traffic, do cars and pedestrians carefully obey the rules (Rule), or do they ignore road signs and take their chances (Situation)? In restaurants, do people eat lunch quickly, check their watches, and rush back to work (Process, Schedule), or do they visit with others in a relaxed way (Network, Flow)? Do junior people carry luggage and hold doors open for their bosses (Endowment), or do bosses carry their own briefcases and open doors if they reach them first (Achievement)?

Casual Interaction

You can ask people questions that point to particular cultural tendencies. Answering a request for directions with step-by-step instructions suggests a Process orientation, while a vague response such as, "Over there, by the library," indicates a Network orientation. If a local agrees that people in their city are law-abiding, you can confirm Rule orientation. Stories about people's daily experiences are full of useful information.

Visiting Institutions

An institutional visit provides many opportunities for gathering information. Do discussions describe how the present situation relates to past experience (Thoroughness), or focus on recent developments and future plans (Opportunity)? Do responses take the form of brief, precise answers (Process) or lengthy digressions (Network)? Are senior managers older males from headquarters (Endowment), or do they include a mix of ages, genders, and ethnicities (Achievement)? Are decisions made quickly by a designated decision maker (Independent), or through lengthy consensus building with multiple parties (Group)?

Attending Meetings

Meetings can be a rich source of cultural information, especially if you have a chance to ask questions. Do presentations provide context in a rambling format (Network) or follow a predetermined structure (Process)? Do people arrive haphazardly and leave frequently to take calls (Flow), or are they on time and focused on the discussion throughout (Schedule)? Are new ideas vetted behind the scenes prior to a meeting (Indirect), or are they initiated and debated in the meeting itself (Direct)? Do discussions lead to a handshake (Situation, Network) or a contract (Rule, Process)? Do young people play a prominent role (Achievement), or do older people lead discussions and call on younger ones as appropriate (Endowment)?

Using a mix of these techniques, you can complete a Counterpart Profile relatively quickly. A single meeting, especially if held in your counterpart's offices, can reveal most, if not all, of the group's cultural leanings. (Remember that three to five observations per dimension are recommended for a sound profile.) As you practice identifying tendencies, it will be easier to recognize them, and you'll complete your analysis faster each time.

The charts below will tell you what to look for in public and work-related contexts. Use them to think analytically about your experiences and create your Counterpart Profile. The more examples you have for each dimension, the better, because people's attitudes toward a dimension may vary depending on the context. People who are very law-abiding in traffic (Rule) may underreport earnings on their income tax statement (Situation). Getting three to five examples for each cultural dimension will help ensure that your observations are consistent and the profile is useful. Even so, a Counterpart Profile should always be viewed as a work in progress. The more you interact with others and the longer you live in a new place, the more nuances you'll see. But even assessing just one or two examples per dimension will help you formulate questions for deeper analysis.

To complete your Counterpart Profile, look for the characteristics described below as you interact with your counterpart to identify their cultural tendencies, and fill out the chart on page 63.

Recognizing the Cultural Tendencies

INDICATORS FOR CLARITY

Indirect	Direct

Behavior in Public Places	
Indirect	**Direct**
Clerks in retail stores may be reluctant to acknowledge that they don't carry a particular item.	Clerks in retail stores will acknowledge that they don't carry a particular item.
Disagreement is not overtly expressed in public.	Disagreement may be overtly expressed and overheard in public.
Conversations	
Personal opinions that might offend are avoided, so conversation with new acquaintances is superficial.	Personal opinions may be expressed freely in conversation with new acquaintances.
Expressed opinions may be softened by terms such as "I think," "It seems to me," "I wonder whether," etc.	Opinions are likely to be stated as fact.
Negative responses are avoided or expressed minimally as doubt—or even agreement—rather than disagreement.	Negative responses are considered acceptable, and people express disagreement openly.

3

Indirect	Direct
Body language, tone of voice, sarcasm, or humor may convey a negative response while statements avoid overt disagreement.	People indicate disagreement openly and provide justification for it.
A response may begin with praise, followed by criticism, to soften negativity.	Criticism and disagreement are voiced without softening.
Written Materials	
In advertisements, personal contact is recommended. ("Call this number," or, "Come to this location.")	In advertisements, impersonal action is recommended. ("Visit our website," or, "Send an e-mail for information.")
Information in public media is couched in background and context.	Information in public media is conveyed succinctly.
Product packaging in stores refers indirectly or euphemistically to medical conditions and details of personal hygiene.	Product packaging in stores explicitly mentions medical conditions and details of personal hygiene.
Meeting Structure and Interaction at Work	
Organizers establish general agendas and expect to follow them loosely.	Organizers establish detailed agendas and expect to follow them closely.
Problems and conflicts are tabled, to be discussed later.	Participants discuss problems and conflicts until a decision or agreement is reached.
Matters for group discussion may be reviewed and decided in private settings, then "rubber-stamped" in public meetings.	Matters for group discussion are likely to be introduced, debated, and decided in public meetings.
Presentation Format and Delivery	
Concepts are explained rather vaguely or through examples or stories, and answers to questions may include considerable context.	Concepts are clearly defined, and answers to questions are concise.

Indirect	Direct
Presentations are rambling and may include history and storytelling.	Presentations are orderly and precise and convey specific information.
Speakers focus on context and leave the conclusion to be determined by the listener.	Speakers may introduce their position or conclusion first, followed by justification and details.
Audience questions may be tangential, and speakers may allow themselves to be pulled in new directions.	Audience questions are likely to be closely related to the topic; if not, speakers will redirect back to the topic.
Organizational Structures and Policies	
Managers motivate employees through positive feedback and personal example.	Managers guide employees through positive and negative feedback and correction.
Poor employee performance is managed by lack of promotion, shame, exclusion, or decreased responsibilities.	Poor employee performance is acknowledged verbally and managed through criticism, reduced compensation, or termination.

Pointers for Investigating This Dimension

It may be difficult to spot Indirectness in people who are interacting with their peers or subordinates. Knowing that Indirectness increases with hierarchy may help you recognize it. People are always more direct with their inferiors than with superiors, and in Endowment environments, this tendency increases. If someone claims to be Direct, consider whether they would criticize a ridiculous suggestion made by their boss.

INDICATORS FOR EMOTION

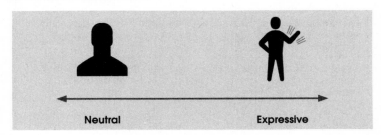

Behavior in Public Places	
Neutral	**Expressive**
People tend to speak quietly and in a subdued manner.	People tend to speak loudly and in an animated manner.
Nonverbal behavior—such as facial expressions and hand gestures—is restrained.	Nonverbal behavior is active.
Laughter and expressions of emotion are minimized.	Laughter and expressions of emotion are easy to observe.
Cell phone calls are handled quietly, with speakers moving away from others while talking.	Cell phone calls may be disruptive, with speakers speaking loudly near others who are conversing.
Conversations	
People tend to avoid expressing their feelings and reactions until they get to know others well.	People are relaxed about sharing their feelings and reactions with casual acquaintances.
Conversations are even in tone and relatively quiet.	Conversations are illustrated by hand gestures, loudness, and laughter.
Written Materials	
In advertisements and articles, persuasion is based on "factual" information.	In advertisements and articles, persuasion appeals to the emotions.

Neutral	Expressive
Descriptions emphasize objective detail, the order of events, and other factual information.	Descriptions include emotional information such as popular reaction to facts and the writer's attitude or opinion.
Visual content has emotionally neutral impact.	Visual content has strong emotional appeal.
Meeting Structure and Interaction at Work	
Arguments appeal to logic.	Arguments appeal to emotion first and may be supported with logic.
Descriptions are concise and factual.	Descriptions are rich in adjectives and detail.
People speak evenly during disagreements.	People speak loudly and with more gestures during conflict.
Joking is infrequent, even in relaxed situations, and responses are quiet.	Joking is common in relaxed situations, and responses can be loud and disorderly.
Presentation Format and Delivery	
Presentations are even in tone, with few gestures and little facial expression.	Presentations are illustrated by hand gestures and variation in tone.
Presenters persuade by making logical arguments.	Presenters persuade by engaging emotions.
Presenters answer questions directly, providing information requested with little elaboration.	Presenters engage actively with questions, elaborating on answers in detail.
Organizational Structures and Policies	
Corporate culture encourages focus on work and minimizing disturbance of others.	Corporate culture allows personal expression and some intrusion of noise and interruption.
People describe their work in terms of duty and commitment.	People describe their work in terms of passion and expression of identity.

3

INDICATORS FOR STATUS

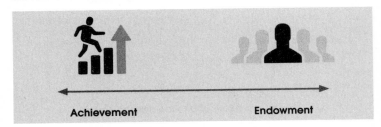

Behavior in Public Places	
Achievement	**Endowment**
Interaction between juniors and seniors is relatively informal.	Interaction between juniors and seniors is relatively formal.
Bosses manage their own belongings and environment.	Juniors may carry seniors' belongings, open doors for them, drive them, etc.
Conversations	
Seniors interact with juniors as relative equals.	Seniors take a teaching or parental tone when talking with or about juniors.
Seniors may acknowledge their own lack of information or expertise.	Seniors are unlikely to acknowledge their own lack of information or expertise.
Seniors and juniors exchange information relatively equally.	Seniors do most of the talking; juniors listen respectfully.
Written Materials	
Personal accomplishments and awards are listed on business cards and mentioned in written materials.	Title, division, and company affiliation are listed on business cards and mentioned in written materials.
Advertised products and services promote upward mobility through performance.	Advertised products and services promote getting the most out of relationships.

Meeting Structure and Interaction at Work	
Achievement	**Endowment**
Participants are introduced and seated in any order.	Participants are introduced, and may be seated, in order of seniority.
When high-level people are present, their manner is relaxed and interactive.	When high-level people are present, their manner is formal and scripted.
Meetings are relaxed in tone. Clothing may be informal, and new acquaintances may use first names.	Meetings are formal in tone. Clothing is likely to be formal, and new acquaintances may use last names or titles.
In mixed groups, juniors and seniors talk to one another about topics of mutual importance or interest.	In mixed groups, juniors and seniors speak with equals, and juniors convey questions or comments to their seniors as appropriate.
Junior participants ask questions, provide relevant information, and introduce suggestions at will.	Junior participants ask questions, provide relevant information, and introduce suggestions as directed by seniors.
Presentation Format and Delivery	
Presentations are relatively informal, with active exchange of information among participants.	Presentations are relatively formal and are directed to senior participants, who ask most of the questions.
Seniors listening to a presentation will be alert.	Seniors attending a presentation may appear to disregard it.
Organizational Structures and Policies	
Leaders may be young and come from any walk of life, gender, ethnic background, or religious group.	Leaders are likely to be older males and may come from a particular social stratum, ethnic background, or religious group.
Employees are rewarded and promoted on the basis of performance relative to their job description.	Employees are rewarded and promoted on the basis of influence, effectiveness, and length of service.

3

Achievement	Endowment
Education and expertise acquired outside the company, such as degrees, are highly valued in employees.	Familiarity with the company culture through long service is highly valued in employees.
Junior and senior employees have relatively similar work environments and advantages.	Seniority entails perks such as separate restrooms, offices with doors, company cars, and club memberships.
Founding members have similar status to others and may move on to other ventures as a company grows.	Founding members have high status and tend to stay with the company.
Companies promote an image of innovation and change.	Companies promote an image of stability and reliability.
Junior employees may earn more than their managers as a result of performance-based incentives.	Managers earn more than their employees based on seniority.

Pointers for Investigating This Dimension

It's not always easy to recognize Endowment characteristics. An entrance exam-based university system may sound egalitarian, but in many countries, only wealthy families can afford the expensive preparatory schools that guarantee a student will pass the exam. A good way to spot Endowment tendencies is to consider the positions and behavior of young people and women in organizations.

INDICATORS FOR INVOLVEMENT

Network ←————————————————→ Process

3

Behaviors in Public Places	
Network	**Process**
People may ignore strangers, avoiding eye contact or acknowledgment.	People may greet and engage with strangers through eye contact and smiling.
Greetings and conversations with acquaintances in unplanned encounters are lengthy.	Greetings and conversations with acquaintances in unplanned encounters are brief.
People give general, vague directions, sometimes with nonspecific reference to landmarks.	People give detailed directions, making reference to streets and numbers.
Clerks in retail stores may guide customers personally or recommend other places to buy items they don't carry.	Clerks in retail stores provide information succinctly.
People consider their homes private and conceal them behind walls, fences, and shutters.	People consider their homes part of their surroundings and build them relatively open to public view.
Conversations	
Explanations contain stories involving digressions and elaborate context before reaching the conclusion.	Explanations are organized chronologically, with few digressions, and may begin with the outcome or "punch line" followed by details.

Network	Process
Speakers provide context and may make lengthy digressions when answering questions.	Speakers provide specific and precise answers to questions.
Written Materials	
Text and images on products emphasize results and emotional benefits.	Text and images on products provide information about contents, ingredients, and nutritional qualities.
Elaborate contextual information may be provided, including historical background and personal opinion.	Information and descriptions are succinct, focusing on the delivery of facts or arguments.
Written materials convey emotional content through wordy, flowery, or poetic language.	Written materials use precise language for clarity.
Structure may involve lengthy descriptive paragraphs.	Structure includes bullets and lists with succinct paragraphs.
Text may cover the page in nonlinear arrangements.	Text tends to be laid out in linear form.
Colors are bold and diverse, with graphics splashed around the page.	Colors are restrained, and graphics are arranged within shapes or borders.
Meeting Structure and Interaction at Work	
Greetings are time-consuming and may include questions about current activities, family, and social engagements.	Greetings are relatively brief and formulaic.
Meetings begin with lengthy social interaction, and business discussion may occur at the very end or not at all.	People "get down to business" quickly in meetings and socialize afterwards if there is time.
Meetings may be organized through a general statement of goals. Discussion may wander from planned topics.	Meetings are organized according to an agenda whose points are followed in order.

Presentation Format and Delivery	
Network	**Process**
Presenters tend to speak in generalities.	Presenters tend to convey information explicitly.
Answers are general, and may not address questions directly.	Answers are succinct, precisely addressing questions.
Speakers talk about issues generally, referring to history and philosophy and illustrating with stories.	Speakers address issues directly, sticking to the matter at hand and illustrating with brief examples.
Presenters may refer to loosely structured notes or presentation material and improvise as they go.	Presentations are highly structured, and presenters follow the format closely, with little improvising.
Presenters are easily diverted to related topics and tangents.	Presenters stick to agendas and talking points, redirecting tangential questions back to the original topic.
Organizational Structures and Policies	
Job descriptions and criteria for advancement are general and vague.	Job descriptions and criteria for advancement are detailed and specific.
Promotions are based on employees' effectiveness in teamwork and relationships with colleagues and managers.	Promotions are based on employees' performance relative to specific duties.
Employees engage in group work and social interaction, possibly after hours.	Employees focus on individual tasks and may have little social interaction with one another.
Employees display photos, souvenirs, and other personal objects in the workplace.	Few personal articles are displayed in the workplace.

3

INDICATORS FOR COLLABORATION

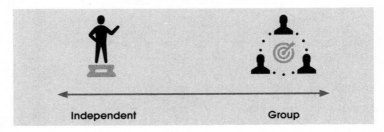

Behavior in Public Places	
Independent	**Group**
People often spend leisure time alone.	People usually spend leisure time in groups.
People demonstrate individual personality through their clothing and behavior.	People blend in with others in their clothing and behavior.
People often eat alone in public, and individual seating is common in restaurants.	People rarely eat alone in public, and large group seating is common in restaurants.
People order individually in restaurants.	Everyone may order the same thing, or one person may order for everyone in restaurants.
Meals are served in individual servings eaten by one person.	Meals may be served in group portions shared by everyone.
Conversations	
People demonstrate individual attributes such as wit and charm.	People present themselves as affiliates of their group and try to appear upstanding.
People freely express personal opinions, which may not conform to majority views.	People avoid casually expressing opinions that conflict with majority views and take care to identify them as personal opinions.

Independent	Group
Personal hobbies and areas of interest may be discussed with strangers.	Individual preferences and activities may be reserved for conversation with intimates.
Written Materials	
Promotional materials are written to appeal to the "decision maker."	Promotional materials are written to appeal to all concerned with a decision.
Advertisements (e.g., vacation packages) are geared to individuals and couples.	Advertisements (e.g., vacation packages) are geared to groups.
Meeting Structure and Interaction at Work	
One person may represent an organization in negotiations.	Multiple people with relevant knowledge and expertise represent an organization in negotiations.
The top-ranking negotiator has decision-making authority in meetings or negotiations.	Decisions are made by groups that include representatives of relevant organizations.
Negotiations are usually carried out by the same person or group over time.	Negotiating teams change members, adding and subtracting people based on the topic of discussion.
In negotiations, those present make decisions.	Negotiators break to check with others or hold separate meetings to get consensus.
Decisions are made quickly.	Decisions take a long time and may involve building consensus within large groups.
An individual's answers to questions may reflect personal opinions.	An individual's answers to questions indicate group consensus.
People may guess or estimate when answering questions outside their expertise.	People check with or defer to others rather than answer questions outside their expertise.

3

Independent	Group
There is a difference between personal opinions and "official" answers, which should come from an expert.	All answers are official answers and are confirmed with the group beforehand.
Presentation Format and Delivery	
One or two presenters cover diverse material.	Multiple presenters cover topics in their area of expertise.
Presenters may speculate on questions outside their area of responsibility.	Presenters defer to others or check and return with answers when asked questions outside their area of responsibility.
Organizational Structures and Policies	
Employee attrition is considered natural, and people with similar skills replace outgoing members.	Employee attrition is considered an indication of a problem in the team or company and handled as a social issue.
To solve problems, individuals develop solutions and promote their ideas to others.	To solve problems, groups meet to discuss. Each member contributes, whether or not they have a solution.
Decision making is majority rule or top down.	Decision making is consensus based.
Representatives dress and behave in ways that express their individuality.	Representatives dress and behave in ways that emphasize company affiliation, including organizational logos or jewelry.
Projects are staffed with people with relevant skills. Groups are disbanded when projects end, and individuals are reassigned to new projects where their skills are needed.	Project teams are cultivated for effective dynamics. When projects end, teams remain intact and new projects are assigned to them.

Independent	Group
Individuals complete tasks on their own and then integrate their work with that of other group members.	Individuals complete tasks in close collaboration, possibly with all members in the same room. Integrating work is constant throughout a project.
Individual contributions are recognized and rewarded.	Individual contributions are not separated from the results of a team.
Innovation and revolutionary thinking are highly valued.	Contribution to existing models is highly valued.

Pointers for Investigating This Dimension

The language of business complicates things because companies everywhere emphasize the importance of team performance, which may sound like Group orientation. But while teams are valued everywhere, Independent- and Group-oriented teams have very different characteristics. People often mistake Network tendencies for Group orientation. Good indicators of Group tendencies include a strong preference for eating or spending private time with others, not expressing personal opinions, and not making individual decisions, even about oneself.

INDICATORS FOR AUTHORITY

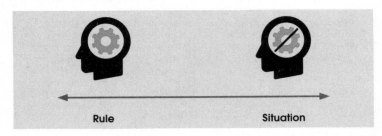

Rule   Situation

Behavior in Public Places	
Rule	**Situation**
Dress and behavior are conservative and reflect the values of the environment.	Dress and behavior are idiosyncratic and express individual preferences.
People are respectful of rules and policies.	People may make excuses for breaking rules according to the situation. ("I'm in a hurry," "Just this once," "It won't hurt anyone," "It's a silly rule.")
Traffic tends to be orderly. Lanes are indicated. Signs use direct language and are not defaced or ignored.	Traffic tends to be haphazard. There may be no markings or signs, or these may be defaced or ignored.
People wait for the light and cross at intersections.	People cross against the light or jaywalk.
People wait their turn in orderly lines.	People mass in groups or cut in line.
Signs issue orders and describe penalties.	Signs appeal to human nature and values.
Public transportation operates on time.	Public transportation operates haphazardly.
People pay for tickets and sit in their assigned class.	People avoid paying and move up in class.
Buildings and streets are clean.	Buildings may be covered in graffiti, and streets may be dirty.

Rule	Situation
People take responsibility for keeping public areas clean.	People litter public areas.
People may instruct others or criticize rule breaking.	People ignore it when others break rules.
Conversations	
People tend to adhere to societal norms and government policy in expressing themselves.	People express individual views and opinions and may criticize social convention or government policy.
Written Materials	
Instructional signs issue orders and describe penalties.	Instructional signs appeal to readers to do the "right thing."
Meeting Structure and Interaction at Work	
People follow similar rules and procedures regarding arrival time, behavior during meetings, and responding to questions.	There is individual variation in arrival time and behavior during meetings. Individuals express their own opinions freely.
Based on an assumption that rules will be followed, legal documents are carefully worded.	There may be lengthy discussion about measures to make sure rules are followed, regardless of the terms of documents.
NDAs, MOUs, and contracts are implemented to guarantee partner compliance.	Strong relationships are considered the best way to ensure partner compliance.
Negotiations proceed in an orderly manner, with agreement at the end.	Negotiations may be stopped frequently and return to previous points. Issues may be reopened at the end to renegotiate additional concessions.
Presentation Format and Delivery	
Presenters tend to stick to specific talking points and observe time limits.	Presenters tend to diverge from specific talking points and may go over time.

3

Rule	Situation
Presentations are likely to be planned and rehearsed.	Presentations may be largely unscripted, with spontaneous digressions.
Questions and answers stick closely to the original topic.	Questions may be tangential, and presenters may allow themselves to be pulled into new topics.
Organizational Structures and Policies	
Policies are clearly specified, displayed, and referred to.	Rules and policies are not emphasized, even where they exist.
Rules apply equally to everyone.	Rules apply less to senior and influential people or groups.
Job descriptions and criteria for advancement are clearly articulated.	Job descriptions are vague, and advancement is determined by relationships with coworkers and seniors.
Contracts are lengthy, detailed, and carefully worded.	Contracts are relatively short, general, and vague.
Contracts are followed closely once in place.	Contracts are considered a guide, to be renegotiated when conditions change.
A trusted partner is one that honors commitments.	A trusted partner is one that has been tested over a period of time.

INDICATORS FOR ACTION

| Opportunity | Thoroughness |

Behavior in Public Places	
Opportunity	**Thoroughness**
People appreciate recent buildings and art, which are valued for their innovation and vitality.	People appreciate old buildings and historical sites, which are valued for their history and preserved with care.
Tour guides emphasize recent accomplishments over past history.	Tour guides emphasize past glory over modern innovation.
Conversations	
Descriptions and explanations tend to focus on the present and future.	Descriptions and explanations tend to refer to history and tradition.
Written Materials	
Organizational materials emphasize current and recent performance and plans for the future.	Organizational materials emphasize past history and philosophy as a context for current and future plans.
Promotional materials emphasize innovation, uniqueness, and opportunity for upgrades.	Promotional materials emphasize history of value, reliability, and service.
Meeting Structure and Interaction at Work	
Moving quickly and efficiently is prioritized.	Caution and thorough analysis are prioritized.
Current opportunity and threat are emphasized.	Continuity and reputation are emphasized.

Opportunity	Thoroughness
Relationships are rather utilitarian and based on current needs. When old relationships fail, new ones are easily made.	Relationships are long lasting and carefully maintained. Resentment results when they are allowed to lapse.
Presentation Format and Delivery	
Presentations focus on the present and future, without much discussion of the past.	Presentations emphasize the past and may include lengthy historical descriptions.
New ideas are introduced as a chance to improve on the present.	New ideas are introduced as a chance to build on tradition or recreate past success.
Organizational Structures and Policies	
The need for quick responses to opportunity and threat is a motivator for change.	The desire to maintain continuity and reputation is a source of caution.
The current situation and future opportunities are the focus of decision making; today's conditions are unique.	The past is always the standard in decision making; future actions could harm a carefully built reputation.
Product innovations and upgrades are considered the way to attract and retain customers.	Product reliability and customer service are considered the way to attract and retain customers.
Sales cycles are designed to be short for incremental performance improvement.	Sales cycles are designed to be long for sustained financial performance.
Employee bonuses and raises are awarded soon after performance to encourage short-term achievement.	Employee bonuses and raises are awarded well after performance to encourage long-term customer retention.
Strategy involves constant analysis of recent performance to modify direction quickly.	Strategy tends to favor staying on course through ups and downs and letting results play out over time.
Changes are justified in terms of today's environment and current opportunity.	Changes are justified in terms of recreating past success.

INDICATORS FOR ORGANIZATION

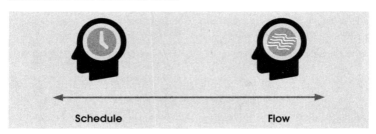

Schedule   Flow

3

Behavior in Public Places	
Schedule	**Flow**
People walk briskly and purposefully, referring frequently to timekeeping devices.	People walk in a relaxed, unhurried manner or hurry as if late.
Public transportation operates according to published timetables, and vehicles depart and arrive as scheduled.	Public transportation may operate without published timetables, and vehicles may not depart and arrive as scheduled.
People eat relatively quickly during the workday, keep track of the time, and leave soon after eating.	When eating during the workday, people are relaxed and may linger after finishing the meal.
Conversations	
Conversations may be brief and hurried, and participants may seem limited by other appointments and activities.	Conversations may be lengthy and relaxed, and participants appear unconcerned about getting to other appointments and activities.
People maintain awareness of the time.	People relax and forget about the time.
Written Materials	
Timetables for transportation systems, store hours, and parking rules are prominent in written materials.	Timetables for transportation systems, store hours, and parking rules may not be included in written materials.

Schedule	Flow
Instructions and lists are ordered logically or chronologically.	Instructions and lists are ordered somewhat randomly.
Information is provided to help organize the reader's thinking.	Information is provided to make the reader aware of options, components, and problems.
Meeting Structure and Interaction at Work	
People are generally on time or slightly early for meetings.	People arrive at various times during meetings.
Attendees arriving late apologize and join the meeting with as little disruption as possible.	Attendees arriving late may disrupt the meeting with greetings and may not apologize for lateness.
Meeting participants focus on the discussion with little other activity.	Participants may take phone calls and enter or exit the room in the course of meetings.
Meeting agendas are detailed and followed closely.	Meeting agendas are general and followed loosely.
Tasks are divided into segments, and work on the first segment begins immediately.	Tasks are divided into phases, and the majority of the work may be done toward the end.
Presentation Format and Delivery	
Speakers proceed point by point, and materials are highly structured.	Speakers ramble, and materials may be vague and general.
Speakers proceed methodically and stay on topic.	Speakers change topics, adding new material or addressing tangents.
Speakers stick close to written materials.	Speakers improvise.
Questions are answered succinctly.	Questions may result in digressions.
Organizational Structures and Policies	
Company history is perceived as a linear sequence of events.	Company history is perceived as a coalescing of events.

Schedule	Flow
Employees and partners are expected to meet deadlines regardless of circumstances.	Meeting deadlines is perceived as beyond human control.
Schedules are detailed, linear, and specific. When changes occur, schedules are rewritten.	Schedules are general and flexible to accommodate changes, which are perceived as inevitable.
Schedules and milestones are adhered to closely.	Schedules and milestones may change frequently throughout a project.
Missed internal deadlines are considered cause for concern, and efforts are made to return to the original schedule.	Missed internal deadlines are considered normal, and resources are reallocated to meet the final deadline.
Last-minute changes are considered disruptive and problematical.	Last-minute changes are considered natural and unavoidable.

Recording Your Observations

Once you've completed your observations for your Counterpart Profile, write them down to help you remember what you've observed. Reflecting on the context of various observations will give your profile more detail and nuance over time.

Here's an example: You notice that people attending a business event in your counterpart country are exceedingly formal, using titles and showing deference for seniors. Based on this experience, you conclude that the country is Endowment oriented. The following week, you attend a similar event where people dress and behave casually, using first names and interacting with all comers as equals. How do you interpret this conflicting information?

Considering the contexts of the two events might give you additional information. Maybe the two events included representatives of different types of companies—large ones vs. small ones or established ones vs.

young ones. Maybe they included different categories of people—executives vs. lower-level workers or urban employees vs. those from rural areas. Recording the context of your observations helps you get the most information possible and allows you to revise your profile as needed.

Below is a format for recording your observations and their context, along with a few examples. By making these kinds of notes, you will have continued access to the building blocks of your Counterpart Profile.

Cultural Tendency: Achievement/Endowment

Observation 1:

Attended a reception hosted by the Capital City Primary Industries' Association. Dress was quite formal, and our host used titles such as "Director So-and-So." Junior attendees stayed in the background while their seniors talked, and one directed me to give my business card to his boss first when I approached him. Strong Endowment orientation here.

Context:

The event took place in an expensive hotel. The companies represented were among the oldest and most established in the capital city. Interesting that most of these companies are suffering now that government subsidies are declining.

Observation 2:

Attended a reception hosted by the Capital City Entrepreneurs' Association. Dress was relatively informal—some people took their jackets off. No one seemed to be using titles, and I heard a couple of CEOs use one another's first names. Junior attendees joined in the conversation. Relative Achievement orientation here.

Context:

The event was held in an upscale club. The companies represented were young and innovative, from the rapidly growing entrepreneurial sector. Seems there's quite a difference between the traditional, government-subsidized firms and these young companies.

You would not want to "average" the results of these two observations, since they refer to different types of companies. Instead, you might use different symbols on your profile for the two.

Constructing Your Analysis

- Your initial analysis will be preliminary. Cultural systems are complex and constantly evolving. You can strengthen and revise your profile with continued time and exposure.

- The more sources of information you refer to, the stronger your analysis will be. Researching a destination beforehand will suggest cultural tendencies to look for. Reading about history, geography, and political structures will help you recognize how these factors contribute to its cultural profile.

- Remember that every cultural tendency is present in every social group, although certain tendencies will be stronger in certain groups, and people display different traits in different situations. Don't force your counterpart into a cultural box.

- When you note a contradiction—significant differences in two organizations in a single city, for example—explore the possible reasons. External factors such as influence from a partner or customer, a leader's educational background, and different ages or ethnicities may be contributing factors.

- A counterpart may have little or no preference for either end of a dimension. People are often "in the middle," so don't assume you will always find extremes.

- One counterpart may demonstrate opposing tendencies in different contexts (just as you probably do). If you find this sort of conflict, avoid choosing just one tendency or "averaging" results—look for explanations for why both exist.

- Observe behavior in as many situations as possible. Include people of various ages and socioeconomic groups in stores, business meetings, restaurants, and traffic.

- If your counterpart is a place, take care not to document tourist culture. To observe local people, look for neighborhoods where they live, shop, and work.

- Be aware of context. Don't conclude that people in a certain country have a casual attitude toward time just because you see some relaxing in a park—parks generally encourage relaxation. (If they seem unhurried at work, you're on to something.)

- Remember individual variation. One person's behavior or opinion is not a basis for typing a population. Observe several people in the same situation, or ask several people the same question.

- When faced with conflicting evidence, ask knowledgeable people about local tendencies. A coworker or hotel concierge can be helpful, but be careful not to rely heavily on reported information. Local "experts" may be biased or provide formulaic answers, so they should be used as tiebreakers, not primary sources.

- Don't overgeneralize. If your information comes from a particular city, agency, or company, don't assume the rest of the country will be the same. Visiting more than one location will give you a better idea of broader tendencies.

Your Counterpart Profile

For each cultural dimension, mark the chart below based on your assessment of your counterpart. This is your Counterpart Profile, a snapshot of the cultural tendencies and preferences of the person, group, or place you are analyzing. Comparing it to your Personal Profile will give you an idea of where you may encounter confusion and conflict.

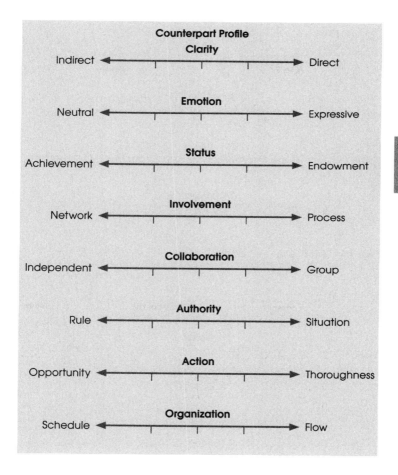

3

Comparing Your Profiles

Now that you've completed your own profile and one for your counterpart, compare the two for similarities and differences. Create a Composite Profile using different symbols for your two profiles.

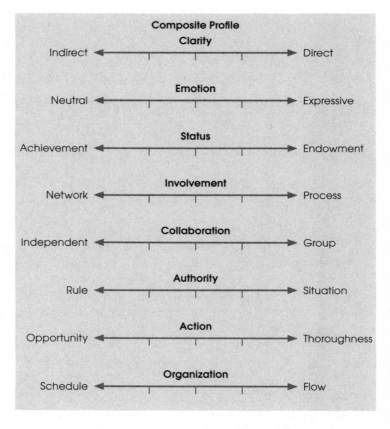

Now you can see the cultural differences between the two of you. For dimensions where your marks are close together, cultural difference probably won't be an issue. For ones where there is more space between marks, there's greater potential for confusion and conflict.

Chapters 4–6 explain the eight cultural dimensions in detail through scenarios and detailed descriptions. If you're pressed for time, focus just on those dimensions that show significant differences between you and your counterpart. Chapter 7 will show you how to interpret your Counterpart Profile to anticipate behaviors and how differences lead to problems.

The ARC System
Part II: Recognize

4

The Communication Dimensions

hapters 4–6 describe how various people view the world and the confusion and conflict that can result when people with differing cultural tendencies work together. If you don't have much time, focus on the "critical" dimensions where you and your counterpart are relatively far apart on your Composite Profile.

The description of each cultural dimension includes:

1. A scenario illustrating problems between people with different cultural scripts;

2. A chart describing the two cultural tendencies associated with each dimension;

3. A summary of the advantages and disadvantages of each tendency, as well as the benefits of integrating them;

4. An analysis of the scenario.

Clarity and **Emotion**, the two dimensions that are most important in communication, affect the way we understand one another in collaboration and negotiation. When people have different expectations of **Clarity**, communication methods may seem confusing, devious, overbearing, or insulting. When norms for **Emotion** aren't shared, people may participate unequally in discussions and problem-solving activities. In my work with intercultural teams, these two dimensions are often responsible for misunderstanding and conflict, and communication is the place to start.

Cultural Dimension 1: Clarity

Scenario 1: The Good Idea

Werner Hess, a marketer for Munich-based Protégé Computers, is visiting Protégé's Japanese subsidiary in Tokyo. His ideas for marketing the next release have gotten a good response in the home office, and company executives are ready to use them in their new advertising campaign. He's excited about sharing his marketing materials with the Japanese office and hopes the marketing program can be implemented in Japan with few changes.

Werner's meeting with Protégé Japan's marketing director, Kenji Tanaka, has gone smoothly. After some social conversation, Werner is ready to present his ideas. He makes the marketing presentation that received such good results at home. When finished, he looks at Kenji. "So, Kenji-san, please give me your assessment of the new marketing plan." Kenji looks down at the papers in front of him. He clears his throat. "Well, I think it's a good idea, but there might be some problems." Werner is ready for this, expecting that changes would be necessary to adapt his ideas to the Japanese market. "What sort of problems do you mean?" he asks. Kenji stares at his hands on the table. "Ah, I think there might be some difficulties." "What kind of difficulties?" repeats Werner. "If you think the scorpion image is too sinister, we could change that, or I could rework the way it's portrayed on the cover—whatever you think is appropriate. If it's the translation of the efficiency concept, we can talk about that." There's a long pause. Kenji finally says, "I think it's okay. I'll show it to our management. I'll do my best. Thank you, Werner-san."

Although Kenji's behavior seems less positive than his words, Werner decides to take the response at face value. He tells Kenji that he needs an answer by the following Friday so that his office can get started on any modifications to the advertising campaign. Kenji nods and thanks him again.

When Werner presents the results of his visit to management back at headquarters, he recounts Kenji's comment that it was okay as written and his promise to show the marketing plan to his management. Werner's manager, Mr. Fischer, is pleased that things are going forward and that the presentation was a success.

Three weeks pass with no word from Tokyo. Mr. Fischer finally calls Kenji's manager, Mr. Hashimoto, and is told that the proposed marketing plan is inappropriate for Japan and that they would prefer to create a new set of materials. Frustrated, Mr. Fischer reports to his team that Kenji apparently either changed his mind or wasn't authorized to make the decision in the first place—or maybe just wasn't being honest. Werner's team doesn't understand why Kenji hasn't responded before now. Now they're back at square one, and the launch date for the ad campaign will be delayed.

Clarity Tendencies: Indirect and Direct

4

Scenario 1 illustrates conflict based on different approaches to **Clarity** in communication. *Indirect* and *Direct* tendencies determine the way people communicate in sensitive situations, particularly ones involving conflict. For Indirect speakers, the goal is to maintain a pleasant surface tone and avoid overtly embarrassing anyone. (This is expressed as "face" maintenance in some cultural environments.) A motto for Indirect speakers might be "If it wasn't stated, there's no harm done." Although they may use nonverbal behavior, sarcasm, or humor to express their true intent, Indirect speakers avoid overtly stating a position that could cause offense— sometimes even to the point of stating that they agree when they don't— and resolve disagreement privately or through intermediaries. Thais have strong Indirect tendencies, and highly Direct visitors to Thailand may think they are much more popular with their hosts than they actually are.

For Direct speakers, the purpose of communication is to convey facts and information. They get to the point quickly and express disagreement openly. They resolve disputes by presenting arguments for their position and criticizing their opponent's position. Direct speakers see people as being separate from their ideas, and challenging an idea isn't considered a personal attack. In the Netherlands, a country known for Direct communication, detailed questioning and blunt disagreement are the preferred method of communication and cause no personal offense.

CHARACTERISTICS OF THE CLARITY TENDENCIES

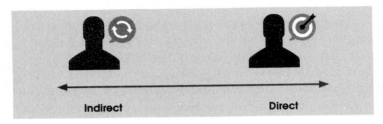

Indirect   Direct

Perspectives, Motivation, and Goals	
Indirect	**Direct**
Developing relationships is valued in business dealings.	"Getting to the point" is valued in business dealings.
Social etiquette and harmonious communication are valued; details can be worked out if a relationship is maintained successfully.	Direct exchange of information and content is valued; relationships are expected to withstand disagreement.
Issues are negotiated in terms of people and personalities. Business is not done with people one dislikes.	People and personalities are separated from negotiating issues. There is no need to like one's business partners.
Negotiation is seen as a ritual with a strong social component that develops relationships and establishes compatibility.	Negotiation is seen as a practical way to make decisions and establish procedures.
Direct communication is seen as confrontational and lacking in sophistication.	Indirect communication is perceived as devious and passive-aggressive.
Surface harmony is considered a cooperative goal, even when engaging in sarcasm or humorous ridicule.	Clarifying issues and reaching decisions is considered a cooperative goal.
Form is valued over function; concessions may be made in the name of harmony.	Function is valued over form; harmony may be sacrificed to reach a good decision.

Behavior and Communication	
Indirect	**Direct**
Participants tend to speak cautiously, with a goal of ensuring that everyone present saves face. Negative input is rarely offered.	Participants tend to speak clearly, with a goal of conveying information. Opinions are voiced readily.
Messages are interpreted based on contextual cues. Hidden meanings are expected and looked for.	Input is usually taken at face value. Subtext and covert signals are not expected in conversation.
Negative messages are transmitted through subtle signals—such as body language, tone of voice, or vagueness. Negative opinions often are not expressed verbally.	Disagreement is not taken personally. Negative input is offered directly, with the assumption that others will do the same.
Presentations are nonlinear and may involve tangents and digressions.	Presentations are clear and proceed through material in a linear manner.
Presenters provide general, philosophical, and historical information. Listeners avoid asking direct questions that might embarrass others.	Presenters are explicit about each point. Listeners ask detailed questions and receive specific answers.
"Yes/no" questions are considered confrontational and too direct; it is preferred to sound people out indirectly.	Participants ask direct questions and expect to be asked direct questions in return.
Elaborate language that avoids conflict is perceived as gracious and sophisticated.	Elaborate language that avoids conflict is considered manipulative and deceptive.
Clear language that expresses conflict of ideas is considered clumsy and insulting.	Clear language that expresses conflict of ideas is considered honest and constructive.
Closed-door meetings are seen as necessary and appropriate for sensitive matters.	Closed-door meetings are seen as an indication of untrustworthiness.

4

Indirect	Direct
People expect to spend time on social preliminaries before discussing business with a new partner.	People expect to begin talking business right away and get to know colleagues in the course of a project.
Cautious discussions are expected to take time, and participants arrive prepared to give it.	Participants arrive prepared to talk about precise details and expect meetings to proceed rapidly.
Organizational Structures and Processes	
Intermediaries may be used to resolve disagreements to avoid confrontation.	Disagreements are dealt with by the relevant parties.
Decisions are often made before meetings by networking with participants; meetings provide official ratification.	Decisions are usually made during meetings through discussion and debate.
Specific mechanisms such as ritualized drinking provide opportunities to speak freely.	Direct exchange may occur in any context.

Advantages and Disadvantages of Each Tendency

INDIRECT

Indirectness has the benefit of managing conflict tactfully. Indirect speakers work hard to frame their communication in a way that avoids overt conflict while subtly getting the point across. Indirect communicators are experts at identifying subtexts and subtle signs of emotion and responding effectively. They are also good at managing interpersonal relationships on teams when nerves are frayed, and they can be relied on to handle difficult situations with tact and diplomacy.

On the other hand, the complex maneuverings of Indirect speakers take more time, and their lack of clarity can cause confusion, especially in intercultural interactions. Direct colleagues may miss subtle expressions of disagreement, while indirect speakers who seem to say "yes" but don't follow through may be perceived as unreliable or untruthful.

Their behind-the-scenes methods of gaining support for their ideas may seem devious, and Direct speakers may perceive them as manipulative or passive-aggressive.

Indirect speakers may be easily hurt, too. They can feel insulted by honest criticism of their ideas and, rather than risk more unpleasantness, may withdraw and refuse to participate.

DIRECT

Directness has the advantage of clarity and efficiency. Direct speakers' opinions are easy to understand because they are stated openly. Because they consider people to be separate from their ideas, Direct speakers voice criticism freely and accept critiques of their own ideas without feeling personally attacked. Misunderstandings are sorted out quickly, and adjustments and improvements are made rapidly. Direct speakers are good at getting to the bottom of problems, and on a team they can be relied on to take action.

At the same time, Direct communicators' overt self-expression may be seen as pushy and overbearing by less Direct counterparts. Their ready criticism of others' ideas may cause offense, while they may express impatience with the more elaborate strategy needed to communicate with Indirect colleagues. Because they are unused to looking for subtext, Direct speakers may miss subtleties and ignore tactful signals of disagreement or frustration. In an Indirect context, Direct communication may be perceived as tactless and uncouth.

Synergistic Potential

Teams and partnerships that successfully integrate these two tendencies benefit from the clarity and efficiency of Direct individuals and the interpersonal sensitivity of their Indirect colleagues. Direct members can appreciate the Indirect adeptness at recognizing subtle signs of disagreement, avoiding resentment, and managing sensitive issues tactfully, while Indirect members can look to Direct counterparts to introduce difficult topics and clear up confusion.

Analysis: The Good Idea

Werner Hess's Direct perspective leads him to assume that Kenji will be comfortable telling him what he thinks of the new ad campaign. He's used to receiving frank appraisals of his ideas, which he doesn't take personally; he and his colleagues frequently debate one another's suggestions in order to reach the best solution, giving and taking criticism without offense. He considers this sort of joint exercise most efficient and would be surprised to learn that others find it excessively confrontational.

Kenji Tanaka's perspective is very different. In his company, developing new initiatives and preparing them for broader discussion is handled largely outside of formal meetings. Once a new idea is sufficiently vetted, it can be discussed and modified during formal meetings without debate, an elegant solution that avoids conflict. Introducing a new approach without advance preparation would be considered risky and confrontational.

The meeting with Werner was excruciating for Kenji because the normal methods of introducing an idea behind the scenes hadn't been used. When Werner blurted out his request for a "yes" or "no," Kenji faced the prospect of humiliating Werner with his negative reaction. He did his best to be polite, conveying through body language and tone of voice that the response was negative so that Werner could withdraw the proposal on his own and avoid losing face.

But Werner didn't get the message. His manager's subsequent call was a shock. The Tokyo office had assumed that the matter was closed, and the phone call caused further embarrassment. Kenji's manager, Mr. Hashimoto, was forced to say outright that the ad campaign was inappropriate for Japan. This sort of unsophisticated communication was painful and embarrassing, and Mr. Hashimoto assumed that Werner's manager, Mr. Fischer, would apologize for the misunderstanding. Instead, Mr. Fischer insinuated that Kenji had made promises he had not kept, an insulting suggestion that left Mr. Hashimoto furious.

This sort of exchange is common between Direct and Indirect entities. One side feels that it can't get clarity or an honest answer, while the other feels that it is constantly forced into embarrassing or humiliating exchanges.

Cultural Dimension 2: Emotion

Scenario 2: Just Being Friendly

When Teresa González was first notified about her assignment in Prague, she called her mother and two brothers immediately to tell them the exciting news. Teresa's first assignment outside her native Argentina would be the Golden City! But now that she's been there a while, Teresa feels less excited. The museums and architecture are all that she expected, but she feels unable to connect with the Czechs she's met in her work.

Before she left, Teresa imagined all the friends she would make in Prague. She was sure that her natural friendliness and enthusiasm would be huge assets, and she's made every effort to engage the Czechs she's met. But her coworkers seem to regard her as a little strange, and a few even seem to avoid her. She doesn't understand it. During her first week of work, when she saw someone she knew in the coffee room each morning, she would smile and wave and call out to them cheerfully. But instead of returning her enthusiastic greeting, people seemed to cringe a little. She noticed that Czechs were subdued when they greeted each other, shaking hands and smiling a bit, but talking in low voices and moving quickly on to their work. Teresa was used to kissing friends on the cheek, with big hugs for close friends. But no matter how hard she tried to engage them with questions about themselves and their families, her Czech colleagues typically wanted to end the discussion sooner than she did. Teresa soon noticed that she was always the loudest person in the group.

Teresa wonders whether the company culture of the Prague office might be responsible. The managers there seem grim and reserved—maybe they're intimidating her colleagues. She asks her supervisor, Helena Nováková what she thinks of company morale. Helena proudly points out that the company just won an award for being one of the top employers in Prague. She is astonished by Teresa's concerns and adds that people outside the company are just as quiet. Teresa must acknowledge that this is true; people seem to talk in a reserved manner everywhere she goes, and strangers appear to dislike her exuberance as much as her coworkers do. Later that day, during an animated conversation on her cell phone, she notices a small group of bystanders staring at her with disapproval. She has observed that Czechs don't talk on their phones much in public, so maybe that was the problem.

Helena has seemed friendly enough up to now, but during a coffee break the next day, she takes the opportunity to tell Teresa that she would benefit by working more and talking less. Her constant attempts to engage her colleagues in conversation are causing concern that she isn't serious about her work, and her loud comments and "wild" hand gestures are out of place in a business environment. Teresa is horrified. The quality of her work has never been criticized before, and she can't believe that being pleasant is damaging her reputation. Czechs are just unfriendly, she decides. You can't make friends with them, and there's no point in trying.

Emotion Tendencies: Neutral and Expressive

Scenario 2 illustrates conflict arising from differing perspectives on the **Emotion** dimension. The cultural tendencies that characterize this dimension are *Neutral* and *Expressive*. These tendencies describe the degree of emotion people convey in interaction. People with a Neutral orientation don't make their feelings and emotions obvious. They use minimal gestures and facial expressions and a moderate tone of voice. Problems are discussed with close friends and are not communicated in business situations. An example is Sweden, where public self-expression is muted and "bringing problems to work" is considered unprofessional.

Expressives convey their feelings and emotions clearly. They use active gestures and facial expressions, and their tone of voice varies with their feelings about a topic. Problems are discussed publicly and may be communicated in business situations. An example is Egypt, where friends kiss on the cheek and people talk about personal problems openly in the workplace, sometimes becoming emotional and suspending work to discuss them.

CHARACTERISTICS OF THE EMOTION TENDENCIES

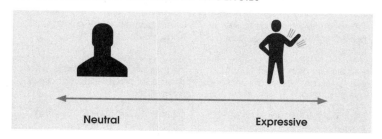

Neutral   Expressive

Perspectives, Motivation, and Goals	
Neutral	**Expressive**
Emotional displays are perceived as unprofessional and indicating immaturity or a lack of self-control.	Controlled emotions are interpreted as a lack of commitment or engagement.
People interact in a way that shows dignity and avoids disturbing others.	People interact in a way that helps people connect, meet emotional needs, and get their own needs met.
Showing one's feelings is seen as risky as it may give others an advantage.	Hiding one's feelings is seen as unfriendly, devious, or closed-minded.
The emphasis is on equity, mutual competition, and performance.	The emphasis is on equality, solidarity, and quality of life.
Behavior and Communication	
Physical contact and strong body language are avoided.	Physical contact and strong body language are common.
A moderate tone of voice and body language are used during disagreement.	Participants become animated when disagreement surfaces.
People listen quietly and may perceive interruption as offensive.	People enjoy brainstorming and speak enthusiastically, at times overlapping with others.

4

Neutral	Expressive
Open-ended questions are paired with controlled body language.	Direct questions are asked with enthusiasm.
People are comfortable with silence in conversation and may use it to think.	People are uncomfortable with silence in conversation and will try to fill it.
Direct confrontation is avoided and little feedback is given.	Confrontational and challenging actions are commonplace and overt feedback is provided.
People tend not to express what they are thinking or feeling, sticking to facts or logic.	People speak freely about ideas, opinions, and feelings.
Participants tend to move towards goals in a linear manner.	Participants show empathy and understanding of other's position, changing course as needed.
Organizational Structures and Processes	
Rewards and promotions are tied to job performance.	Rewards and promotions are tied to interpersonal effectiveness.

Note that in some countries, a neutral demeanor is considered appropriate for the workplace, and even people who are naturally quite expressive will appear neutral while at work. In more social contexts, their expressive nature will be more evident.

Advantages and Disadvantages of Each Tendency

NEUTRAL

Neutral people remain calm in the face of crisis and separate facts from feelings when they make decisions. They work quietly without a great deal of fanfare, allowing others to focus without interruption. They tend to keep their problems to themselves and get things done with little drama. They are good at sorting out problems in a crisis.

However, people with strong Neutral tendencies can also seem cold and distant, and their lack of expression may be perceived as a lack of engagement. They can be difficult to read, making Expressives feel insecure and uncertain about their opinions and motives. On an Expressive team, Neutrals may contribute less than others, especially if they are also Indirect.

EXPRESSIVE

Expressive people are easy to read and understand. They don't hold back their emotions, so it's easy to recognize their mood. They tend to enliven meetings and often will articulate problems that Neutrals feel uncomfortable mentioning. By providing the social "glue" that holds a team together, they can help resolve conflict.

At the same time, Expressives can unintentionally dominate conversations by "overcontributing." Often uncomfortable with silence, they may fill pauses by talking. Neutral colleagues sometimes feel there is no "space" to participate, and constant conversation may overwhelm people who need quiet to think. Neutral counterparts may be insulted by the Expressive tendency to interrupt, and energy and enthusiasm may be perceived as immaturity or a lack of self-control. Their preference for physical closeness or touching may be inappropriate in Neutral contexts. Expressives who are also Direct may come off as overbearing.

Synergistic Potential

Integrating Expressiveness with Neutrality yields partnerships that are both dynamic and controlled, with all members contributing value. Expressive participants can be relied on to create an energetic dynamic and get discussions going, while trusting their Neutral colleagues to help keep them focused and realistic.

Analysis: Just Being Friendly

Teresa González's outgoing style worked well for her in her native Argentina, but the more Neutral Czechs were unprepared for her exuberant behavior. Teresa equated friendliness with overt shows of enthusiasm and did her best to express goodwill by approaching colleagues in an energetic manner. Her waving and calling out to colleagues in public seemed to her a normal way of indicating her happiness to see them, and she failed to understand their embarrassed reactions.

Although they may be quite dedicated to their work, people with Expressive tendencies feel a need to connect with others at an emotional level and tend to socialize on the job. They value sharing details of their lives with colleagues, take time to reconnect after weekends or holidays, and congratulate or sympathize with coworkers, even if it means working a little later to finish a project. They expect frequent interpersonal interaction in both work and casual environments.

Neutral colleagues can seem cold, boring, and difficult to read to their Expressive counterparts, who are unused to deciphering what others are thinking. The lack of feedback from her colleagues caused Teresa to behave more demonstratively in an effort to elicit a response, which, unfortunately, just made them withdraw further.

Teresa's Neutral coworkers found her rather appalling. The first time she hugged Helena, her supervisor, Helena was so startled that she almost shoved her away. People with Neutral tendencies may consider exuberant shows of emotion childish and suspect that extreme Expressives lack self-control. Teresa's colleagues found her constant questions about their lives and families inappropriate and intrusive. They felt that such discussions were out of place at work, where a serious, businesslike demeanor is more appropriate. And, in addition to seeming a little hysterical, Teresa's behavior was considered annoying at times. Loud phone conversations and public displays of emotion can be seen as a breach of etiquette in Neutral environments and considered rude, selfish, or immature. In spite of her solid work, these factors caused Teresa's colleagues to question her competence.

5

The Cooperation Dimensions

The three cultural dimensions described in this chapter, Status, Involvement, and Collaboration, explain the way people cooperate at the individual, group, and organizational level. Different attitudes toward Status can result in confusion about hierarchy and reporting structures. Differing approaches to Involvement can make it hard for teams and companies to form and maintain relationships. And when norms for Collaboration aren't shared, there will be different expectations for how groups are organized, processes are implemented, and team members connect with one another. The Cooperation dimensions cause problems for collaboration at every level, from small projects to corporate mergers and acquisitions. Modifying policies and procedures to meet the needs of a particular project or relationship can ease tensions and greatly improve group dynamics.

Cultural Dimension 3: Status

Scenario 3: No Match for Me

Manolo Cárdenas is proud of his work at Sandoval Pharmaceuticals. His undergraduate degree from Universidad de Chile, the country's most prestigious university, has served him well in creating ties with potential customers. Over the years, he has held positions in a variety of functional areas at Sandoval, and at age fifty-three he can expect a promotion to vice president before he retires. His colleagues consider him to be the embodiment of Sandoval ideals, and in recognition of his experience and judgment, he's been named head of a negotiating team to manage a joint venture with a Norwegian company, Albertsen Orthotics. The partnership will design a next-generation orthotics product using technology developed by Albertsen.

Manolo thoroughly understands his own company's mission and approach. For the joint venture's design project, he expects to rely on junior people for input on technical and financial aspects; his own specialty is fitting the project into Sandoval's corporate vision. He's proud of this prestigious assignment and the responsibility it involves, and he looks forward to working with a Norwegian counterpart—a senior colleague like himself who can teach him about business and culture there.

Manolo's counterpart at Albertsen, Bergit Folstad, has been very busy lately. A thirty-two-year-old PhD in biomechanics, she's moved up quickly at Albertsen, where she recently led two of the company's most successful product design projects. An acknowledged expert in her field, she was the obvious choice to negotiate the joint development project with Sandoval. Having been with Albertsen for only two years, she is proud to have earned their trust, and she feels well positioned to make informed decisions about the complex technical aspects of the project. As long as the two companies' technologies can successfully mesh, she reasons, she can work out other details without too much trouble.

But trouble quickly ensues. To begin with, Bergit is surprised to learn that her counterpart holds only an undergraduate degree in biology and has spent the past eight years in marketing. In fact, he's never had responsibility for a technical project. And once negotiations begin, her fears are confirmed—he has almost no technical knowledge of the product they're designing together. She can't understand why Sandoval would send a bureaucrat to supervise a technical project, and she wonders whether the Chilean partner really understands what they're committing to.

Manolo is equally upset. He is appalled at his negotiating partner. She's young and inexperienced in his opinion, and has been with her company for only two years. What's more, she's just a technical person with a very narrow area of expertise. What could she know about the history or structure of the pharmaceutical industry, or her company's relationships with its customers? He's outraged that Albertsen would match his seniority, rank, and experience with this "whiz kid." Are they trying to insult him? From their first meeting, Bergit has behaved aggressively, constantly asking questions and voicing unrequested opinions. She seems to have no respect for his seniority or position. He really doesn't know how he can work with her.

Status Tendencies: Achievement and Endowment

Scenario 3 illustrates conflict arising from differing perspectives on **Status**. The cultural tendencies associated with how people gain status are *Achievement* and *Endowment*. In Achievement-oriented environments, an individual's personal accomplishments and track record are the basis of status. An example is the way U.S. audiences embrace athletes and celebrities who have achieved recent success and move on to new ones once they decline.

5

In Endowment environments, status is based on inherent characteristics such as family name, wealth, influential connections, political affiliation, ethnic background, gender, or age. Personal accomplishments are less important than in Achievement environments. An example is India, where social and occupational castes play an important role when it comes to education, marriage, and professional advancement.

CHARACTERISTICS OF THE STATUS TENDENCIES

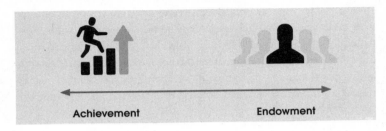

Perspectives, Motivation, and Goals	
Achievement	**Endowment**
Respect is earned by demonstrating professional competence and achieving results.	Respect is bestowed on people from prestigious backgrounds and those with high-level connections or seniority.
People's perceived value derives from their talent, initiative, and accomplishments.	People's perceived value is based on their influence with others due to seniority, connections, and credentials.
An individual's history of accomplishing important goals determines the amount of respect they receive.	Titles, indicating status and position in the organization, determine the amount of respect individuals receive.
People strive to accomplish relevant objectives to improve their status over time.	High-level people strive to live up to the status bestowed upon them; others do their best within the limitations of their status.
Older managers are suspected of being out of touch.	Young leaders are perceived as lacking in experience and sophistication.
High-level people may feel impatient with counterparts who have connections or seniority rather than expertise.	High-level people may feel insulted when paired with talented counterparts who lack seniority or lineage.

Behavior and Communication	
Achievement	**Endowment**
Names are used more than titles during interaction. First names may be used from the beginning.	Titles (Dr., Ms., Director General) and last names are used during interaction.
Juniors and seniors interact freely and as relative equals.	Juniors show deference; seniors take the role of mentor.
Each party may speak at length on topics they are knowledgeable about.	Juniors speak less; seniors' comments are viewed as more valuable.
Input is designed to convey information efficiently; feelings are secondary.	Input is designed to honor age and titles; superiors' mistakes aren't pointed out.
Presentations emphasize concrete examples and data.	Presentations emphasize history and context.
Content is valued over style; the terms of the deal are more important than interpersonal relations.	Style is valued over content; conveying appropriate respect is a critical aspect of cementing a deal.
High-level people may acknowledge areas of weakness and ask others for input.	High-level people are expected to be knowledgeable and avoid admitting areas of weakness.
Organizational Structures and Processes	
Promotion to managerial positions depends largely on track record.	The majority of managers are older men.
Employees are expected to take personal initiative.	Employees are expected to follow instructions.
Employees bear responsibility and receive credit for results.	Seniors bear full responsibility and take credit for results.
Decision making is decentralized.	Decision making is centralized.
Teams are led by subject matter specialists and experts.	Teams are led by people with seniority and cross-functional experience.

5

Achievement	Endowment
Rewards are based on performance.	Rewards are based on position and seniority.
Job descriptions and evaluation criteria are specific and detailed.	Job descriptions and evaluation criteria are general and fluid.
Pay is a function of performance and skill acquisition.	Pay is a function of growth through promotion.
There is limited distinction between levels of status other than salary.	Status comes with benefits (e.g., company car, expense account, and executive gym).
Skills and performance are rewarded financially soon after results.	Company loyalty is rewarded financially over the long term.
People leverage new skills by changing employers frequently, increasing their salaries each time.	People increase their salaries through promotions within a company. Changing employers may be difficult or impossible.
Within a company, bonds are loose, with junior members changing teams as new opportunities present themselves.	Within a company, factions are common, and when a senior mentor loses favor, their protégés may suffer as well.
Family hiring and promotion are perceived as risky and nepotistic. Family-run businesses are uncommon.	Family hiring and promotion are perceived as a source of loyalty and continuity. Family-run businesses are common.

Advantages and Disadvantages of Each Tendency

ACHIEVEMENT

Achievement leaders have made their way to the top through ability and initiative and are likely to be intelligent and motivated. They tend to be egalitarian as managers and provide incentives to their subordinates to meet company goals. Achievement employees work hard to distinguish themselves and move up the ladder by making strong contributions.

At the same time, young leaders who are successful in one area may be moved quickly into new positions where they have little knowledge or ability. Older employees' experience may be disregarded in favor of youthful energy, resulting in a loss of institutional memory. Opportunities for rapid advancement may cause employees to compete with their teammates and managers rather than cooperate with them. Endowment colleagues may resent their assertive demeanor and conspicuous displays of success.

ENDOWMENT

Endowment leaders use the influence associated with their birth or personal connections to benefit their employers. They take mentoring seriously and carefully cultivate their juniors. They tend to be sophisticated, well educated, and diplomatic. Endowment team members are respectful and loyal and work hard for their superiors in order to earn their favor.

However, people may move into top positions through seniority or prestigious affiliations rather than motivation or talent. Privileged leaders may consider themselves above the rules that apply to others and treat subordinates with disdain. Talented employees who are young or lack connections may become frustrated, and companies may suffer from stagnant management that lacks vigor and innovation.

Synergistic Potential

Integrating Achievement and Endowment tendencies enables organizations to reap the benefits of both experience and vigor. They can count on energetic Achievers to advance ambitious proposals, which can be honed and polished through the insights of experienced Endowment members to prevent youthful mistakes. A balance between vertical and egalitarian reporting structures gives all members a chance to contribute, maximizing loyalty and avoiding excessive jockeying for position.

Analysis: No Match for Me

Manolo Cárdenas comes from an Endowment-oriented environment. The sources of his self-esteem and prestige at Sandoval are his family background, which made it possible for him to attend top schools; the connections he made at university; and his wise use of these advantages. The gray hair he's acquiring at age fifty-three is a source of added status that earns him deference and respect, both socially and in business. He has built a reputation based on his many years of work for his employer, and he has used his personal influence to benefit the company and society as well. He oversees Sandoval's corporate giving to charity and serves on the board of a national museum. He's proven himself worthy of his privileged lifestyle and increased his prestige and influence throughout his life. He's proud of his family name and his role in maintaining its status.

Sandoval's top management chose Mr. Cárdenas based on his seniority and experience, a typical approach for Endowment companies. He doesn't pretend to be a technical expert—personal connections and big-picture acumen are what make him valuable to the company. He can draw on the expertise of junior employees who specialize in technical fields if he needs to. He expected to be paired with a counterpart of similar social standing and experience—someone he could relate to and create a lasting relationship with. In his company, young employees—no matter how talented and skilled—wait their turn as they learn the ropes while being mentored by senior managers. Management notes their progress and assigns more prestigious assignments later in their careers. The wise ones accept senior managers' instructions graciously and avoid direct challenges to their authority, since advancement is based largely on management's opinion. However impatient they might be, trying to rush things would be inappropriate. In any case, it would be unnatural and demoralizing for employees to have a boss younger than themselves.

Bergit Folstad is from an Achievement-oriented environment where talent and initiative have boosted her career, short though it has been. Her intelligence and competence set her apart early on, and she was able to get an excellent education despite coming from a lower-class family. In fact, her modest background motivated her to achieve so much so soon and helped make her such an outstanding producer. And her employer's policies and structure made it easy for her to move ahead. Bergit was hired to fill a position where responsibilities were clearly articulated. She was told what percentage of her time she was expected to devote to each type of activity. Between scheduled performance reviews, her compensation was based on her performance relative to clearly defined objectives. In this environment, Bergit worries little about cultivating relationships—what matters is execution, something she excels at.

Albertsen is happy to reward Bergit's productivity because its management wants to keep her as long as possible. In Achievement-oriented business environments, expertise like Bergit's is highly valued, and employees may be hired in at any point in their careers. Each assignment will add to her skill and expertise, and Albertsen can be sure that competitors will try to lure her away. Bergit's management wants to keep her motivated and challenged, and since her expertise fits well with the Sandoval project, she's the obvious choice. Achievement companies tend to choose team leaders on the basis of subject expertise rather than company experience, and Bergit's technical knowledge and product design skills make her an excellent candidate for the project.

Bergit is aware of Mr. Cárdenas's reaction to her. Whatever his objection is, surely the way to overcome it is by establishing her credentials. She addresses this problem in typical Achievement fashion, by engaging him in conversation and striving to demonstrate her competence. At their first meeting, she mentions her past successes in an effort to impress him. That same night, she sends him an article she wrote on a technology relevant to the project. Unfortunately, this strategy just makes things worse.

From Mr. Cárdenas's perspective, the issue is not whether Bergit is technically competent. Seniority and experience, not technical competence, are what makes someone a leader, and he perceives her as an upstart. Given her age and gender, he feels that she should defer to his seniority rather than showing off her knowledge, and her attempts to impress him fall flat.

Of course, Bergit isn't without prejudice, either. Mr. Cárdenas is below her in terms of education and expertise, the things she values most highly. From her perspective, he's risen up the ranks just by sticking around for thirty years—not much of a career in her opinion. She doubts whether he's qualified to manage the complexities of the deal and finds it easier to talk to the technical people he brings with him when they meet.

Cultural Dimension 4: Involvement

Scenario 4: Making Friends

Ji-Won Park had really looked forward to her Houston assignment. The chance to live in the United States for a year, travel, and make new friends seemed like a dream come true. But six months into her assignment, the experience isn't exactly what she was hoping for. She doesn't feel she's made any real friends and cannot understand how Americans think. She misses her friends and family back in Korea, where she always had someone to talk to.

Being called "Ji-Won" by virtual strangers felt very odd, but Ms. Park accepted the American use of her first name to fit in, and things seemed to go very well at first. Texas has a reputation for friendliness, and the Americans she worked with seemed outgoing—even excessively so. They smiled at strangers on the street, chatted in line at the grocery store, and said "thank you" constantly to waiters in restaurants. Everyone seemed to interact freely and have many friends. Ji-Won was excited about meeting new people and developing close ties with her coworkers. At the Seoul office of her employer, the employees were like a family. They knew each other's spouses and the details of their daily lives. They spent time together after work as well, going out for meals or drinks and exercising at a local gym. When her boss moved to a new house, he asked the office staff to help with the move. Although Ji-Won could have found other things to do with her morning, she was willing to make the effort. The boss is the boss, and anyway, she and her coworkers expected to help one another out with projects and problems. She understands that work and private life can't be separated, and she doesn't think they should be, given the amount of time people spend together in the workplace.

At least that's Ji-Won's opinion. The Americans she works with seem to see things differently. Their friendliness appears to be on the surface. At work, they talk little about their family lives or personal problems. They focus on the task at hand and only interact to discuss business issues. When work is over each day, they hurry home. Ji-Won tried to make friends with Rebecca, who works with her in marketing. But Rebecca is busy with activities of her own—playing tennis with one group of people, knowing another through her son's school, and going sailing on the weekends with friends from her church. At home, these are things Ji-Won would do with a single, close-knit group of people. Rebecca did invite Ji-Won to her sailing class, but Ji-Won doesn't enjoy sailing. She's joined a gym but feels uncomfortable striking up a conversation with strangers the way Americans seem to do, and she hasn't made a single close friend.

Ji-Won complains to Rebecca that her coworkers aren't as warm as in Korea. Rebecca seems surprised that she even cares. "Why would you want to hang around with people from the office anyway?" she asks. "We see enough of these people at work. I want to choose my own friends!" Ji-Won is discouraged. She can't understand the way Americans think about relationships.

Involvement Tendencies: Network and Process

Scenario 4 illustrates conflict arising from differing perspectives on **Involvement**. The cultural tendencies that characterize the Involvement dimension are *Network* and *Process*. They describe the relative importance of relying on deep personal relationships vs. moving through a process to meet personal goals and accomplish tasks.

Network-oriented people cultivate deep relationships as a kind of currency used to get things done. They invest heavily in other people they can call on for help, and whom they help in return. They make friends slowly and choose them carefully, since they will introduce their new contacts to others in their existing network and keep them for a lifetime. In Network-oriented environments, close friendships often date back to childhood, and the line between corporate and personal relationships is blurred. Managers may hire relatives and give friends their business, and they expect similar favors in return. People with Network tendencies make decisions based on how they affect the whole network.

In Network environments, relationships are consistent across contexts—the boss is always the boss, no matter where an encounter takes place. Partnerships are based on trust and developed with caution over time. Chinese organizations are known for their Network orientation and insisting on a lengthy getting-to-know-you period while parties size one another up as future partners.

For Process-oriented people, relationships are casual and based on shared interests. Although they will have a core group of very close friends, they may have many casual friends among various social groups, and they may lose contact with current friends if they move away or change hobbies. In Process environments, policies promoting workplace fairness prohibit basing decisions on relationships. Since friendship doesn't require the exchange of favors, it's less risky. People make new friends easily and are more apt to interact with strangers.

Organizational roles don't extend outside the workplace, and people's relative status depends on the situation—an employee might have higher standing than her boss in a social organization she chairs, for example. Partnerships are developed based on shared goals among the parties, and organizations protect their interests through carefully worded agreements rather than relationships. In Process-oriented Canada, for example, partnerships advance quickly on the basis of contracts, which can be extended if shared interests continue.

CHARACTERISTICS OF THE INVOLVEMENT TENDENCIES

Perspectives, Motivation, and Goals	
Network	Process
People and groups prefer to build relationships first and then consider doing business.	People and groups go quickly to business discussions; personal connections matter little.

Network	Process
Social interaction with partners is important. Relationships are built through personal interactions such as dinner invitations and personal questions.	Lengthy social and personal discussions are considered inappropriate in professional contexts.
People demonstrate reliability by developing common ground with potential partners.	People demonstrate reliability by highlighting their organization's performance and track record.
Employees have personal relationships with one another and perceive their workplace as a community.	Employees have casual relationships with one another and a contractual relationship with their employer.
Representatives emphasize the history of their organization and its function as a social group.	Representatives emphasize objective aspects of their organization's performance such as numbers and financial data.
Relationships and seniority transcend legal structures in ensuring job security—being liked is the best insurance.	Legal structures and performance are the most important factors in job security; relationships and seniority are no insurance.
Work relationships extend outside the workplace, and relative status of coworkers is maintained across contexts.	Relative status of coworkers is situational and depends on the context.
Behavior and Communication	
Meetings begin with lengthy social preliminaries, and participants get down to business afterward.	Meetings begin with business discussions, and participants socialize afterward if time permits.
Presentations begin with context, followed by a conclusion and summary.	Presentations begin with a summary, followed by details.
Presentations may ramble. Speakers digress from the agenda to accommodate the questions and interests of all concerned.	Presentations are linear. Speakers stick to agendas to accomplish business efficiently.

5

Network	Process
Participants expect to spend time on connected topics because all are related.	Participants expect to address principal topics specifically and individually.
Speakers persuade through storytelling and engaging the audience at a personal level.	Speakers persuade through logical arguments that convince the audience.
Speakers give complex responses, explaining history and nuances before stating the conclusion.	Speakers give concise answers, followed by nuanced explanations if asked for more information.
People socialize with close friends in a variety of contexts and maintain them throughout their lives.	People socialize with various groups based on shared interests and activities and change friends as their interests evolve.
Smiles, eye contact, and personal information are reserved for friends.	Strangers interact relatively freely and make new, casual friends easily.
People are careful about making new friends, who will have the right to call on them for favors.	Friends have few rights over one another, so new friendships pose little risk.
Face-to-face interaction is considered most effective.	Phone calls or e-mail are considered most efficient.
Organizational Structures and Processes	
Companies establish little bureaucracy; there are few rigid rules.	Companies establish administrative structures and systems with rules and controls.
Meetings are loosely structured because everything is related and there are many ways to reach objectives.	Meetings are tightly structured because the goal is to move in a straight path towards objectives.
Hiring practices may prioritize personal affiliations such as relationships with company executives, a common educational background or hometown, or relatives in the company.	Hiring practices prioritize skills, education, and credentials relative to specific positions. Care is taken not to give any candidate an unfair advantage.

Network	Process
Professional relationships are maintained outside work through social interaction.	Social needs are met largely outside the workplace.
Seniors may presume on juniors to perform support duties outside of work.	Juniors have no responsibility to seniors outside of work.
Financial incentives are based on the strength of relationships and contextual factors, such as number of dependents.	Financial incentives are based on performance relative to clearly defined expectations.
Companies may address employee needs by providing housing or compensation for personal hardship.	Companies support all employees equally, primarily through salary and related financial benefits.

5

Advantages and Disadvantages of Each Tendency

NETWORK

Because they need to know and trust the people they deal with, Network-oriented companies and individuals take partnership seriously and can be counted on to do their share once they have committed. Network team members are good at providing the social lubricant necessary for a smooth team dynamic. In communication, their awareness of context and external factors can help prevent single-minded thinking. Employees' performance is evaluated in the context of their overall situation, facilitating compassionate treatment.

At the same time, it may take so long for Network-oriented organizations to reach the level of trust they require for collaboration that Process-oriented partners suspect they aren't truly committed. Network-oriented participants' inclination to socialize and digress can create inefficiencies in meetings, and their tendency to prioritize personal networks over rules and principles can lead to favoritism and legal irregularities.

PROCESS

Because they rely on legal structures rather than long-standing relationships to ensure the reliability of their partners, Process-oriented companies create and dissolve partnerships as needed for maximum flexibility. Their meetings are well organized and get quickly to the point, and their rational approach helps them come quickly to solid, fact-based decisions. Honoring rules and principles facilitates legal compliance and fair treatment for employees.

However, this focus on tasks and outcome can prevent Process-oriented teams and partnerships from bonding thoroughly. Because their business relationships are deal-based rather than deeply committed, partners may not support one another in difficult times. Since there is no strong social component in their team dynamics, Process-oriented members can reach stalemates when they disagree, and a heavy reliance on agendas and models can lead to inflexibility and difficulty adapting to fluid conditions.

Synergistic Potential

Integrating Network and Process tendencies results in closely knit organizations that accomplish work efficiently. Process-oriented procedures drive the action and keep discussions on target, while a Network-oriented atmosphere fosters cohesion and minimizes stalemates and disputes. Process-based policies ensure fairness and compliance, while Network-oriented systems engender loyalty and a sense of belonging. Parties to partnerships support each other through give-and-take in times of difficulty while upholding contractual obligations.

Analysis: Making Friends

Network-oriented Ji-Won Park expected that she would develop deep friendships among her coworkers in the United States based on their shared experience in the workplace. It was confusing to her that, although people appeared friendly and willing to engage, the deeper relationships she hoped for never seemed to develop. Network-oriented people tend to have a strong sense of privacy. They admit a relatively small number of people into their "inner circle" and spend a majority of their social time with this group, treating strangers as largely irrelevant, anonymous "others." Ji-Won's new colleagues' apparent friendliness struck her as insincere, as if interacting superficially with everyone but deeply with no one. Although Rebecca seemed willing to be friends with Ji-Won, her own social life was too fragmented to accommodate Ji-Won's desire for closeness, which left Ji-Won feeling hurt.

Process-oriented Rebecca was just as confused. She liked Ji-Won and tried to help her integrate into her social circle. But rather than take advantage of the outlets Rebecca suggested, Ji-Won seemed to want social opportunity to come to her and expect her colleagues to embrace her just because they work together. People with a Process orientation may have a few very close friends and family members that they rely on for deeply personal interaction, but they're accustomed to sharing various aspects of their lives with a diverse group of social partners based on their preferred activities. Since having children, Rebecca and her husband grew away from many of the couples they knew before becoming parents, socializing more with people whose children attended school with theirs. This feels natural, as they have more interests and problems in common with this group, at least for now. Process-oriented people strike up relationships with new people through "small talk" and shared activities. Rebecca didn't know how to help Ji-Won, who lacked these skills and seemed insecure and needy to her American colleagues.

Cultural Dimension 5: Collaboration

Scenario 5: Inside Scoop

Anne McCollough is the leader of a Canadian software design team working on a project with a team from her company's Japanese subsidiary. Anne is proud of her group and its work, and when the team leader from the Japanese partner comes to visit, she volunteers to show him around. The two teams haven't had much interpersonal interaction so far, and

Anne hopes to facilitate more efficient communication by helping them integrate.

Yamada-san is a young, friendly programmer from Tokyo. He seems interested in the work that the Canadians are doing, and Anne feels they're getting along well. During the morning, she gives Yamada-san a general tour of the company premises. Over lunch, the two discuss their families, work histories, and personal interests. Yamada-san seems impressed by the fact that Anne is a technical leader for her team, which consists mostly of men. He mentions being a fan of jazz music, and she suggests a nearby jazz club as well as a toy store where he can buy gifts for his children. She's working hard to be a good host.

After lunch, Anne and Mr. Yamada discuss their recent work on the project. To make her guest feel like more of an insider, Anne mentions a colleague's recent illness, the scheduling difficulties that has caused, and how everyone has pitched in to stay on schedule. To further indicate their cooperation and teamwork, she mentions that she's been staying late to help another team member who's working on a particularly difficult component. As the quality of their work clearly shows, the team executes well in the face of challenges, and Anne is very proud of this. To help Yamada-san feel that he knows each of her team members, Anne finishes by describing the excellent work two of them have recently done on a device driver. Now he knows the whole team. As he leaves, Anne feels that she's made a new friend.

When her manager asks to see her the following week, Anne is stunned at his news. The Japanese team manager called him to express concern about the lack of morale on the Canadian side. He's worried about Anne's lack of confidence in her coworkers and her indications of laziness and incompetence on her team. Under the circumstances, he feels it would be best if the team reported directly to him, and he's planning to request that her manager be removed from the project.

Anne is horrified. She can't understand how Mr. Yamada could have inferred such negative things from what she said. And regardless of anything he might have misunderstood from her comments, her team's excellent performance should speak for itself. She doesn't understand why her boss's leadership is being questioned and can't imagine how she could have been misinterpreted so completely.

Collaboration Tendencies: Independent and Group Orientations

Scenario 5 illustrates conflict arising from differing perspectives on **Collaboration**. The cultural tendencies of the Collaboration dimension—*Independent* and *Group*—describe the ways responsibility and reward are allocated, decisions are made, and teams interact internally and with one another.

In Independent groups, work is divided into smaller tasks assumed by individuals, who first work individually and combine their contributions afterward. Individuals receive credit or blame for the quality of their contribution. Individuals are often given decision-making authority. In the United States, for example, being acknowledged and rewarded for individual performance is considered an important motivator.

On Group-oriented teams, there is less division of responsibility, and the whole group receives credit or blame for project outcomes. People complete tasks in close proximity so they can be in constant contact. Decisions are made by consensus, and all group members must agree before moving forward. In Japan, a country with Group tendencies, work groups carefully maintain the appearance of equal contribution by all members, and singling out an individual for praise or criticism is considered inappropriate.

5

CHARACTERISTICS OF THE COLLABORATION TENDENCIES

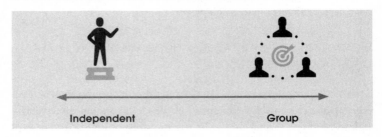

Independent   Group

Perspectives, Motivation, and Goals	
Independent	Group
Focus is on individual action, personality, talent, and achievement.	Focus is on group cohesion, mutual support, and contributing to group performance.
The performance of teams and companies is valued above all else. Internal friction may be tolerated if a team performs well.	Teams and companies carefully cultivate the appearance of harmony and consistency, which affects perceptions of their performance.
Turnover on teams is considered acceptable as long as replacements with equivalent skills can be found.	Turnover on teams is perceived as a sign of internal problems because loyalty and in-group experience are difficult to replace.
Behavior and Communication	
Individuals tend to speak for themselves, giving personal opinions and ideas.	People speak as group representatives, refraining from personal opinions. One member may be chosen to speak for the group.
People may speculate and hypothesize when in doubt.	People are likely to delay answering and seek confirmation when in doubt.
Being alone is considered peaceful, and constant interaction may be exhausting and overwhelming.	Spending time with others is considered healthy; working and eating alone may cause feelings of isolation.

Independent	Group
Individual preferences are emphasized. People make their own choices and express opinions freely.	The group dynamic is emphasized. Individuals forgo personal preferences and adopt the group position as their own.
Persuaders try to identify and influence individual opinion leaders or decision makers.	Persuaders present their case to all specialists present, assuming each will have a role in making the decision.
Nonconformity to norms and policies is tolerated and equated with uniqueness and creativity.	Conformity with norms and policies is valued, and nonconformity is equated with deviance and unreliability.
Team members tend to work individually and bring work together to integrate.	Team members tend to work together throughout a project.
Phone calls or e-mail are considered most efficient.	Face-to-face interaction is considered most effective.
Team boundaries are softened to allow groups to merge for joint projects.	Boundaries and formality between partnering teams are maintained.
Problems are mentioned early to partners to facilitate joint solutions.	Problems may be withheld from partners to preserve the team image.
Competence is demonstrated through superior results, and internal conflict and difficulty "make colorful stories."	Competence is demonstrated through an outward show of unity, and internal conflict is kept within the group.
Weak team members are easily spotted and replaced. Strong members rise quickly to leadership positions.	Weak team members are protected and nurtured to preserve the team dynamic. Strong members work to advance the team's success, waiting for promotion.
People tend to change companies and occupations in the course of their careers.	People tend to stay within established networks throughout their careers.

5

Organizational Structures and Processes	
Independent	**Group**
Responsibility for negotiation may be held by an individual who requests input from others at will.	People with expertise in relevant functional areas share negotiating responsibility.
Decisions are often made by individuals without consulting others. Implementation may be delayed while internal support is developed.	Decision making is consensual and involves checking frequently with others. Once made, decisions have internal support and are quickly implemented.
Teams are formed as needed to aggregate skills for particular projects and may not involve personal ties.	Teams cultivate strong internal relationships and bonds of trust, often lasting beyond projects.
Teams are considered vital to the organizational mission. High-performance teams capitalize on diverse skills and ideas.	Teams are considered vital to the organizational mission. Highly performing teams integrate diversity into a close-knit whole greater than the sum of its parts.
Individual targets are established, and each member has specific responsibilities.	Group targets are established, and all members are fully responsible.
Individuals are recognized and rewarded.	Groups are recognized and rewarded.
Performance-based pay is the norm.	Service- and seniority-based pay is the norm.
Individual review determines salaries.	Collective bargaining determines salaries.
Compensation is based on individual performance relative to predetermined targets.	Compensation is consistent across cohorts. Individual bonuses and commissions are avoided.
Technology innovations tend to come from specialists acting alone and are likely to be patented.	Technology innovations tend to be made within an existing company and are less likely to be patented.

Advantages and Disadvantages of Each Tendency

INDEPENDENT ORIENTATION

Independent-oriented employees move readily from one project team to the next throughout their careers, contributing their expertise on particular projects. Since collaboration doesn't require close ties between individuals, teams assemble quickly, and poor performers are easily recognized and replaced. Owing to their relatively weak team boundaries, Independent teams integrate comfortably with one another, exchanging information as needed for smooth collaboration. The appointed executives in Independent organizations make decisions quickly and efficiently.

On the other hand, poor decisions (more likely when negotiators are individuals) may cause internal conflict, delay implementation, or damage partnerships. Members of teams with a poor dynamic may focus more on personal advancement than the group result. Since individuals do more of their work alone, integrating contributions or covering for sick colleagues may be more difficult. In meetings with outsiders, Independent team members may express personal opinions rather than speaking for the group, which can cause confusion and give the impression of internal disorganization or disagreement.

GROUP ORIENTATION

Group-oriented teams invest heavily in developing internal bonds for maximum productivity. As members get to know each other over time, teamwork becomes increasingly efficient and productive. Because groups receive credit as a whole, individuals prioritize group results, with a minimum of self-interested behavior. Thanks to cross-functional interaction, members can pick up one another's work as needed. Team members speak in one voice "for the group," avoiding confusion. Decisions are quickly implemented, having been approved by all relevant parties beforehand.

Decision making itself in Group-oriented organizations is time-consuming, however, and delays may be misinterpreted by Independents as stalling or a lack of interest. Bold ideas may be weakened during the lengthy process of consensus building. In teamwork, a group's carefully maintained façade may hide poor individual performance and perpetuate weaknesses. Because they maintain strong group boundaries, teams may be mistrustful of their partners and refuse to share information. Group-oriented teams may also delay notifying collaborators of problems until the last minute, making it difficult for partners to assist them or redirect their efforts in a timely manner.

Synergistic Potential

On projects that integrate Independent and Group orientations, each team operates efficiently and cohesively on its own, while interfacing smoothly to share information and offer mutual support. Policies that support integration assist Independent teams in exhibiting a unified demeanor and help Group-oriented teams become comfortable working across boundaries and creating bonds with their partners.

Analysis: Inside Scoop

Anne McCollough's Independent orientation places relatively little emphasis on group boundaries. Most of the people on her team didn't know one another before this project, and they expect to eventually move on to other teams. They are committed to the quality of their own work and the ultimate product, but their group is a collection of individuals rather than a family. Independent teams tend to merge relatively easily with one another and expect strong information flow between collaborating teams, which is why Anne worked so hard to get to know Mr. Yamada.

Mr. Yamada had very different expectations. His team had worked together for three years, and as new projects came and went, the team remained in place. Group-oriented teams tend to be inwardly focused, and while individual members may make friends with members of other groups, boundaries between collaborating groups remain strong and information exchange is managed carefully. Group-oriented team members maintain an outward appearance of unity and harmony, and internal disagreements, problems, and variations in competence are carefully shielded from outward view. Dropping this façade is seen as a sign of serious problems—that things are so bad that group members can't even fake it. So although Anne's team performed very well from a technical perspective, the fact that she "aired her dirty laundry" to an outsider signaled to Mr. Yamada that things were really bad.

In highly Group-oriented environments, individuals receive equal credit regardless of their individual contribution. Managers know who their strongest employees are, and rewards await strong producers later in their careers. But singling someone out for praise or criticism is considered inappropriate. Anne breaks this rule when she mentions one team member's illness and another's need for help—and identifying the good work of two others is just as bad in Mr. Yamada's eyes, as it insults the rest of the team.

Anne is mistaken in thinking she can make Mr. Yamada feel like an insider, and he would be astonished to know this was her expectation. From his perspective, a good partner should remain a relatively unknown quantity, producing good work while maintaining a professional distance. The inside information he receives from Anne, far from reassuring him, convinces him that her team's functionality has broken down at the most basic level.

Given Mr. Yamada's experience, his report to his manager is not surprising. He's seen what appear to be indications of serious dysfunction. He doesn't know how the team managed to produce quality work under these circumstances, but surely they will not continue to do so, and it was his job to alert his manager to the problem. Since group morale is the leader's responsibility, the Canadian manager has clearly failed, and the obvious solution is to replace him.

5

6

The Structure Dimensions

The three dimensions discussed in this chapter, Authority, Action, and Organization, describe the approaches organizations and individuals take to planning and execution. Misalignment regarding Authority (how much structure is appropriate and how strictly legal agreements are enforced) can derail partnerships and strain teams. Differing norms for Action (the criteria for making decisions and moving forward) often lead to mismatches in strategy and timing. And conflicting approaches to Organization cause problems for planning and project management. Conflict on the Structure dimensions creates problems at every level of collaboration, but integrating differences yields partnerships that are both flexible and responsible with stable yet responsive strategies.

Cultural Dimension 6: Authority

Scenario 6: Managing Surprises

Ishani Arjan is baffled and indignant. In her twelve years working for Malik Engineering in Delhi, India, she's never encountered the kind of unfeeling inflexibility she's seeing in Malik's new Swiss partner. And it's not because she lacks international experience. She's negotiated deals with companies in Malaysia, China, Greece, and Mexico and considers herself quite knowledgeable about contract negotiation and management. But this new partner, Uster Controls, is unusually difficult, and as Malik's head negotiator, Ishani is responsible for sorting things out.

It all started during negotiations, she reflects. From the beginning, Uster's legal team seemed excessively thorough and rather impersonal—specifying practically every possible problem that could arise in the relationship and assigning a penalty for any delay. It seemed a bit ridiculous to Ishani, and became a sort of joke to her legal staff. Who could know all the things that might happen to delay the joint project? Between the weather, currency fluctuation, political shifts, and economic changes, there were just too many variables. That's why partners need to be flexible and work together, they reasoned. But it was clear that Uster was serious, and Ishani's management wanted the contract, so they proceeded with the detailed specifications. If things changed after signing, they could always renegotiate the terms. Or so she thought.

Uster's general counsel, Pascal Blattner, is astonished to get Ishani's call. Just three months after negotiating a sound contract, she's asking him to waive the penalty for late delivery of a critical component for Uster's most popular commercial refrigeration system. Delivery will be late, Ishani explains, because of transportation problems caused by a late monsoon season. She argues that the problem doesn't qualify as *force majeure*, since it's due in part to weak infrastructure, which isn't covered in the contract, and claims that the penalties outlined for late delivery will create hardship for the company if enforced. Pascal points out that Malik's negotiators agreed to the terms of the contract—there is really nothing more to discuss as far as he's concerned. If Malik didn't approve of the late delivery penalty, they shouldn't have signed in the first place. But Malik had not counted on the roads being closed in October, which is very unusual, Ishani explains, when they agreed to the contract. In the name of their partnership, she asks Uster to renegotiate the delivery terms. Otherwise, she says, Malik will suffer from the deal—a bad way to begin a new relationship.

Pascal is unimpressed. What about Uster's suffering from disappointing its customers? It's not Uster's fault that Malik failed to factor in monsoons. But of greater concern to him is Malik's lack of professionalism. In business, you must stand by your word, no matter how painful it might be. This will be a good lesson for Malik, he tells her. Next time, the company will know to make better decisions. In the meantime, it may suffer, but that's the nature of business.

Ishani is appalled. She'll have to relay this message to her managers, and they may question her judgment in authorizing the contract. She can't understand the rigidity of this new partner and wonders whether the collaboration is a mistake.

Authority Tendencies: Rule and Situation

Scenario 6 illustrates conflict arising from differing perspectives on the **Authority** dimension. The cultural tendencies that characterize attitudes toward authority are *Rule* and *Situation* orientations. Rule-oriented people believe that people should be respectful of rules and authority for everyone's benefit. They feel that breaking rules is irresponsible, and making exceptions sets dangerous precedents. Rule followers will obey rules they disagree with just to keep things stable and willingly follow them even when there is no supervision by authorities. Switzerland, where pedestrians wait for the signal to cross the road even when there is no traffic, has strong Rule tendencies.

Situation-oriented people believe in following rules selectively, based on the situation, and sometimes make exceptions. ("I'm in a hurry," "This is a silly rule," "I'll do it just this once.") They may refuse to follow a rule they consider pointless or one imposed by an authority they don't respect. In extreme cases, they may be suspicious of rules and authority in general. In Situation-oriented Russia, for example, rules are unlikely to be followed willingly unless people respect the given authority and accept the validity and necessity of the rules.

CHARACTERISTICS OF THE AUTHORITY TENDENCIES

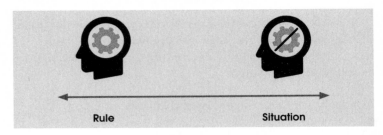

Rule   Situation

Perspectives, Motivation, and Goals	
Rule	Situation
Business deals proceed quickly and according to set guidelines.	Business deals take a long time to finalize and involve changes and surprises.
People follow rules and assume others will as well.	People break rules and expect others to do the same.
Business dealings are based on mutual benefit and are enforced legally.	Business dealings are only possible when strong supporting relationships are present, and these count more than legal agreements.
People tend to feel that there is only one truth or reality.	People tend to feel that there are multiple perspectives on reality.
Trustworthy people honor their promises.	Trustworthy people can be relied on to help when needed.
Rules, policies, and regulatory structures help avoid ambiguity and uncertainty.	Rules, policies, and regulatory structures may create unfair constraints and unnecessary complications.
Loyalty is earned by organizations with solid principles and reputations.	Loyalty is given to personal contacts rather than the organization itself.

Rule	Situation
Developing and enforcing legal agreements is the best way to manage risk.	Developing trusting relationships is the best way to manage risk and ensure that partners follow their promises.
Specific terms in contracts are needed to cover all possible contingencies.	Vague contract wording allows parties to adapt to the unexpected.
Contracts should be followed regardless of any changes in the business environment.	Partners should be responsive to changes in the business environment. Signed contracts should be modified if conditions require changes.
Behavior and Communication	
People follow even rules they dislike or consider pointless to maintain order.	People circumvent rules they dislike or consider pointless to assert their independence and meet their goals.
Unpopular rules are followed willingly, even without supervision or likelihood of detection.	Unpopular rules are followed only under supervision or likelihood of detection.
Rules are carefully applied to everyone to ensure equal treatment and avoid resentment.	Friends, family, or high-status people receive preferential treatment to maintain social structure and relationships.
Meetings begin and end according to schedule.	People may arrive late. Meetings end when business is concluded.
People may become suspicious that their time is being wasted in drawn-out business dealings.	People may become suspicious that the other party is hiding something when business is rushed.
Negotiators stick close to their targets when making offers and conclude agreements when terms are acceptable.	Negotiators may "high-ball" or "low-ball" when making offers and come back at the end of a deal to seek additional concessions.

6

Organizational Structures and Processes	
Rule	**Situation**
Organizations strive for consistency and uniform procedures when dealing with all constituencies.	Organizations build informal networks and create special deals for some constituencies.
There is a relatively high degree of bureaucracy; rules are followed and enforced.	There may be a relatively low degree of bureaucracy—where rules do exist, they may be ignored.
Procedures are centralized throughout an organization.	Branches have greater autonomy.
Organizational representatives behave according to rules and procedures.	Organizational representatives have relatively great freedom to improvise.
Job descriptions are specific and detailed to ensure fairness.	Job descriptions are general to allow for flexibility.
Employees complete work according to specific criteria.	Employees contribute wherever needed.
Promotion is based on performance.	Promotion is based on fit with the team and relationship with the supervisor.

Advantages and Disadvantages of Each Tendency

RULE

Because they value stability so highly, people from Rule-oriented environments impart order in everything they do. They are dependable and work hard to avoid missing an obligation. They come prepared to meetings and keep careful track of their progress on projects. They take rules seriously and adhere to the letter as well as the spirit of the law. They are reliable about fulfilling contractual obligations, and they expect the same from others.

At the same time, since Rule-oriented team members tend to operate in structured, predictable environments, they may have difficulty adapting to more fluid contexts. Minor rule breaking by a partner may be interpreted as unreliability or evidence of unethical tendencies. Rule-oriented corporations may be heavily bureaucratic and contractual. They may react slowly to changing conditions and fail to understand the need for flexibility with partners that operate in less stable environments.

SITUATION

Because they tend to value relationships and outcomes over rules, Situation-oriented team members are master problem solvers. They do well in fluctuating conditions, using interpersonal networks to work around problems. They are experts at finding ways around rules that are unfair or pointless. They change directions easily, demonstrating flexibility in the face of challenges. Situation-oriented companies are willing to make sacrifices for their partners to maintain relationships that will serve them in the long term.

At the same time, Situation-oriented team members may have difficulty with structure and bureaucracy, ignoring rules and procedures whose purpose they don't understand or value. They may circumvent rules to repay a favor or give preferential treatment to friends or family members. Situation-oriented companies may take contracts less seriously than Rule-oriented partners, expecting contract terms to relax if conditions change, even after they are signed.

Synergistic Potential

Integrating Rule and Situation tendencies helps organizations create stability without rigidity. Rule-oriented collaborators' preference for promoting reliability through structure guides the development of useful policies and procedures. Situation-oriented provisions help minimize bureaucracy and instill flexibility.

Analysis: Managing Surprises

Ishani Arjan's Situation-oriented background did not prepare her to deal with a strongly Rule-oriented partner. She was used to establishing longstanding relationships with companies that consider ongoing give-and-take a natural part of business, even after a contract is signed. In her home country of India, fluctuations in the natural environment and physical infrastructure frequently create logistical and financial problems, and in such a fluid business environment partners expect to share the burden when crises arise. In fact, in some of the countries Ishani has dealt with, a contract is more of a midpoint in a negotiation than the final step. Her experiences led her to assume that postcontract changes are common throughout the world.

Pascal was equally surprised. His experience in a highly contractual environment failed to prepare him for Situation-oriented attitudes toward legal agreements. In Pascal's view, a contract is the ultimate statement of two parties' commitment to action, and negotiations end when the contract is signed. The concept of a binding legal agreement makes no sense to him if the partners don't take it seriously.

Rule- and Situation-oriented organizations manage risk in different ways. Pascal's company created strong financial, physical, and legal infrastructures. It mitigated risk through detailed contracts spelling out each party's obligation and invoking legal penalties when partners don't deliver. If Uster itself were unable to deliver, it would never occur to Pascal to ask a partner to reconsider a signed contract—his word is his bond, and such a request would damage their reputation. Uster's use of detailed contracts makes it easier to do business with unfamiliar new partners and form relationships based on opportunity, which may or may not be long term. Because he was confident in the contract with Malik, Pascal did not see this problem coming.

Situation-oriented organizations perceive legal structures as constraining and may not trust authorities to resolve conflicts fairly or in a timely manner. They mitigate risk by developing trusting relationships with partners before agreeing to do business. In all the previous partnerships Ishani negotiated, each party accepted responsibility for helping the other with unexpected hardships—after all, each stood to benefit from mutual support over time. Malik's contracts were vaguely worded to provide maximum flexibility, and where a long, trusting relationship existed, some deals were even based on verbal agreements.

Cultural Dimension 7: Action

Scenario 7: No Closure

Brian O'Connor has designed a "match made in heaven" for his native city of Fullerton, Australia—or at least so he thinks. Brian is in charge of attracting new manufacturers to Fullerton's technology sector. The region's growing status as a manufacturing center is attractive to technology companies in diverse industries, and when Fullerton's city government announces that it will offer tax incentives through the end of next year for electronics companies to build facilities there, Brian starts looking for candidates. When he hears that RK Components, a Hong Kong electronic components supplier, is looking for a new manufacturing location, he convinces his management to send him there for a meeting.

Brian schedules three days of discussions with RK's directors of facilities and expansion, and everything starts off smoothly. His primary contact there, Mr. Wang, suggests two additional days of dinners and cultural activities, but Brian is on a tight budget and knows his boss wouldn't appreciate him spending time on tourist activities. He sticks to his agenda, describes the many benefits of Fullerton to his hosts, and heads home.

Several weeks later, Brian is gratified to learn that, based on his presentation, RK Components considers Fullerton one of their top three locations. Feeling triumphant, he expects an announcement to follow quickly—RK must decide soon to take advantage of the tax incentive.

But to Brian's surprise, RK seems hesitant about moving forward. Mr. Wang stays in touch, but rather than talking about the specifics of the deal, he asks endless questions about Fullerton's history as a manufacturing center—which company came in which year, who the general manager was at each facility—questions that take time to research and seem largely irrelevant. Mr. Wang says RK's decision must take into consideration the company's tradition and reputation. He seems to question Fullerton's appropriateness, not due to a lack of amenities, but simply because it's less familiar than its two other rivals. Mr. Wang hints that it may not be "durable" as a location. Brian doesn't understand his concern. Fullerton is well established as a center of electronics. All objective measures suggest that the city is a slightly better candidate than its competitors, and the tax incentive is an added attraction.

Mr. Wang, for his part, feels nervous. He wishes Brian had stayed in Hong Kong until his colleagues had gotten to know him thoroughly. Brian is young and mentioned being new to economic development; before, he worked in marketing for a real estate company. Who knows how long he will stay in his current position? Mr. Wang's superiors expect Brian to be there to make introductions for RK executives and troubleshoot any problems that arise. Brian is RK's principal point of contact with Fullerton, and company management will base its decision in part on its impression of him. But Brian seems overly focused on getting a commitment and gives little assurance of what will come after RK makes the investment. And he seemed in such a hurry during his trip. Is the city's economy really as stable as he claims? Will Fullerton's industrial sector really materialize?

Why didn't Brian spend more time in Hong Kong, given the significant investment he was requesting, and why didn't he provide more background information about Fullerton? He brought facts and figures and impressive brochures but contributed little historical information beyond the past five years. RK has been building a reputation for over fifty years. Mr. Wang doesn't want to be responsible for undermining this solid track record. Without a good sense of Brian or Fullerton, he can't be sure RK's investment won't end up being an embarrassment. It's wiser to choose a more familiar location. Even without the tax incentives, it's better to be safe than sorry.

Action Tendencies: Opportunity and Thoroughness

Scenario 7 demonstrates conflict based on different perspectives on **Action**. The cultural tendencies that characterize attitudes in this dimension are *Opportunity* and *Thoroughness*. They describe approaches to developing relationships and designing strategies. For people with an Opportunity orientation, the present and future (where they are now and where they're going) are what matters most; what has happened in the past is largely irrelevant. Opportunity strategies focus on the near term, and people move quickly to take advantage of new opportunities, avoid problems, or recover from mistakes. In decision making, intuition and quick results are valued. Relationships are developed to meet specific goals and may not last in the long run. In India, for example, companies change direction frequently as conditions change, without focusing much on the past.

For people with a Thoroughness perspective, history and tradition are always in mind, and present conditions and future actions are considered with regard to the past. Strategies focus on preserving tradition, recreating past success, and avoiding past mistakes. In decision making, detailed analysis and thoroughness are valued over speed. Relationships are developed slowly to ensure success over time. In China, a country with strong Thoroughness tendencies, changes in direction are made carefully. Existing relationships are used where possible, and new ones are developed slowly.

CHARACTERISTICS OF THE ACTION TENDENCIES

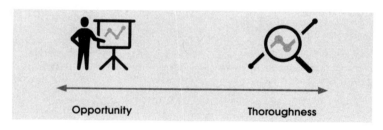

Opportunity   Thoroughness

6

Perspectives, Motivation, and Goals	
Opportunity	Thoroughness
The present and immediate future are the focus. The past is seen as largely irrelevant.	Tradition and history inform any decision about the future. Continuity with the past is considered vital to new initiatives.
Authority stems from recent accomplishments.	Authority stems from a history of accomplishments, even if none are recent.

Opportunity	Thoroughness
Short-term results and the bottom line are emphasized. Relationships can be created as needed relative to these.	Strong relationships are the basis for future results. Nothing can be achieved overnight.
A primary goal is to create new value and achieve new success.	A primary goal is to continue or recreate past success.
Deadlines and milestones are considered paramount.	There is a perception that things happen in due time.
Ability, expertise, and performance are desirable characteristics in an employee.	Age, experience, and wisdom are desirable characteristics in an employee.
Customers are seen as instrumental to the success of a new initiative. "We should try to attract new ones."	Customers are viewed as relationships to be maintained. "We must not lose current ones."
A bad strategy is not a disaster as long as a productive change in direction can be made quickly.	A bad strategy is very serious and likely to result in a loss of credibility, regardless of later changes.
Time efficiency is important; past a point, continued study yields diminishing returns.	Thorough study and exhaustive analysis are critical and may continue for an extended period of time. There's no such thing as too much knowledge.
Behavior and Communication	
Recent performance is constantly analyzed in case the current direction needs to be modified.	A long-term focus is maintained through ups and downs, letting results play out thoroughly.
Organizations may assume risk to take advantage of a window of opportunity.	Organizations may forgo opportunities in uncertain situations.
Presentations focus on the present and the future.	Presentations focus on history and reputation.
Persuasive arguments focus on facts, statistics, and the value of opportunity.	Persuasive arguments focus on history, tradition, and the value of continuity.

Opportunity	Thoroughness
Customers reward innovation and new product features.	Customers reward reputation, consistency, and service.
Representatives strive to close negotiations quickly.	Representatives expect lengthy meetings as two sides come to terms.
Organizational Structures and Processes	
Negotiators may be reassigned without disruption to the proceedings.	The relationship with a negotiator is crucial, and replacements are considered highly disruptive.
Relationships are based on current needs. When old relationships lose importance, new ones can be made.	Relationships are carefully maintained. Allowing them to lapse would create resentment, and enemies are forever.
An employee's success derives from individual performance.	An employee's success derives from relationships with coworkers and superiors.
Employees are promoted and rewarded based on recent accomplishments.	Employees are promoted and rewarded based on professional growth and relationships developed.
Bonuses and raises follow recent performance to reward incremental success.	Bonuses and raises lag behind recent performance to reward long-term strategy.
Rules and processes are designed to encourage efficiency and achieve goals.	Rules and processes are designed to encourage consistency and continuity with the past.

Advantages and Disadvantages of Each Tendency

OPPORTUNITY

Opportunity-oriented businesspeople are forward-looking, innovative, and decisive. They take initiative in identifying possibilities and creating strategy. People are assigned to teams and projects based on their skills and experience, and members come and go. Opportunity companies are nimble and responsive. They are quick to adapt to changes in markets and take advantage of developing prospects, providing new options and features to their customers and creating and dissolving partnerships as needed.

But because they focus on the present and future, people with Opportunity tendencies may fail to learn from the past, making mistakes that could be avoided. They may take unnecessary risk if they feel the "window of opportunity" is closing. Opportunity companies tend to focus on short-term profit over long-term stability. Constant turnover may limit continuity on teams and projects. Changes in direction and leadership may lead to incoherent strategies and unstable product offerings.

THOROUGHNESS

Because they look constantly to past experience when making decisions, Thoroughness-oriented businesspeople are good at recognizing recurring patterns and avoiding past mistakes. They value thorough analysis and make decisions only after painstaking reflection. Because they are willing to forgo short-term success in favor of long-term stability, they tend to create strategies and partnerships that help their organizations survive difficult times.

At the same time, Thoroughness-oriented individuals and teams can become bogged down in research and fail to take initiative. Without near-term reward for performance, top employees may lose motivation. "Paralysis by analysis" can prevent companies from adapting to changing environments and capitalizing on opportunity.

Synergistic Potential

Organizations that successfully integrate Opportunity and Thoroughness perspectives are flexible, responsive, and willing to invest in the analysis needed for sound strategic decisions. Opportunity collaborators can be trusted to recognize possibility and propose responses to change, while Thoroughness partners will consider the implications of decisions carefully to synthesize sound, innovative strategies.

Analysis: No Closure

Brian O'Connor's Opportunity orientation shaped his marketing strategy, which emphasized current conditions and short-term incentives. By promoting these, Fullerton attracted several innovative young technology companies over the past two years, and Brian expected RK to be impressed as well. Mr. Wang's Thoroughness criteria were quite different, however. His company's strategy was one of gradual change. RK navigated Hong Kong's rapidly changing economic environment by carefully developing and maintaining a reputation for excellence. Success derived from a strong corporate vision, wise direction by seniors, sound partnerships, and gradual movement in new directions while maintaining legacy and tradition.

Mr. Wang doesn't want to be responsible for any unpleasant surprises. His supervisors—as well as RK's partners, shareholders, and customers—expect sound business decisions based on thorough research. The cost of a hasty decision could be very high. In Thoroughness-oriented environments, memories endure, and a lapse in consistency would affect relationships with these important constituencies. Mr. Wang would rather pass up the Fullerton tax incentives than make a bad recommendation.

Mr. Wang was disturbed by Brian's behavior during their meetings in Hong Kong. Brian's youth and relative inexperience counted against him in Mr. Wang's view. And rather than address these concerns, Brian raised new ones about his seriousness by refusing to extend his stay long enough to develop a trusting relationship or talk adequately about Fullerton's history.

Brian failed to anticipate these problems because his strategy had worked so well up to now. The younger and smaller companies he attracted before had Opportunity tendencies themselves. They invested less in their location than RK would and found the short-term attraction of tax incentives compelling. Their business model prioritized experimentation and redirection, and their partners and investors approved of leveraging Fullerton's offerings. These companies also considered Brian less important than Mr. Wang did—they were less interested in him personally than in the structural benefits he represented. After arriving in Fullerton, they made their own connections in the business community based on their technology and product offerings, and they expected to have little more to do with Brian.

Cultural Dimension 8: Organization

Scenario 8: Taking It Easy

Alard Brouwer has to admit it: As much as he looked forward to working in Spain, he's finding it a bit frustrating. His family and friends keep commenting on his great luck in getting a Barcelona assignment, so it's difficult to explain that instead of having a wonderful vacation, he's feeling tense and annoyed. At home in the Netherlands, he'd heard plenty of jokes about Spaniards' relaxed attitude toward time. While that's fine in a vacation destination, it's a different matter when it comes to getting things done.

To start with, meetings rarely seem to take place as planned. For his first meeting, Alard arrived ten minutes early in order to distribute the agenda and handouts. As the manager of a software design project, he wanted to set a good example. But he needn't have bothered. He sat and chewed his nails as the time went by, wondering whether the others had missed his meeting announcement somehow. The next person to arrive, Diego, was ten minutes late. He entered the room talking on his cell phone and didn't even apologize. The others trickled in after that, dawdling and visiting with each other, seemingly unaware that they were wasting time.

As Alard has since learned, this is how meetings in the Spanish branch start in general. Throughout the meeting, participants move away from the agenda and discuss peripheral issues that take them far from the point, so that by the time the discussion is finally over, the meeting has run late. No one seems to mind, however—everyone is prepared to just push other appointments back. In Alard's home office, if business isn't concluded when the meeting time ends, another meeting is scheduled or problems are worked out via e-mail and phone calls. This constant rescheduling is destabilizing and makes him feel unnerved. How does anything get done in this chaotic environment?

The attitude of his coworkers toward customer deadlines is lax as well, in his opinion. He arrived at the first project meeting with a detailed timeline, expecting to discuss various milestones and intermediate deadlines, but was surprised at his colleagues' lack of interest in the details. When he pressed them, the systems architect, Constanza, finally spoke up. "Whatever you've inserted there is fine," she said. "Unexpected things will come up, so there's no point in getting too focused on details. We should just try to be flexible and adapt to changes." Alard was astonished at this attitude. Yes, of course surprises will come up, but when they do, the plan should be revised accordingly to keep the project on track. Alard considered Constanza's point of view unprofessional and has worried about the team's commitment to on-time delivery ever since.

At the same time, he must admit, their performance has been impressive in a number of ways. When the customer was late with design specifications, Constanza and Diego worked late for an entire week to get the next version of the product ready. They didn't complain, and seemed surprised when a relieved Alard thanked them for their hard work. Constanza made a couple of remarks about the virtues of flexibility, implying that Alard is perceived as a bit rigid. He believes they consider his insistence on punctuality a nuisance, and he can't understand it. How did they get anything done before he arrived?

Organization Tendencies: Schedule and Flow

Scenario 8 illustrates conflict arising from differing perspectives on **Organization**. The cultural tendencies that characterize the Organization dimension are *Schedule* and *Flow*. These describe different approaches to organization and planning. Schedule-oriented people perceive time as linear, with events occurring one after the other, and they organize their time this way as well. They begin and end meetings on time, organize tasks sequentially, and have a strong commitment to sticking to plans. An example is Germany, where punctuality is highly valued and plans are carefully developed and implemented.

Flow-oriented people perceive time as a complex system, with events occurring simultaneously. Meetings in Flow-oriented companies may begin and end late, with people using their computers and taking phone calls throughout. Plans may be changed frequently and are less important than maintaining relationships. In Italy, known for its Flow tendencies, appointments may be delayed and strategies modified repeatedly in response to change.

CHARACTERISTICS OF THE ORGANIZATION TENDENCIES

Schedule   Flow

Perspectives, Motivation, and Goals	
Schedule	**Flow**
Time is viewed as a sequential process, with events occurring one after another.	Time is viewed as flexible and chaotic, with events occurring simultaneously.
Time has substance—it can be measured, saved, and wasted.	Time is intangible—it's a characteristic of the activity taking place.
Time is managed by referring to clocks and calendars.	Time is allocated based on opportunity and obligation.
Schedules are considered serious commitments.	Schedules are viewed as goals to be met if conditions permit.
Commitment to appointments is a high priority.	Commitment to an activity or conversation is a high priority.
Schedule changes by others are viewed as indications of a lack of commitment.	Schedule changes by others are viewed as natural and unsurprising.
Changes to plans are viewed as disruptive, and the later the change, the more disruptive it is.	Changes to plans are viewed as inevitable, and late changes are accommodated.

Schedule	Flow
Getting everything done is a priority.	Giving everything adequate time is a priority.
Interruptions are viewed as disruptive and impolite.	Interruptions are considered unavoidable.
People prefer a quiet working environment where they can focus on individual tasks.	People prefer a dynamic working environment where they can multitask.
Behavior and Communication	
Planning tends to be complex and complete, and is reworked when conditions change.	Planning tends to focus on goals, with details left vague to accommodate changes in conditions.
Appointments are moved or canceled reluctantly, due to serious impediment.	Appointments are freely moved or canceled according to opportunity and convenience.
Commitments are made sequentially: "We will do this, then that."	Commitments are made together: "These are the things that need to happen."
Estimated time for each task is considered when making commitments. There are twenty-four hours in a day.	A day's commitments take as much time as they take, perhaps more than twenty-four hours.
People tend to focus on one task before moving on.	People tend to work on multiple tasks at a time.
Tasks are divided into equal parts and completed incrementally to finish projects before deadlines.	People focus on what is most interesting or urgent at the moment. Using deadline pressure as a motivator, they may work harder toward the end to complete projects.
Interpersonal interaction is constrained in order to prioritize schedules.	Appointments are missed in order to prioritize interpersonal interaction.
Phone calls or e-mail are considered most efficient.	Face-to-face interaction is considered most effective.

6

Organizational Structures and Processes	
Schedule	**Flow**
Work environments are orderly and methodical.	Work environments are dynamic and may seem chaotic.
Processes and procedures are specific and are followed by employees.	Processes and procedures are general and may be disregarded.
Project management plans are detailed, and internal milestones are specific.	Project management plans are general, and internal milestones may not be specified.

Advantages and Disadvantages of Each Tendency

SCHEDULE

Schedule-oriented team members are punctual and organized. Their focus on schedules makes them natural timekeepers for team projects. They approach work in a structured manner, moving through it efficiently. Because they value reliability, Schedule-oriented individuals, groups, and companies can be counted on to discharge their responsibilities and meet deadlines.

But due to their dependence on structure, Schedule-oriented individuals and teams may have difficulty with fluid environments. Repeated revisions of their detailed plans can make them frustrated and anxious. They dislike last-minute changes and may resist even constructive ideas that are introduced late. Schedule-oriented companies are less prepared for business in unpredictable environments, where they may be blindsided by external events.

FLOW

Flow-oriented individuals and teams are good at allocating resources wherever needed. Untroubled by changes in direction, they adapt to fluid environments. They are creative troubleshooters who can be relied on to find pathways around obstacles in times of crisis. Flow companies have networks of partnerships to help them manage unexpected events effectively.

Because they work at an uneven pace, however, people with Flow tendencies may feel constrained by detailed schedules. Schedule-oriented colleagues may perceive their late arrival and multitasking during meetings as indications of disrespect. Since they focus more on outcomes than on process, they may miss internal deadlines and earn a reputation for flakiness or incompetence. The unpredictability of Flow-oriented organizations may create concerns about their stability and strain partnerships.

Synergistic Potential

Organizations that integrate Schedule and Flow tendencies accomplish work in a timely, predictable manner while demonstrating creativity in problem solving. Schedule-oriented participants organize and track projects, ensuring accountability for deliverables and deadlines, while counting on their Flow-oriented colleagues to overcome obstacles, troubleshoot issues, and develop creative solutions to unanticipated problems.

Analysis: Taking It Easy

6

The scenario above illustrates conflict in the Organization dimension. Alard's highly structured Schedule approach to time management and planning emphasized reliability and predictability, and he found the fluidity of his new environment unnerving. Schedule-oriented people value punctuality and structure. Alard associated lateness with a lack of commitment and organization, and his colleagues' relaxed attitude to meetings made him nervous. He placed value on detailed agendas, expecting them to help structure meetings and ensure efficiency, and he always sent them to the team in advance with a request for changes. They consistently failed to respond, however, instead bringing up new topics during the meetings, which Alard found irresponsible.

To his Flow-oriented colleagues, Alard's approach seemed restrictive and inflexible. Given that conditions change and important relationships must be prioritized, in their view the shortest path from start to finish is not necessarily a straight line. Responding to change requires flexibility, and no one should expect their day to go exactly as planned. Alard's coworkers think of meeting times as estimates. If they arrive on time, so much the better. While they're waiting for colleagues to catch up, they can make phone calls or fill out expense reports. If they're late, their colleagues will be doing the same. There's not only a "Plan B" if things don't go as expected—they're ready to respond to changes with Plans C and D if necessary. Given these complexities, once people are together, it makes sense to discuss an issue to its conclusion. If other meetings need to be rescheduled, that's no problem, as others are prepared to modify their plans as well.

Alard's Schedule-oriented approach to managing projects is quite different. Schedule-driven project planning involves dividing activities into segments with a timeline for accomplishing each. Internal milestones are carefully scheduled to minimize surprises. Each segment is tracked carefully, and unexpected problems are factored into a revised plan. Flow-oriented schedules are flexible and assume that internal delivery dates will change, possibly multiple times. In the early phases of a project, people take a relaxed approach, working harder toward the end to meet deadlines.

Part of Alard's confusion is that while his colleagues seem uncommitted and disorganized by his standards, they come through in the end—a Flow characteristic. The Flow approach has its own logic, and his colleagues aren't as grateful for his organizational acumen as he thinks they should be. Sometimes, in their view, flexibility is a more useful attribute.

Some Common Misperceptions about Cultural Tendencies

As people become familiar with the cultural tendencies in this framework, they sometimes make mistakes based on their own orientations. The most common is to think that people with certain tendencies will all have certain characteristics—that Situation-oriented people are all lawbreakers, for example. It's important to recognize that people with every cultural tendency demonstrate the full range of human behavior—but often with different motivations.[1] The descriptions below should help you avoid some common misconceptions.

Clarity: Indirect/Direct

Direct speakers tend to find it very difficult to understand their Indirect counterparts. For Direct speakers, saying what you mean is the easiest course, while Indirect evasiveness seems cagey and dishonest. Remember that Indirect speakers are actually trying to be polite, and blurting out criticism can be quite painful for them. Indirectness is one of the most difficult tendencies to unlearn, so simply saying, "Please be direct," to them will not be enough—it's a little like saying, "Feel free to slap me every time I make a suggestion you don't like."

Indirect speakers tend to confuse Directness with a lack of sophistication or even intelligence. The fact that Direct speakers are unfamiliar with the delicate art of verbal parry or face-maintenance says nothing about their native ability in other areas, and they can learn Indirect formulas with a bit of coaching.

The single most concise solution when dealing with disagreement—for people with either tendency—is to begin with thanks and praise and follow with criticism. Thanking a counterpart for their suggestion helps Indirect speakers feel they have made the necessary gesture towards politeness before moving on to criticism. Direct speakers can learn to begin with formulaic thanks and find at least one positive comment to soften the criticism that follows.

Status: Achievement/Endowment

Achievers tend to think their Endowment counterparts are less hardworking than they really are. They reason that people at the top don't need to work to advance themselves, while people at the bottom have no incentive

---

[1] To test your skills at recognizing the cultural tendencies, take the quiz on my website at www.deirdremendez.com/practice-quiz

to do so. But whereas Achievers work to move ahead, Endowment contacts work just as hard to live up to their family names, religious ideals, or ethnic backgrounds.

Authority: Rule/Situation

People with Rule tendencies tend to equate the Situation orientation with rule breaking, but many Situation-oriented people are extremely law abiding because they respect the laws in their environment and the authorities that enforce them. Remember, the Situation orientation is about choosing whether to follow rules based on context.

People sometimes assume that authoritarian governments encourage a Rule orientation by imposing many laws and restrictions, but the opposite is often true. Regimes perceived as illegitimate or unfair actually increase people's tendency to disobey through such means as black markets, tax evasion, and antigovernment graffiti. In true Rule-oriented environments, people willingly follow rules—even silly ones when no one is looking—because they accept the authority that governs them.

It may seem at first blush that certain cultural orientations encourage Situation tendencies. Achievers tend to think that Endowment orientation leads to rule breaking, because highly placed people in Endowment environments are above the law, while poor people have little incentive to obey. But there are many examples of rule breaking in Achievement environments due to personal ambition and determination to get ahead. Process-oriented people tend to equate the Network orientation with favoritism and cronyism, which is possible. But history is full of law breakers motivated by commitment to a mission or ideology. Group-oriented people may favor the interests of their group over the law, and Independents may break laws for personal gain. Again, people break rules in every cultural environment, but for different reasons.

Involvement: Network/Process

It is often assumed that people with Network tendencies are friendlier than their Process counterparts because personal connections are so important to them, but this is not always the case. In Network environments, people may reserve smiles and confidences for their circle of friends and treat others with bare civility. People with strong Network tendencies invest heavily in their personal circle, and may not want to expend their "social capital" on strangers. They may be stand-offish with new acquaintances, calculating carefully whether a new contact's connections and influence are worth the obligation they will incur, and keeping in mind that the rest of their network will hold them accountable for the new contact's behavior. Process counterparts may be easier to connect with, at least at a casual level, since they don't perceive new relationships as a burden.

When you're looking for identifiers for the Involvement dimension, people's behavior in the workplace may be misleading. In some places, the importance of efficiency in the workplace causes people to be more Process-oriented than they would be in other contexts, so be aware of this as you create Counterpart Profiles.

Collaboration: Independent/Group

In many Group-oriented societies, an Independent orientation is equated with selfishness; however, in Independent environments it is stressed that each person should assume personal responsibility for doing what is right, even if others are not doing so. In countries with Independent tendencies, action by a single person is often responsible for ending abuses or illegal behavior. Independents make extreme sacrifices just as people with Group tendencies do, but they're more likely committed to principles or to humanity at large than to a specific group.

7

Comparing Profiles

Now that you understand the cultural tendencies for each dimension, you can interpret your own profile and compare it with the one you made for your counterpart.

Here's an example of how to read a profile. Let's say the one below belongs to someone named Kathrin Becker.

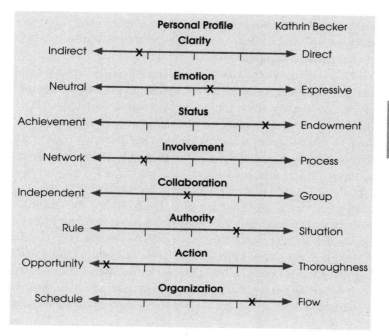

Kathrin's profile shows the following:

- Strong Endowment, Opportunity, and Flow tendencies
- Moderate Indirect, Network, and Situation tendencies
- Weak Independent and Expressive tendencies

Where her tendencies are weak (in the middle of a dimension on the chart), Kathrin will empathize with both perspectives on a dimension and adapt easily to new approaches. Her slight Independent tendency won't be a problem if she encounters new approaches to group work, reward structures, and decision making. She'll be comfortable working alone on assignments and being held accountable for her individual performance, but if she works in a Group context, she'll adapt to working closely with other group members and gaining personal satisfaction from her team's success. In decision making, Kathrin will be able to promote her opinions actively or submit to the wisdom of the larger group as necessary. She's nearly as weak on the Emotion continuum, which means that she'll relate well to both Neutral and Expressive counterparts and adjust her own level of expressiveness as appropriate.

Moderate tendencies, which offer some potential for confusion and conflict, can usually be overcome by explicitly identifying intercultural problems. Kathrin's Situation orientation will cause her to be casual about rule following, and she may feel constrained by excessive bureaucracy. But she'll be willing to obey rules that are valid and important, and where they are not, she can probably bring herself to follow them to please her colleagues, maybe with some eye rolling. Due to her Network orientation, she will ramble a bit in presentations, but if following agendas and getting to the point are important to her coworkers, she should be able to learn to be more concise. She will desire strong relationships with colleagues, but if she finds herself in a context where people have multiple friend groups outside work instead, she'll probably adapt by joining a club or finding another outlet. Although naturally cautious about criticizing others' ideas and easily hurt by overt criticism, she will learn through interaction with Direct colleagues that honest comments aren't intended as personal attacks, and she will learn to be more straightforward to be sure she's understood.

The three dimensions where Kathrin's profile indicates extreme preferences are the most likely to create problems in new environments. Due to her strong Endowment orientation, she may be offended if juniors show her inadequate respect, and she may hesitate to express her opinions directly to superiors out of deference (particularly since she's also somewhat Indirect). In a highly Achievement-oriented context, she's likely to feel that people are aggressive and excessively focused on self-advancement. Very egalitarian environments may be uncomfortable for her. She may seem imperious to junior colleagues whom she doesn't consider her equals, and she may wait for instructions rather than question instructions or take the personal initiative her superiors expect. Kathrin should focus on developing strategies for dealing with Achievement counterparts and environments.

Kathrin's pronounced Opportunity tendency will cause her to be impatient with people who focus on maintaining tradition and require detailed analysis in decision making. She's likely to see Thoroughness-oriented counterparts as old-fashioned and dismiss their concerns. If she makes arguments appealing to Opportunity-based goals, others may perceive her as impulsive and reckless. She should spend some time researching the Thoroughness perspective so she can accommodate their strategic expectations and present new ideas effectively.

Kathrin's strong Flow orientation will make it difficult for her to work successfully with Schedule-oriented colleagues. If she arrives late for meetings, they may question her commitment or competence, and missing deadlines could hurt her reputation for reliability. Her tendency to start with tasks she enjoys and put off less interesting projects may frustrate her colleagues, and their attempts to hold her to detailed schedules might feel suffocating.

In preparing for an overseas assignment, international negotiation, or new team project, Kathrin should reflect on her moderate and strong tendencies. As she completes Counterpart Profiles on her new environment, negotiating partners, or team members, she should look for tendencies different from her own to identify potential problems, prepare for interactions, decipher miscommunications, and resolve conflicts.

Interpreting Your Personal Profile

Now take a look at your own profile and what it indicates about your culture-based preferences, strengths, and weaknesses. Refer to Chapters 4–6 as needed to understand the attitudes, expectations, and behaviors associated with each cultural tendency.

If you're in the middle for most or all of the dimensions, congratulations! You were born to do intercultural work and probably find it easy to adapt to a variety of styles. For you, the goal in using this framework might be to help others avoid surprises and manage conflict between those less flexible. You also have an opportunity to learn how people with extreme tendencies view their world and explain them to each other.

If you have strong preferences, focus on these, anticipating and troubleshooting problems as you go. If you have multiple strong preferences, don't despair—you can overcome them by being intentional as you interact with other profiles. People with strong preferences can actually be excellent intercultural problem solvers because they're often the most conscious of the tendencies and how they work.

Tip: It's a good idea to revisit the self-assessment questions again after you've worked with a new group for a while, because we tend to perceive our own tendencies based on the environment we come from. For example, someone from a very Neutral environment, like Stockholm, might be quite Expressive compared to their colleagues. But this same person might be very Neutral and reserved by the standards of Buenos Aires, where a highly Expressive manner is the rule.

Reading Your Counterpart Profile

You can analyze your Counterpart Profile in the same way you did your own. Focus on your counterpart's strong and moderate preferences. Where tendencies are near the midpoint, your counterpart will be fairly flexible, so it's the extreme ones that matter most.

If your counterpart is a person or small group, the example below will show you how to interpret their profile and predict challenges. If your counterpart is a place or organization, skip to Example 2.

Example 1. Profile of a Person: Kathrin Becker

As an example, let's look at the sample profile for Kathrin Becker again, this time in the role of your counterpart:

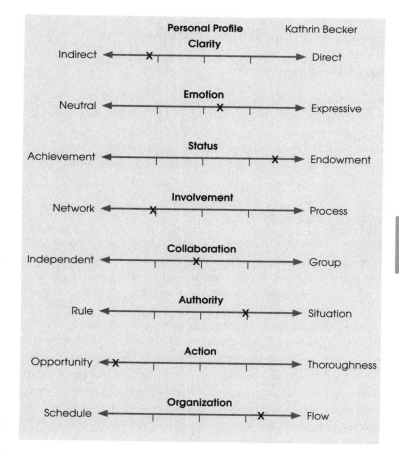

Personal Profile — Kathrin Becker

Clarity: Indirect ←—X—————————→ Direct

Emotion: Neutral ←—————X———→ Expressive

Status: Achievement ←—————————X→ Endowment

Involvement: Network ←—X————————→ Process

Collaboration: Independent ←———X————→ Group

Authority: Rule ←—————————X—→ Situation

Action: Opportunity ←X———————————→ Thoroughness

Organization: Schedule ←————————————X→ Flow

Kathrin's profile indicates weak Expressive and Independent tendencies, moderate Indirect and Situation tendencies, and strong Endowment, Network, Opportunity, and Flow tendencies.

Working with Kathrin

The description below will give you an idea of the way Kathrin would interact with you and other colleagues. This is a preview of Chapters 12–17, which provide more detail on the way cultural tendencies shape different approaches to specific professional contexts and functions.

WEAK TENDENCIES

Kathrin's fairly neutral in the Collaboration dimension, so she'll be comfortable working with you regardless of your own orientation. And given her central position in the Emotion dimension, you can expect to get along whether you're demonstrative or more reserved. You don't need to worry much about these two dimensions in your work with her; she's easygoing for both.

MODERATE TENDENCIES

Kathrin is relatively Indirect, so if you have Direct tendencies, you may have difficulty reading her reactions to your ideas. If she disagrees with you, you should expect positive answers with little follow-through, especially if you're her superior. It may also take you a long time to discover problems she keeps private out of respect or politeness. She may feel insulted or humiliated if others challenge her ideas directly or publicly. While coaching her to function in a Direct environment, you may need to take extra trouble to be sure you're hearing from her and protecting her.

Kathrin's Situation orientation indicates that she'll be a good troubleshooter and a creative thinker. She'll probably be casual about following rules and surprised and dismayed by bureaucracy in the workplace. She may ignore inconvenient procedures that are important to you, so you'll need to convince her that they are important to her success as well.

STRONG TENDENCIES

The four dimensions where Kathrin's profile indicates extreme preferences are the most likely to cause difficulty as she deals with new environments and colleagues. At the same time, each one has benefits to offer. Kathrin's strong Endowment orientation will make her highly aware of her position relative to others. If she is older than you or senior to you, she'll be a good source of historical information, context, and advice. She may also expect you to defer to her judgment and feel insulted if you challenge her ideas. If you're a junior with an Achievement orientation, her behavior toward you may seem somewhat standoffish—unless you report to her directly, in which case she may act as a strong mentor dedicated to helping you learn the ropes and avoid political mistakes. If she is younger than you, particularly if you are male, you may have difficulty getting her to speak her mind openly or give negative feedback. She may wait for direction rather than express her own opinions, even in her area of expertise. If you develop a strong relationship with her, though, you will find her a loyal employee who is eager to learn.

Due to her Network orientation, Kathrin is likely to contribute to a warm office or team dynamic, and she may have a tendency to socialize on the job. She'll collaborate with you more happily if you take time to get to know her, and she's likely to feel isolated if she doesn't have a chance to interact personally with her colleagues.

Kathrin's pronounced Opportunity tendency indicates that she'll be a quick decision maker who is good at innovating to meet her goals. She may become impatient if you emphasize extended analysis and reflection in decision making. She may see your Thoroughness perspective as obsolete and consider your cautiousness exaggerated. Although she might come off as brash and impulsive, her innovative thinking can be an asset if she's well supervised.

Kathrin's strong Flow orientation may make her difficult to work with if you're highly Schedule oriented. Her casual attitude toward start times for meetings and internal deadlines may seem unprofessional to you, and others might see her as lazy or incompetent. Kathrin may feel constricted by rigid scheduling and need some freedom to do her best work. If the reins are loosened a bit, her problem-solving ability and strength at managing complex tasks will be valuable when the unexpected arises.

Example 2. Profile of a Place or Organization: Merubia

To understand how to read a profile of a place or organization, consider the profile below of a fictitious context—a place or organization called Merubia. (This could be the United Territories of Merubia, for example, or Merubia Pharmaceuticals.)

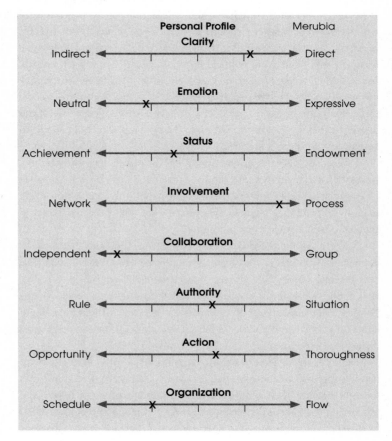

Merubia's profile shows weak Achievement and Thoroughness tendencies; moderate Direct, Neutral, and Schedule orientations; and strong Process and Independent tendencies. What would it be like to interact with people from Merubia?

Working in Merubia

WEAK TENDENCIES

Merubia has a slight tendency toward Achievement. This means that reward and promotion there are based largely on performance, but people also show respect for authority. If you're extremely Endowment-oriented, you may be a bit formal and cautious compared with most people there, but they will probably take your tendencies in stride. The same goes for Merubia's slight Situation orientation. People there will tend to bend the rules a bit to solve problems, but they won't take this to the extreme. Their tendency toward Thoroughness will incline them toward lengthier analysis and caution in decision making, which may frustrate you if you're extremely Opportunity oriented, but since they're fairly neutral for this dimension, they'll probably understand your perspective.

MODERATE TENDENCIES

When you deal with people from Merubia, who have moderate Direct tendencies, you can expect clear communication without much beating around the bush, and they will give you their opinions if you ask for them. They'll disagree with your ideas fairly openly and not take it personally if you do the same. If you're extremely Indirect, they may seem a bit confrontational and even insulting at times. At the same time, you'll always know where you are with them, and their clarity will help you correct mistakes quickly. Since their tendencies here are only moderate, Merubians will likely accommodate requests for a gentler approach.

Due to their moderate Schedule tendencies, they'll generally be organized and punctual. If you're Flow-oriented, you may find this a bit limiting when they are reluctant to deviate from the plan. But Merubians are reliable, and their organizational skills will be a source of stability and predictability in your work together.

STRONG TENDENCIES

Merubia's strong Process orientation will be evident in meetings and social activities. If you're highly Network-oriented, meetings may seem to launch abruptly into serious business, with very little social icebreaking beforehand. Merubians may also seem too narrowly focused on their main agenda points and unwilling to cover related issues. Expect them to be efficient, though—you can build relationships and discuss peripheral items at the end of meetings once business discussion is finished. If you hope your Merubian colleagues will become members of your social circle, you may be disappointed, as they're more likely to make friends outside work through clubs or volunteer organizations. But members of groups that interest you will probably welcome you into their organizations if you should want to join.

Institutions in Merubia are Independent and base reward and promotion on individual performance, which will probably be acknowledged openly. This may make you uncomfortable if you have strong Group tendencies. You will be expected to voice your thoughts publicly without prior vetting, which may make you feel exposed, but you will be amply rewarded for valuable ideas. Merubians will do most of their work individually, with group members meeting as needed to integrate their contributions. You may feel a bit isolated by these practices and want more guidance than you're getting. If your team is collaborating on a project with a Merubian partner, their communication may seem unprofessional by your standards—but don't confuse this with incompetence. You'll find them willing to share information freely with your team to help synchronize both your contributions.

The Critical Dimensions

Comparing your Personal and Counterpart Profiles in Chapter 3 showed you the "critical" cultural dimensions—the ones with strong tendencies and where you're relatively far apart. These dimensions are the most likely to cause problems, and being aware of areas of possible confusion can help you avoid miscommunication and conflict. Chapter 8 shows you how to predict the specific frustrations you and your counterpart are likely to have with one another.

7

8

Predicting Challenges

I n addition to predicting your counterpart's attitudes and behaviors, you can anticipate specific challenges in your work together using the charts below. They indicate how people with strong preferences commonly experience working with those of the opposite tendency. The charts will help predict your feelings about your counterpart and—just as important—how your counterpart will feel about you. They show how applying our own cultural scripts raises concerns and suspicions when we encounter others with conflicting tendencies.

CLARITY: INDIRECT AND DIRECT

Building Relationships	
Indirect	**Direct**
When we try to make pleasant conversation with them at dinner, it seems to confuse them. But we find it inappropriate to talk business at social events.	When we try to initiate business conversations at dinner, they change the subject to something social. When will they get to the point?

Indirect	Direct
They seem well intentioned but lack tact and finesse. It's difficult for them to integrate socially because they miss social signals.	They seem to have a sort of secret code, and everyone knows what everything means—except us. They must be trying to communicate around us.
When there's a delicate situation, they tend to blurt out their opinions, even in public. We must be careful whom we introduce them to—who knows what they might say to someone important?	They don't stand up for their ideas, even to their own managers—let alone their customers. They don't want us to talk to anyone of importance, either. They don't treat us like real partners.

Explaining and Discussing	
Indirect	**Direct**
When we ask a question, they give us a brief answer with little context. The only details they provide are data and statistics. We can't get a good sense of the reasons behind what they say. Maybe they're hiding something.	They don't give straight answers. They talk around the point with history and other tangential information that fails to answer the question. Maybe there's a language problem.
In meetings, they want to go through their bullet points one by one. They don't seem to realize that each issue is related to the others. When we try to explore things fully, they get impatient.	In meetings, they don't stick to the agenda. They go off on tangents and waste time talking about things that are only distantly related to the point.
They seem to want a yes or no answer to every question, no matter how complicated. That would be oversimplifying. You must accept complexity until things are fully understood.	They seem to see every possibility as equally likely. It's hard to manage a dozen scenarios at the same time. Why don't they just choose the most probable and outline a Plan A and a Plan B?

Managing Disagreement	
Indirect	**Direct**
Yesterday their representative asked us point-blank what we thought of his new idea. It was no good, but how could we say that to his face? We said it was "interesting" to keep from embarrassing him. He should have known better than to place us in that situation.	It's hard to get a straight answer from them. I asked what they thought of a new idea, and they said it was interesting, but I could tell something was wrong. The last time this happened, they didn't follow through as promised. Why do they say one thing and do another?
Their team leader asked for suggestions in a meeting, so I made one, and she responded that it wouldn't work. I've never been so humiliated—that's the last time I'll speak out in her presence.	I ask for suggestions in meetings, but they rarely have anything to recommend. If they want to be considered full partners, they'll need to start coming up with useful ideas.
In joint meetings, they understand about half of what we say. They miss all the nuances and take sarcastic comments at face value. They're unsophisticated and, frankly, don't seem very smart.	In joint meetings, they seem to use this secret code of half-statements—or worse, comments that mean the opposite of what is said. It's really confusing and kind of dishonest.
We send signals to let him know when his suggestions are off target, but he doesn't seem to get it. He takes everything at face value.	Instead of telling me the truth, they nod and agree with my ideas, but in a vaguely negative way. Why don't they just say what they mean?
When we meet with their team, members openly criticize their colleagues' ideas. It's embarrassing. They obviously have poor team morale.	People on their team dance around the issues, and it takes forever to get to a decision. They waste time being polite about bad ideas.
They should have run that idea by some key players informally before the meeting. Big ideas should be vetted before they're introduced publicly to consider all the angles and avoid conflict.	Their meetings are very scripted. Important matters seem to have been decided beforehand, and there's very little discussion. They should create a forum for debate.

8

EMOTION: NEUTRAL AND EXPRESSIVE

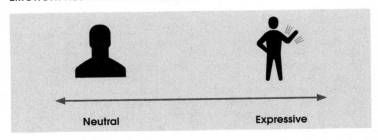

Communication	
Neutral	**Expressive**
They get upset about minor points, and problems escalate from there. Maybe they aren't disciplined enough to partner with us.	They don't seem engaged by anything we suggest. Maybe they aren't really interested in partnering with us.
We had a carefully prepared agenda that contained all the important points. They introduced tangential ideas and pulled us off topic. The discussion went off the rails!	We had a general idea of what we wanted to accomplish, but they forced a linear agenda on us that ignored important related points. Discussions must develop naturally.
Thinking carefully before you speak and waiting your turn is considerate and efficient. Everyone talking at once is impolite and messy.	A free exchange of ideas with everyone brainstorming at the same time moves the conversation ahead. It's a good way to stimulate creative energy.
Interpersonal Relations	
Neutral	**Expressive**
They get excited about minor details—everything is either wonderful or terrible. They overwhelm us with their emotions.	They're so impassive we can't tell what they think of anything. They drain our energy when we interact with them.

Neutral	Expressive
They talk constantly and about nothing in particular. They ask personal questions and tell stories that have nothing to do with business. It's hard to think with so much chatter.	They get standoffish when we try to chat or ask questions. Their silence makes us overcompensate, and we end up doing all the talking.
She wants to hug me and pat me on the back. Even my relatives don't do that!	When I tried to hug him, he seemed to shrivel up. I thought we were friends.
Financial reward and interesting work are important to me. I don't need to socialize with my colleagues—I see enough of them at the office.	Strong relationships with colleagues are critical to a good working environment, but she doesn't seem to value bonding with her coworkers.
At work, they act as if they were home and spend a lot of time socializing instead of working. It seems inefficient and unprofessional.	They seem so tense at work—formal in their dress and manner—and no one smiles. I find them cold and unfriendly.

Resolving Problems	
Neutral	Expressive
They blurt out their opinions on every subject. They seem to have little discipline.	When there's a problem, they're silent. We don't know what's wrong, so we can't fix it.
I wish they would calm down and behave less emotionally. I feel as if an explosion were about to happen at any moment.	I wish they'd express themselves so I could change direction when I need to. I feel like I'm wandering in the dark.
They show little respect for the person speaking—interrupting and adding side comments whenever they think of them. Why can't they be more polite? This behavior is insulting.	We're expected to constantly look for signs like silence, vagueness, and lack of eye contact to know if something's wrong. Why don't they just tell us? It's exhausting.

8

STATUS: ACHIEVEMENT AND ENDOWMENT

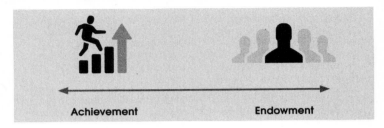

| Achievement | Endowment |

Leadership and Competence	
Achievement	**Endowment**
We chose a technical expert to represent us on this project. They sent someone who's been buried in management for the last fifteen years and knows nothing about the technology. Why didn't they send someone competent?	We sent a senior executive to this negotiation to show how seriously we take it. He knows everything about our company. They sent a thirty-year-old who's been with their company for two years! Are they trying to insult us?
A member of our partner's team really has difficulty accepting my role as manager. He's older than I am, but my education and track record earned me this position.	Our partner team's manager is ten years younger than I am. How can I be expected to trust and respect someone with so little experience? He shouldn't have been promoted so fast.
Engagement and Demeanor	
Achievement	**Endowment**
That company has lagged the market for years. When we offered them a big opportunity, their management took forever to respond. They don't seem to get the current environment—they need new blood and fresh ideas.	That young company exploded on the scene last year, but who knows whether they'll have any staying power? These start-ups come and go all the time—and are often unreliable.

Achievement	Endowment
We tried to establish a friendly, relaxed tone in our first meeting, but they were stiff and formal. Despite our impressive track record, they treated us like we were on trial. These outdated formalities slow things down and are irrelevant to the bottom line.	Our company has been in business for nearly a century, and our main partners take that seriously. But this young group took off their jackets in the first meeting and used our first names. They were disrespectful of our stature—they seem arrogant and immature.
When I interact with their senior manager, he starts a monologue about his own experience and opinions. When I try to contribute to be polite, he ignores what I say and goes back to the monologue. He seems very self-centered.	When I interact with their junior employees, they don't listen politely. Each time I say something, they jump in with a comment of their own. They seem not to respect authority.

Hiring and Performance	
Achievement	**Endowment**
Their management includes three members of the founder's family. How can we know whether they're qualified and competent? Policies preventing nepotism are vital to ensure that qualified people are hired and promotion is based on performance.	They hire job-hoppers from other companies who stay with them for only a few years. How can we expect them to develop any company knowledge? It's essential to hire people like family members whose strong connections to the company ensure loyalty.
When we complain about an incompetent employee at one of our branches, they refuse to discipline her because she's from a prominent family. Why would they hire someone with no qualifications in the first place?	They criticized one of our employees, who comes from a powerful family, as "incompetent." Don't they understand that her connections are more valuable to us—and, by extension, to them!—than if she were a technical expert?

8

Achievement	Endowment
Performance-based compensation is the fairest system. They want to compensate our joint venture team on the basis of seniority, but we'll lose our best employees if we don't reward them for their performance.	Seniority-based rewards are only fitting. They want us to compensate our joint venture team purely on the basis of performance, but then some younger people would make more than the senior employees. That would be an insult.
Their young employees are given little responsibility and must get approval for every decision. If you treat people like children, they'll never grow up. That can stifle creativity in talented people, too.	They test young employees by giving them responsibilities and exposing them to challenges they are unprepared for. This creates risk and a lack of coherence.

INVOLVEMENT: NETWORK AND PROCESS

Network   Process

Building Relationships	
Network	Process
We've been trying to build a relationship during cultural events and meals, but they seem resistant. How else can we get to know them and decide whether they're a good fit?	We came here to do business, and they keep taking us to concerts and banquets. We have to go home soon, and we haven't even started work discussions. Are they serious about this deal?

Network	Process
It's time-consuming to create strong business relationships. It would be a waste of time to skip from one partner to another; we would jeopardize continuity and develop a reputation for instability. We want partnerships that last.	It's easy to create a trial partnership. If things don't work out, end it. Why waste time spending years developing relationships? We change partners depending on who offers us the most at a given time.
It's better to be sure our companies are a good fit than risk a bad relationship. Why are they in such a hurry to talk contracts? We're just getting to know one another.	We don't need to know the names of their children to do business—all we need is a good contract. Why do they keep bringing up these personal topics?
We took them to our manager's country house to honor them and show that our company provides a good living to its employees. But they didn't seem to get the message or appreciate the hospitality.	They drove us out to the country house of one of the managers. He must have wanted to impress us with his wealth. The quality of their products is what we care about—we don't need to spend time touring vain people's homes.
We asked our partner for a special concession, and they turned us down. We've worked together for years now; it's the least they could do for a long-standing partner.	They asked us for a special concession. They need to understand that our terms aren't subject to special deals—all our partners get fair and equal treatment.

Hiring and Promotion

Network	Process
That interviewee had strange expectations. He wanted an exhaustive list of specific job duties. Employees should do whatever is needed, growing and adapting to changes. We evaluate them on compatibility and flexibility.	I prefer knowing exactly what is expected of me. Employers should evaluate the execution of specific duties. Without clarity on the criteria for promotions and raises, how can I be sure the system is logical and fair?

8

Network	Process
As president, I'm proud that our senior management includes family members and close friends—people I know I can trust. That says a lot about the cohesiveness and stability of the company.	We have policies to prevent relatives from working in the same division, and if two employees marry, one has to leave. Nepotism results in favoritism and bad business decisions.

Workplace Relationships	
Network	**Process**
When I asked about my colleagues' families in a meeting, people were surprised. The team leader acted really impatient. She interrupted me and suggested we get down to business. They're so impersonal!	Their meetings start with a lot of socializing and chitchat, and it can take half an hour to get to the agenda. This time wasting makes me doubt their commitment to the project.
I spend as much time with my work colleagues as I do with family members, so it makes sense for us to be close friends. We're more effective at work, too. I feel rejected by the lack of warmth in our partner.	I prefer to choose my friends based on shared interests. I may not have much in common with my work colleagues; I see enough of them at work, anyway. But our partner's employees pressure us to socialize after work.
Their employees work the required number of hours each week and then go home. They have little company spirit, and they don't take advantage of social occasions to build a strong team dynamic.	They go out with each other after work—and even on weekends. They have to take customers out socializing. There's no end to it. When I'm working with them, my family life suffers and I don't have time for my friends.
Our division manager is moving to a new house next week, and of course we're all going to help out. It's inconvenient for some of us, but the boss is the boss. And he helped my brother get legal counsel last year. There's a give-and-take here.	Their division manager is moving next week, and he asked everyone to show up and help. They don't seem to have any boundaries. The hierarchy applies even away from work, and the top people abuse their privileges.

COLLABORATION: INDEPENDENT AND GROUP

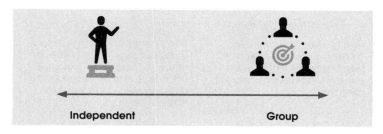

Decision Making	
Independent	**Group**
Why are there so many of them at this meeting? Who has the real negotiating authority? If that person is competent, why are the others here?	Why did they send just one person? How can she have all the knowledge necessary to make informed decisions? Don't they take this negotiation seriously?
Why are decisions taking so long? Are they giving our partnership low priority? Are they stalling? Maybe they're not serious about doing business.	How is this person making decisions so quickly? Is she considering all the angles? Does she really speak for all the business units that will be affected by this agreement? It's a bad sign for things to move this fast.
There doesn't seem to be a decision maker here. They constantly stop and postpone negotiations until they've checked with headquarters. Their method seems very inefficient.	They seem surprised when we stop our negotiation to consult with colleagues. Everyone affected by a decision needs to have input. One person making decisions for a whole company is very risky.
Whenever we come up with a creative suggestion, it takes them weeks to come back with a response. They cannot handle spontaneity.	Whenever they change direction, we must go back to all our departments to discuss the implications. They are capricious and unreliable.

8

Representing the Group	
Independent	**Group**
Nearly every time we take a break, they hold a private meeting. It's as if they're plotting some secret strategy, and it's unnerving.	We must talk among ourselves during breaks to be sure we're all in agreement. Then no one will misrepresent the group's position. Why do they seem surprised?
When I ask even simple questions, they say, "I don't know," or, "I'll check," and then come back later with the answer. Sometimes we just need an estimate. Can't they think for themselves?	If we ask three of them the same question, we get three different answers. Which one is correct? A unified position is the least you can expect from a competent team.
We singled out a member of their team for special thanks to let everyone know what a great job he had done. We want him to get full credit for his hard work, which seems to go unrewarded.	Instead of praising the entire team, they identified only one member, setting him apart from the rest and embarrassing him. His teammates were furious, of course—it was tactless and insulting to them.
Implementation	
Independent	**Group**
They finally agreed to a deal. Now I'll call a meeting at HQ to let everyone know what has been decided. I hope Marketing doesn't object to the deadline for the new collateral.	They were impatient, but we worked things out. Everyone who needs to know about this discussion has provided input. I'm glad we took time to get Marketing on board—now we're ready to move ahead.
It takes them forever to make a decision, so it will probably take them just as long to start implementation. That should give me time to get consensus from our various departments.	They make decisions quickly, so we should be able to ramp up rapidly now that we've agreed. That suits us fine—we got consensus before we agreed to their terms, so we can start immediately.

Team Dynamics	
Independent	**Group**
When this project is over, our team members will go on to various new ones. We respect each other's work, but we don't socialize much after hours—we have our own families and friends. Why do they spend so much time together? They must not have any social lives.	Our team is a close-knit group, and we work hard to stay in tune with one another. The team dynamic is vital to our success, so we spend a lot of time together. Why don't they put more emphasis on their relationships with each other? They must not be very committed.
Our team members work independently, but we come together as needed to compile individual contributions. It's the best way to take advantage of diverse ideas. Their approach seems stifling.	Our team members work together and consult each other constantly. It's the best way to collaborate smoothly. Their approach seems disjointed.
I'm interested in getting to know people from the other team, but they stick to themselves. They're like a club, and they're not that friendly. They must not like us.	My team is like a family. New partners will come and go, so I put my energy into the people I know. Why do they seem so interested in being our friends? Are they trying to spy on us?
If a teammate has a personal problem, I'll help get the work done to move the project forward. I'm proud of my work, and the extra effort is an investment in my future. The opportunity gives me extra visibility, after all.	If a teammate has a personal problem, I'll help get the work done so the team's reputation won't suffer. It's my responsibility, even if it means a sacrifice. They would do the same for me.
I want to make my counterpart on the other team feel like she's part of our group, so I gave her some "inside" information. They can count on us to be friendly.	I want them to respect us as a team, so I'll keep any problems we're having secret. They can count on us to be professional.

8

Independent	Group
They hoard information and won't tell us what's going on internally. If we'd known about that problem, we could have helped. They don't seem to trust us or treat us like real partners.	They ask prying questions and make us uncomfortable. We try to solve problems ourselves. Although we work for the same company, we're still on different teams.

AUTHORITY: RULE AND SITUATION

Rule   Situation

Contractual Relationships	
Rule	**Situation**
They seem to want handshake agreements. The contract wording they suggested was vague and general. An honorable company would be willing to make a contractual commitment.	They seem to want to box us into an airtight agreement. We rely on flexibility from our partners as conditions change, and we accommodate them as needed, too. You need that in a real partnership.
They want us to revise a contract we've already signed. We're prepared to abide by it ourselves—why do they expect us to make an exception for them? A deal is a deal.	We had no way of predicting this change in the market. Why won't they let us out of a deal that now makes no sense? Partners need to help each other.

Procedures and Schedules	
Rule	**Situation**
They seem to be fighting the new process controls we implemented. They try to sneak around them rather than complying. Don't they care about the quality of the product?	There's too much bureaucracy already, and they want to add more. Rules limit flexibility and waste time. Maybe these arbitrary procedures are just a way to control us.
They seem unable to develop or stick to a realistic schedule—we can't seem to nail down delivery dates. Maybe they don't take their obligations seriously.	Schedules are estimates—who can say what's going to come up? They should expect the unexpected and adapt to surprises. Their method seems very inflexible.
We have a schedule for financial reports, and one of our branches consistently misses it. Why can't they just be on time?	Due to our time zone, we can provide the most accurate information a little after the deadline. Do they really value an arbitrary schedule over accuracy?
Consistency and Fairness	
Rule	**Situation**
The procurement manager we work with is also the cousin of their VP, and he's virtually incompetent. Why don't they hold him to the same standards as everyone else?	We all must take care of family members, so naturally people with good connections get special favors. We prioritize family relationships—why can't they?
This partner keeps putting us in awkward positions by asking for special favors. How can we justify making exceptions for them while other partners must stick to the rules?	We've done business with them for years, but you'd think we were complete strangers— they won't give us the slightest concessions. Doesn't our relationship mean anything to them?

8

Rule	Situation
Our new incentive program is fair because it rewards employees for their performance. But one of our branches is fighting it. Don't they see that everyone should meet the same criteria for compensation?	One of our employees recently lost his wife and had a poor sales year as a result. The new corporate incentive program will penalize him even further at this difficult time. Don't they see that this is unfair?
This potential partner claims they can get special treatment because of their government connections. Don't they realize this kind of favoritism is inappropriate, even if they don't do anything illegal? We want to play by the book.	We've spent years on government relations to make the process easier, and this is part of our value proposition to them. Why don't they recognize the usefulness of these connections? They're the only way to get results.

ACTION: OPPORTUNITY AND THOROUGHNESS

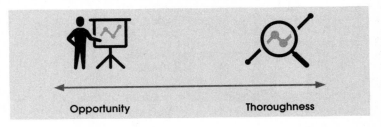

Opportunity   Thoroughness

Strategy	
Opportunity	**Thoroughness**
The past isn't that important. We learn from it, and then we move on. We should constantly look to the future. Decisions must be made quickly. Why can't they move forward?	Any mistakes we make will be remembered for a long time. We must consider the implications of our decisions from every angle. Why are they in such a hurry?

Opportunity	Thoroughness
Achieving good short-term results and opportunity hunting are the ways to establish a reputation. If an idea fails, we'll go in a new direction. Their approach limits innovation.	Building relationships and expanding them carefully over time is the way to establish a reputation. Bad ideas are costly. Their approach is risky and immature.
Our customers want the latest product features, and they'll change suppliers if we don't innovate. If one product is weak, they won't hold that against us if we come out with a winner soon after. Why is our partner unwilling to experiment?	We sell to established customers who want reliability in the form of quality, warranties, and maintenance agreements. Disappointing them has long-term consequences—it may take years to win them back. How can our partner treat these consequences so lightly?

Decision Making and Implementation	
Opportunity	**Thoroughness**
With only three items on today's agenda, we expected quick closure, but they belabor every point. Why is this taking so long?	Many meetings are necessary to conclude the discussion we began today. Each agenda item must be thought through carefully. They seem to undervalue thoroughness.
Meeting deadlines and achieving milestones are vital to our reputation. Our partner should be more specific when it comes to schedules.	Internal milestones are irrelevant if final deliveries are on target. Our partner needs to be more flexible in terms of time.
They claim they can't make a decision one way or the other. We need to move forward or else the deal is off. "Maybe later" isn't an answer we can take back to headquarters. They must not be serious.	The fact that we can't make a decision right now isn't a deal breaker. There's still possibility for the future, but they seem to have a "now or never" attitude. We could never justify this approach to our management.

8

Opportunity	Thoroughness
We have good indications that timing is right for this deal. They want to spend even more time on analysis—there's no end to it. In the meantime, opportunity is slipping away.	There are indications that timing is right for this deal. They want to move forward immediately, but we still need time to consider. If we miss this opportunity, there will be others.
Both teams investigated a question. Ours found an answer in two days, but they insisted on finishing their research. They came up with the same answer after four days but refused to recognize that our process was more efficient.	Both teams investigated a question. Both came up with the same answer, but we spent extra time to ensure we considered every angle. They refuse to recognize that our process was more thorough and complete.

Partnerships	
Opportunity	Thoroughness
We need to get our new partnership in place and begin implementing immediately. The opportunity cost of waiting is high. Why are they so cautious?	Any new partnership must be discussed in the context of our company history and implemented in alignment with tradition. Why are they so reckless?
The pressure we're under to show results in the next quarter forces us to be agile and innovative. We need our partners to be responsive.	The importance of establishing a track record over many years forces us to be cautious and thorough. We need our partners to be patient.
We chose our team based on their ability and expertise. We brought our best to this negotiation. Why did they send these older managers? They aren't close to the product or the customer.	We chose our team based on seniority and experience. Who are these young upstarts on their team? They haven't been around long enough to know anything about the industry or the market.
Why did they get so upset when we reassigned our head negotiator to another project? The new one is competent and well informed.	Just as we were getting to know their negotiator, he was replaced. What did he do to be reassigned, and how do we trust this new person? Something is wrong here.

ORGANIZATION: SCHEDULE AND FLOW

Schedule ←——————————————→ Flow

Schedules and Structure	
Schedule	**Flow**
Because they were late to the meeting, we didn't have time to conclude business before our next appointment. Don't they respect our time? It's unprofessional and insulting.	We gave them our full attention and were willing to spend as much time as needed. But they rushed off to another appointment before we were done. That's really pointless.
We never know when meetings with this partner will start. Why do they say "three o'clock" if they don't mean it? What does "three o'clock" really mean to them?	Appointments are really just estimates. We can't guarantee when a meeting will begin. Rushing one appointment to get to another would be rude and unproductive.
They've rescheduled our meeting three times. They seem to have poor organizational skills.	They're inflexible about appointment changes. They seem to care more about their schedule than having the right people there.
We agreed on a to-do list, but they won't stick to the plan we made. There's no way to predict when things will finish when their team is so disorganized.	The plan they made at the beginning of the project quickly became obsolete, and we've dealt with problems as they've come. Plans are estimates, not manifestos.

8

Schedule	Flow
We missed one of our project milestones. Now it will be difficult to get back on schedule. Our whole plan has been disrupted.	We've done a great job of meeting milestones—only one is incomplete. We may have to work extra hard at the end, but that's just what it takes sometimes.
Getting Things Done	
Schedule	**Flow**
We should take care of this by e-mail—it's faster and less expensive than meeting face to face. There's no need to waste time on small talk. Don't they see that efficiency is what counts?	We should schedule a meeting with them to discuss this. It's important to talk in person when there's so much at stake. Don't they see that good communication is what counts?
After months of work on a proposal, they came up with a new direction at the last minute. We had everything worked out. Why couldn't they suggest this sooner? This will mean a lot of extra work.	We had an outstanding idea, but they complained that adding it so late was inconvenient. A good idea is a good idea no matter when it comes up. They need to get their priorities straight.
They talk on the phone, direct people in the office, and type on the computer all at once. How can they give full attention to our project if they work like this?	They try to control things and deal with each issue in a set order. How can they take care of a complex project if they can only manage one thing at a time?
Their VP took two calls in the middle of our meeting, stopping the discussion both times. This wastes time and is disrespectful of our work. They should focus on the matter at hand.	We have to keep multiple projects moving, so it's natural to take calls during a meeting. They were upset about this, but if they were the ones calling, they'd appreciate our responsiveness.

9

Mastering Cultural Analysis

To build your skills in applying cultural analysis to real-life situations, this chapter provides two scenarios involving cultural conflicts to help you practice identifying the tendencies in action and developing strategies for managing differences. In each one, you'll hear both sides of the story as differences in cultural orientation create confusion and conflict. You can then identify the cultural factors in play, consider how participants might improve things, and observe what each could gain from the other's strengths. The discussion following each one will help you identify any nuances you've missed. A cultural tendency identification quiz is available on my website.[1]

Exercise 1. Scenario Analysis: Collaboration Challenge

Nancy's Perspective

Nancy Bachmaier is having trouble with her new post. Her six-month assignment managing a new international partnership for her employer, Autotech International, sounded like a good chance to gain visibility and enhance her career. But it's turned out to be an exercise in frustration,

---

[1] www.deirdremendez.com/practice-quiz

and possibly a bad career move. Things started out promisingly enough, with the appearance of good will and aboveboard operations on both sides. Now, though, she's concerned that the "relaxed" attitude of the new partner, Kuching Automotive, toward her company's policies may be a serious liability. In fact, an attitude of disdain for every type of rule and procedure seems to prevail at Kuching. Nancy cannot see how the partnership can survive unless things change.

At age thirty-six, Nancy is a rising star at Autotech, and management has given her full support on this assignment. A lawyer with a degree in mechanical engineering, she's negotiated two contracts with European partners and was considered the ideal choice to handle the job's legal and technical components. But she has had run-ins with Affendi Mawar, her counterpart at Kuching, over a range of issues. With each passing week, her confidence in Affendi as a manager has diminished.

The problems began early in the relationship. She worked successfully with Affendi at first, providing information as needed in preparation for contract negotiations. But once it was announced that she would be the project lead on the Autotech side and his direct counterpart, Affendi grew cold and unresponsive. An engineer who moved up the ranks over his many years at Kuching, he is less educated than she is and hardly an innovation leader—essentially a midlevel bureaucrat with no significant technical expertise, in her opinion. Still, he found ways to imply that she was unqualified for her position. She worked hard to gain his respect, completing two assignments in record time, but she had a growing feeling that he disliked her. She didn't know where things went wrong, but he seemed to ignore her efforts to show that she was a top performer.

Nancy told herself she was a professional and could live with the cold shoulder, but the problems just kept coming. During contract negotiations, penalties specified in the contract for late deliveries were consistently pushed to the end of the agenda by the Kuching negotiators. They resisted specific wording and complained about the length of the contract. One commented to her that since only God knew what might come up, there was no point trying to spell out every eventuality. Didn't they understand that the point of a contract is to anticipate eventualities and establish how they'll be handled so there are no surprises? The Kuching negotiators finally agreed to the contract wording, and she thought the matter was put to rest.

A short while later, the price rose for titanium, which is used in several engine parts Kuching supplies to Autotech. Naturally, this would increase Kuching's manufacturing costs. Affendi suggested that they renegotiate the price Autotech would pay based on the new cost of titanium. "What?" Nancy replied in disbelief. "A contract is a contract! Kuching agreed to assume this risk when you signed our agreement. You don't renegotiate contracts every time market conditions change!" Affendi responded indignantly. "How can you expect one partner in a deal to absorb all the loss? You have no respect for relationships! Partners must support each other over the years. If the situation were reversed, we would help you." Nancy was confused. What did he mean by "over the years"? For Autotech, the current project was a one-time deal designed to capitalize on a government incentive program encouraging foreign partnership. Any future collaboration between the two companies would be based on business potential, not friendship. It wasn't Autotech's job to bail Kuching out of self-inflicted difficulty.

As if that weren't enough, friction has been building over Kuching's erratic HR policies. When Nancy asked about the newest addition to the Kuching implementation team, who seemed very young and inexperienced, she was informed that his principal qualification was being the nephew of a Kuching adviser who had helped smooth the way for important business deals. Appalled, she pointed out that putting an unqualified employee on the Autotech project would be viewed as a lack of commitment to the partnership, and requested that Affendi remove him from the team. Affendi repeated his comment that she had no respect for relationships. He moved the young man to another project, but the incident further widened the gap between the two of them.

And now, Nathan Jensen, the Autotech consultant to the project, has just burst into her office. Nathan is teaching local engineers statistical process control methods to ensure that product quality meets Autotech's standards. What he has to report is disturbing. After two weeks of classroom and hands-on training, the Kuching engineers seem to understand the processes, but they aren't using them. They listen politely, but when

Nathan leaves the manufacturing floor, they skip steps and ignore rigorous measurement standards. Two batches of parts have failed inspection, which will result in delayed deliveries to customers. Nathan asked his interpreter what was going on, and she responded, eyes lowered, that the engineers felt that the procedures were "a lot of extra work." Nathan returns home in a week, and once he's gone, the Kuching engineers will be on their own. He wants to know what Nancy will do to get the "incompetent and insubordinate" technical staff to meet quality control standards.

Nancy is at a loss, and walks into the staff lounge to organize her thoughts. Nazira, one of Affendi's project managers, is drinking tea with a few coworkers. Nancy isn't surprised to see her there—as far as she can tell, Nazira does almost no work and spends most of the day on her cell phone. Today, Nazira is beaming and tells Nancy she just received a promotion. Nancy is astonished. She doesn't know how Nazira even keeps her job and is sure she doesn't deserve it. Nazira is attractive and wears expensive clothes. Maybe she and Affendi are having an affair, Nancy thinks. But it doesn't affect the partnership directly, so she decides that this is one battle she doesn't have to fight.

After drinking a cup of coffee, she goes in search of Affendi to check on next month's budget. She finds him in his office, holding Nazira's personnel folder. Nancy can't help commenting that she's heard about the promotion and that, given Nazira's work ethic, she's surprised at the news. He responds simply that Nazira is related to the royal family, as if this were explanation enough. Nancy begins to respond that personal connections are hardly a basis for professional advancement, but stops herself. She has other problems to deal with.

Questions to Consider

A discussion of these questions is provided in the analysis at the end of the scenario.

1. What differences in cultural tendencies do you notice in Nancy and Affendi? How do these differences create conflict? (See Chapters 4–6 to review the attitudes and behaviors typical of each cultural tendency.)

2. How might the conflicts have been avoided if they had understood each other's preferences and approach? What strategies might Nancy have used to interact with Affendi more successfully? What could they do now to improve things? (See Chapter 9 for problem-solving strategies.)

Here's the same story from Affendi's point of view.

Affendi's Perspective

Affendi Mawar can't believe his bad luck. His career was going fine until this "wonderful" new opportunity came up. The deal with Autotech, an international auto parts manufacturer, had the potential to create a significant competitive advantage for his employer, Kuching Automotive. His family hosted a big party to celebrate his being named implementation team lead for this important project. At age fifty-two, he felt he had earned the prestige and could handle the responsibility. Having worked in a variety of departments at Kuching—from engineering to marketing to finance—he knew the company through and through and was trusted by both his superiors and his employees. But he was not prepared for what was coming.

Things actually started out all right. He was happy at first to work with his point of contact at Autotech, a capable young woman, while he waited for them to name a project lead. He looked forward to meeting his counterpart: It would be exciting to have an international colleague and learn about business in another country. So he was shocked and stunned to learn that Nancy, whom he had thought of as an administrative helper, would be his partner. A hundred thoughts went through his mind: Were they trying to insult him? How could this young person—a woman, no less—know anything about the complexities of running a company, of managing employees, of creating lasting partnerships? He almost resigned the day he learned that she had only been with Autotech for three years—she was virtually a novice with the company. And yet Autotech had seen fit to name her as his equal, as if his twenty-six years of building a solid reputation in the industry didn't matter. Sitting in his office, he can feel the blood rushing to his face when he thinks about it even now.

The only thing he could do was swallow his pride and give the deal his best for the good of the company. He decided that he would approach her as he would a daughter, offering her guidance and support. After all, she had much to learn about business and about Kuching. But from the beginning, her attitude was insulting. Instead of treating him like a senior colleague, Nancy behaved as if there were no difference in their age or experience, even trying to compete with him at times. She raced through joint assignments, bringing her portion to him triumphantly when she was done, as if timely spreadsheets were a match for hard-earned experience and wisdom. She caused him to lose face with his superiors on two occasions with this blatant showing off.

And what Autotech calls partnership seems more like indentured servitude for Kuching, he thinks bitterly. This attitude became apparent early on during contract negotiations. The Autotech lawyers descended like a horde of locusts, establishing complex milestones for Kuching to meet and inserting penalties for every possible breach of their terms. His colleagues were stymied. No one can predict the will of God and guarantee exactly how things will go. But everyone knows this, they had reasoned, so Autotech probably writes in all these penalties just to satisfy the legal people—and then everyone can relax. They were wrong, unfortunately. The price for titanium skyrocketed, dramatically increasing the production cost of three crucial parts. Affendi called his contacts at two of his current partners and explained the situation. One, a long-term associate, immediately agreed to split the extra costs. Kuching had done the same for them two years earlier, and Affendi knew he could rely on reciprocation. The other partner, a newer one with a formal contract in place, assured him they would relax the terms of the contract to address the problem. After all, he said, the relationship needed to be insulated against fluctuations today so it would survive until tomorrow.

But when he contacted Nancy Bachmaier at Autotech, he was told that the Autotech contract was fixed and he would be held to its terms. He couldn't understand this attitude. Nancy seemed to be thinking only in the short term—oblivious to the implications of her behavior in years to come. Affendi could hardly face his superiors when he told them the news. The cost increase cut heavily into their margins, and he worried that delivery dates, which are affected by so many factors beyond his control, would also be missed with resulting penalties. He is sleeping poorly and losing weight.

And the problems didn't stop there. Nancy protested his hiring an adviser's nephew, as if she had no conception of how relationships work. The man brokered two deals that brought Kuching RM65,000,000 in business. The least Affendi could do was give the adviser's nephew an entry-level job—how could he refuse, and why should he? Investing in a relationship with someone so influential was well worth it. But Nancy was so insistent that he moved the boy to another project. It's been a lot more work keeping an eye on him there, but Affendi gave in just to appease her.

As if all that weren't enough, a new problem has surfaced. Autotech sent a consultant to implement new quality control processes at Kuching. The training he was to provide was one reason Kuching agreed to the strenuous terms of the contract—it would put Kuching ahead of its competitors in product quality. But the consultant, Nathan, had no social skills. He never bothered to create any sort of relationship with the engineers or explain the reasons behind the processes—it was just, "Do this, and this, and this." He spewed out rules and policies and procedures and expected them to obey like robots. But people aren't robots, and the engineers have come to dislike Nathan. Since they have no personal motivation to stick to his rules, they're apathetic about the new processes and have cut some corners. Affendi may be able to help patch things up once Nathan is out of the way—but here comes Nancy again to complain on Nathan's behalf. Now he has two insensitive colleagues to deal with!

On top of it all, she casually comments that he shouldn't have promoted Nazira, one of their most valuable assets. Having a member of the royal family on their staff is a huge benefit to Kuching. With a few phone calls, she can open doors that were closed to them completely before. Of course she doesn't have a work ethic. Kuching has plenty of "worker bees"—they hired Nazira for her connections! It took him two years to hire someone with just the right social and political positioning, and she has already made three strategic introductions for him. And he has to justify this to an arrogant young girl? The situation is nearly intolerable.

Analysis

How does hearing Affendi's side of the story affect your initial interpretation of the situation? You may notice that the cultural tendencies of each participant seem unreasonable when viewed from the other's perspective, but make more sense when you see the story from their own point of view. That's because the scenario gives background on the cultural environments of each participant, where their respective behavior is normal and rational. In most intercultural interactions, people don't have the benefit of this information, and neither side makes any sense to the other.

Below is an analysis of the cultural tendencies that contribute to the conflict in the scenario.

1. Achievement/Endowment (Status dimension)

    The mismatch in Nancy and Affendi's backgrounds and their lack of mutual respect results from different perspectives on **Status**. Nancy's Achievement orientation values credentials and performance, while Affendi's Endowment tendencies cause him to prioritize experience, loyalty, and seniority. Nancy's strategy for gaining Affendi's respect—to work hard and demonstrate her competence—is an Achievement-oriented strategy that just seems like showing off to him.

    Nancy's conflict with Affendi over Nazira, a relative of the royal family, also reflects differences on this dimension. Nancy doesn't accept Nazira's family connections as a legitimate basis for moving up in the company, thinking she should earn promotions through competence and hard work. Affendi rewards Nazira based on the usefulness of her influence—a different definition of value, but one that she fulfilled.

2. Rule/Situation (Authority dimension)

    Differing attitudes toward **Authority** are responsible for confusion during the companies' contract negotiations. Autotech's Rule-oriented contracts surprise Kuching's Situation-oriented negotiators, who are used to loosely structured contracts that offer mutual flexibility. They are unprepared for Autotech's rigid enforcement of the contract's unfavorable terms when conditions change, and Autotech equally surprised by their request to renegotiate.

The Authority dimension also shows up in the case of Nathan, the Autotech consultant who can't convince the Kuching engineers to follow his detailed procedures. Nathan, who is Rule-oriented himself, assumes that the Kuching engineers will accept that the rules are valid and recognize his authority as visiting consultant. Kuching's Situation-oriented employees, however, are suspicious of arbitrary rules and need a good reason to follow time-consuming procedures. Nathan fails to explain why each step is important, so they lack the information necessary to make that choice.

3. Network/Process (Involvement dimension)

When Nathan treats the Kuching engineers like "robots," he violates their expectations regarding **Involvement**. Creating a personal relationship with the engineers would have helped him gain their compliance, since the Situation orientation values relationships over rules. Nancy's conflict with Affendi over the adviser's nephew is also an example of differences for this dimension. Autotech's Process approach bases hiring decisions on credentials and experience, and Nancy considers it an affront that someone without appropriate skills was assigned to the joint project. Affendi's Network orientation places high value on Kuching's relationship with the adviser, and he believes the benefit of the adviser's goodwill justifies the trouble of managing the nephew. Since this sort of give-and-take is expected in a Network environment, not hiring the nephew could damage their relationship.

These cultural tendencies are also responsible for the disagreement over Nazira, the relative of the royal family. Nancy considers personal connections an inappropriate basis for hiring and promotion decisions. In her Rule- and Process-oriented view, using connections to get ahead in business while doing little work is dishonest. But in Affendi's Network environment, Nazira's status and influence are an important business tool. In his view, motivating Nazira to continue creating value for Kuching justifies the promotion.

4. Opportunity/Thoroughness (Action dimension)

Autotech and Kuching have different goals based on their tendencies in the **Action** dimension. Affendi assumes that the desire for a long-term association will motivate Autotech to renegotiate the titanium clause in their contract; in a Thoroughness environment, mutual give-and-take is an important part of ongoing relationships. But Nancy views the current project with Kuching as a one-time deal with no guarantee of future collaboration. In her view, any future deals will be motivated by favorable conditions, and if those are lacking Autotech will find other partners. On this basis, Autotech has little incentive to help Kuching with the problem.

Coping Strategies

Nancy and Affendi did little to understand one another. Clearly, they should have spent far more time explaining themselves and their company practices and asking about one another's. Beyond this, there were things they could have done to minimize tension and achieve synergies. Here are a few examples:

1. Achievement/Endowment

    A more sophisticated Nancy would have realized that Affendi did not see her as an equal. To lessen the perceived mismatch, she could ask a senior, preferably male, Autotech executive to introduce her formally in her new role, describe her qualifications, and express his trust in her. Nancy would also know that an older Endowment male like Affendi would expect a young, female colleague to treat him as a respected elder. She might address this expectation by showing respect for his age, experience, and stature; asking him questions about his life and career; and listening more than she talks. She might point out that as a newcomer to her surroundings, she has much to learn and would appreciate his guidance. When it comes to disagreements, rather than challenge him directly, she could use indirect verbal strategies to soften her position and avoid insult. None of these style-related strategies would damage Autotech's bottom line, and the goodwill they'd generate would greatly smooth her interaction with Affendi. Having an adviser who knows the ropes at Kuching would be enormously beneficial to her as well; she has much to gain from making him her advocate.

Nancy failed to recognize the value of connections and influence in an Endowment environment. Understanding how social influence advances Kuching's agenda would have helped her see that performing tasks is not the basis of Nazira's contribution. Understanding Affendi's decision to promote Nazira would lessen Nancy's frustration and allow her to evaluate Affendi's competence more accurately.

For his part, if Affendi had more experience with the Achievement orientation, he would have understood Nancy's great motivation to succeed in their joint project. For her, this project is an important rung on the ladder of success, and advancement depends heavily on her performance. Teaching Nancy the way Kuching operates and explaining its systems to her would be tremendously valuable for both of them. If Nancy perceived Affendi as a helpful advocate, she would be more likely to treat him as an adviser than an adversary.

Nancy's goal-oriented approach could be useful to Affendi as well. As an outsider to his system, she could push for innovations that he himself cannot. Nancy's ambition makes her a valuable agent for change. In any case, she's doing her best to prove herself, and he can count on her to be a hard worker.

2. Rule/Situation

If Nancy had understood Situation-oriented attitudes toward legal systems, she would have known that Kuching's management was unprepared for the level of detail and specificity in Autotech's contracts. She might begin by describing Autotech's legal environment and letting Kuching know that their joint contract would be taken seriously, but that they could incorporate language to protect it from certain developments after signing. Walking the Kuching lawyers through the contract would help them understand the commitment they were making. In response to the titanium crisis, she might also have supported Kuching's position and tried to gain at least a few concessions from Autotech. And learning how Kuching and its other partners work to support each other would be good training for Nancy.

Understanding Kuching's Situation and Network orientations would have helped Nancy anticipate the engineers' reaction to the

Rule- and Process-oriented approach of Nathan, the Autotech consultant. She could help Nathan develop personal relationships with them and explain the rationale behind the procedures to convince the engineers to follow the new policies.

If Affendi had been more familiar with Rule-oriented contracts, he might have explained the fluidity of Kuching's environment and asked Nancy to ask Autotech's legal department for more flexibility. He might advise Kuching's negotiating team to include detailed provisions in the contract to limit their liability in case of external problems. To gain her support for renegotiating their contract due to the titanium market change, Affendi might take more time to explain Kuching's expectations of partnership and mutual support. Learning Autotech's approach to contracts would also give Affendi valuable knowledge for future partnerships with Rule-oriented companies. And by recognizing Nathan's Rule and Process tendencies, Affendi could coach Nathan in gaining compliance from the Kuching engineers.

3. Network/Process

Given that Nancy is working in Kuching's facility, understanding the business environment there could save her a lot of frustration. Familiarity with Network-oriented hiring and promotion practices would have enabled her to see the logic of supporting relationships and the importance of personal influence. Hiring the adviser's nephew served a business purpose for Kuching, and although Nancy might prefer moving him to another project, recognizing that this was a strategic long-term decision could help her deal with the situation more tactfully. Explaining Autotech's credential-based staffing practices would give her a policy-based reason for requesting the move and lessen the personal nature of the confrontation.

With an understanding of Nancy's Process-based expectations, Affendi could have predicted her reaction and assigned the nephew to a different project in the first place. He would also be prepared to explain Nazira's place in the system and the reason for her promotion in spite of her apparent lack of productivity.

4. Opportunity/Thoroughness

If she had understood the Thoroughness approach to partnership, Nancy could have properly explained Autotech's goals to Kuching. She could clarify for Affendi that Autotech's goal was to capitalize on short-term government incentives and that future projects would be considered on the basis of similar opportunity. Understanding that there was no guarantee of a lasting relationship would help Kuching's management assess the value of the partnership and prevent false expectations. If Affendi had understood Autotech's Opportunity-based expectations, he could have ensured that the project contract protected Kuching from the unexpected and designed a plan for gaining maximum benefit in the short term.

Exercise 2. Scenario Analysis: Negotiation Nightmare

Frank's Perspective

Frank Bergman is tired. The past three weeks have been a strain, with little improvement in sight. Despite his best efforts, negotiations with Manaus Software, a promising potential supplier, seem to be going nowhere, and he wonders whether it might be better to forget about the deal and look for a new prospect. He hates to give up on Manaus's promising new software offering, but the CEO, Daniel Silva, seems so unstable that Frank wonders whether it's safe to proceed.

The partnership was Frank's idea. As CEO of Avesta Software Solutions, he'd first read about Manaus's new procurement software in a trade magazine. It seemed an excellent complement to his own company's e-business offering to its customers at home and abroad, and Manaus seemed to lack an international distributor. He contacted Daniel, Manaus's CEO, to say that Avesta might be interested in bundling his product with their own for sale to international customers.

Daniel's response was enthusiastic. Manaus was looking for an international partner, and Avesta's customer base seemed an excellent fit. After some e-mail correspondence, plans were made for Daniel to visit Avesta in person. Frank sent a draft of Avesta's standard contract for Daniel to look over in preparation, and everything proceeded smoothly until shortly before the visit itself. Prior to Daniel's trip, Frank had asked for some company information, which took Manaus weeks to send despite repeated reminders. The bios he had requested for Manaus's board of directors barely arrived in time for Daniel's visit. And Daniel was strangely unresponsive about Frank's suggested product rollout schedule. Daniel had given him only vague responses, so Frank was still waiting for his answer at the time of Daniel's visit.

Daniel seemed a bit nervous about coming to meet with Avesta from the beginning, but this didn't seem so surprising, since it was his first discussion with an overseas partner. Frank's staff had made careful arrangements for the trip, and everything was well organized, so he assumed Daniel would relax in time. But Daniel's anxiety seemed to increase during their discussions, and his behavior was odd in other ways as well. To Frank, he seemed full of nervous energy, talking nearly continuously from the moment he arrived. On his first day in their offices, he effusively praised the climate, the scenery, and Avesta's physical plant and asked Frank one question after another, some of them unnecessarily personal. He wanted to know about Frank's family, his hobbies, and even what he liked to do on vacation. Every time there was a pause, Daniel opened a new personal topic. It got to be a bit much, and Frank suggested they talk business. After all, Daniel hadn't come such a long way to chat about vacations. But keeping Daniel on track proved difficult. Every topic devolved into tangential discussions that Frank found distracting and even confusing. Daniel seemed unwilling—or unable—to get to the point.

When they finally got around to discussing the product rollout issue, Daniel announced that Frank's proposed schedule had been approved by Manaus, as if this belated response were some sort of accomplishment. Frank thanked him and explained that since his original proposal, there had been some adjustments to Avesta's forecast for the Asian market, which would move the rollout forward by a week. Daniel became visibly agitated at the news and seemed to be at a loss. "Well, I'll have to get back to you about that," he stammered. "What do you mean, get back to me? When?" asked Frank in surprise. "Well," said Daniel, "once I return, I'll need to discuss this change with my associates." Frank was astonished. Daniel had come all this way to discuss terms, and now that he was here, he needed to go home again before giving an answer. This was the beginning of Frank's concern that Daniel wasn't all he appeared to be. His unbusinesslike manner, his inability to make decisions—it didn't add up. Frank wondered whether Daniel was CEO in name only, with someone else running things from behind the scenes.

In the course of their meetings, Daniel's indecisiveness continued. Each time Frank suggested some novel or creative idea, Daniel would become nervous and confused. He would refuse to respond, mumbling something about needing time before he could answer. The third time this happened, Daniel seemed angry that he was even being asked to make a choice. His clenched jaw and stiff posture through the rest of the meeting alarmed Frank. Daniel seemed to alternate between excessive geniality and angry frustration. If he couldn't manage a professional demeanor during routine negotiations, how would he handle any serious problems that might come up during their partnership?

And it wasn't just decisions that were delayed. During his three days of discussions with Avesta, Daniel was late to two meetings. The second time, he was talking on his phone when he entered the conference room and, still talking, shook hands with Frank while finishing the call. He didn't even bother to apologize as he sat down—he just smiled and began his usual banter about the weather and his lovely breakfast at the hotel.

Frank was dismayed with the lack of progress of the meetings. Everything took longer than it needed to, and Daniel returned home with half of Frank's agenda still unresolved. Daniel promised to follow up, and now that he's home again, some points have finally been addressed, but many others have not. Frank's pricing proposal apparently poses some sort of difficulty, but Frank can't figure out what's going on. He's asked repeatedly for Manaus's response, or at least an explanation of what's taking so long, but Daniel has been slow in answering his e-mails, and recently stopped responding to him altogether. When Frank finally picked up the phone and called him yesterday, Daniel's assistant, sounding flustered, said that Daniel was out of the office and couldn't say when he'd be back. Clearly, there's something wrong at Manaus.

Questions to Consider

A discussion of these questions is provided at the end of the scenario.

1. What cultural tendencies do you notice in Frank and Daniel? How are they creating conflict? (See Chapters 4–6 to review the behaviors typical of each cultural tendency.)

2. How might the conflicts have been avoided if Frank and Daniel had understood each other's preferences and approach? What strategies might they have used to interact with one another more successfully? What could they do now to improve things? (See Chapter 11 for problem-solving strategies.)

Here's the same story from Daniel's point of view.

Daniel's Perspective

Daniel Silva is conflicted. Avesta's offer to take his company's star product to new markets seemed made to order. Daniel was pleased to find that Avesta's reputation, both in its home market and abroad, was excellent— just the sort of partner he was looking for. But the relationship isn't taking shape as he had hoped, and Daniel feels increasingly concerned about Avesta's intentions. Daniel is seeing worrisome behavior in his potential partner, and he isn't about to enter an agreement with a company he doesn't trust.

The idea of an international expansion makes Daniel nervous. He's built his business by developing strong relationships with top-tier partners in his home market, and his reputation is spotless. Replicating this success with international partners will be much more difficult, and he intends to proceed with caution. Frank Bergman's behavior has only added to his concerns.

Daniel first noticed Frank's strange attitude shortly before his trip to meet with Avesta. Frank seemed in a hurry even then, barraging Manaus with questions and expecting immediate answers. Daniel didn't respond right away; there was no rush to get into deep details before the two executives had even met. Daniel eventually asked his assistant to provide the information, and even after that, Frank still seemed irritated. This impatience continued when he and Daniel met face to face. At the first meeting, Daniel's principal goal was to get to know Frank and understand Avesta's company philosophy. He would no more rush into a business deal than he would a marriage, and making sure Frank was a person of competence and integrity was his first priority. If the two companies were a good fit, business would follow in good time, but for now the point was to develop a sense of whether the two could work productively together.

Frank's expectations were clearly different. Daniel arrived brimming with good will, but Frank seemed stiff and formal. He offered little in the way of conversation, and from the beginning, Daniel found him rather cold and hard to read. He seemed to lack enthusiasm for Daniel's ideas, even the ones he agreed with. Frank wasn't exactly negative either, at least not overtly, but several times he bluntly cut Daniel off and redirected the conversation. And he was equally blunt whenever he disagreed, pointing out problems with Daniel's suggestions with no attempt to soften his criticism. In addition to lacking warmth, he was completely tactless.

Daniel arrived at Avesta ready to share the vital details about his family, his career, and his company. But Frank wasn't very interested in this open-book approach; in fact, he resisted Daniel's best efforts to establish a personal connection. He avoided questions about his background and family life, repeatedly steering the conversation to business. Thinking back on it now, Daniel wonders whether Frank has something to hide.

Daniel's sense of apprehension has been strengthened by other factors as well. During their business discussions, Frank seemed determined to stick to a narrow agenda, and when Daniel brought up related issues, he dismissed them as irrelevant. Daniel's experience in business has taught him the importance of understanding the broader context of every business deal—and that thoroughness is especially crucial for international relationships. Frank's impatience to get to the point is unnerving to

Daniel. Maybe Avesta is trying to take advantage of Manaus. Frank certainly hasn't treated Daniel like a friend and partner—he seems to value the schedule over their relationship. He acted tense and annoyed any time Daniel was a few minutes late, especially once when Daniel had to finish an urgent call from his marketing manager just prior to a meeting. If he's this inflexible now, what will happen when something unexpected comes up?

The most disconcerting thing of all is that Frank keeps rushing Daniel on important decisions. Although it's too early to talk about timelines, he tried to accommodate Frank's desire to discuss the topic. When Frank sent him a proposal for a product rollout, Daniel assembled his logistics team and called a meeting with his product localization partners. He explained Avesta's proposal and asked everyone in the group to weigh in. After several discussions, it was agreed that the rollout schedule was feasible, and the group put together a plan for moving forward. This took time, of course, and Daniel was unable to answer Frank's question with certainty before his trip. This seemed to annoy Frank, who clearly expected an immediate response once again. But what was most mystifying was Frank's behavior when Daniel formally accepted his proposal. No sooner had Daniel told him the rollout was approved than Frank had come up with a different schedule, making another request for an immediate response. Daniel was astonished at this frivolous change of direction and Frank's lack of consideration for his need to confer with partners and staff. He seemed to be pushing Daniel toward a snap decision.

After two more incidents like this, Daniel began to question Frank's reliability. He might be Avesta's CEO, but he couldn't know everything that was going on at the company. Where was he getting all these spontaneous ideas? He didn't seem to be conferring with anyone internally before he made these offhand suggestions. And Daniel couldn't be expected to answer responsibly without discussing the issues with his colleagues. Daniel couldn't decide whether Frank was trying to trick him or was just being irresponsible, but either way, this wasn't a healthy sign.

Now that Daniel is back at home, the problems have continued. The pricing strategy Frank proposed is inappropriate for several reasons. To avoid a confrontation and clue Frank in on the problem, Daniel gently explained his company's overall strategy and their pricing policies in their home market. Rather than take the hint and modify the proposal, Frank kept pushing for an answer. The situation became so embarrassing that last week Daniel stopped answering Frank's e-mails altogether, a clear signal to Frank that it was time to back off. Frank still didn't get it; in fact, he became even more confrontational, calling the office and demanding to speak with him directly. Daniel told his assistant to say he wasn't in, but he's beginning to feel harassed.

Daniel isn't sure what's going on, but he's seeing some serious warning signs at Avesta. He needs a partner he likes and trusts—someone with a sense of give-and-take—and Frank is proving to be demanding and inflexible. Rushing into contract negotiations with a partner he barely knows is counter to good business sense, and Daniel won't be pressured into making hasty decisions. Despite Avesta's solid reputation, this deal is beginning to look shady.

Analysis

How does hearing Daniel's side of the story affect your initial interpretation of the situation? Again, a person's culture-based behavior makes more sense when you consider his or her own point of view.

Below is an analysis of the cultural tendencies contributing to the conflict in the scenario.

1. Indirect/Direct (Clarity dimension)

   The **Clarity** dimension is one important source of confusion. Frank misses the Indirect signals Daniel is sending about the pricing proposal. As a Direct communicator, Frank fails to catch Daniel's subtle indication that the proposal is flawed. The contextual information Daniel provides to clue him in seems largely irrelevant to Frank, and rather than recognize that something is wrong on his end, he simply repeats his request for an answer. Frank's Direct manner is confrontational and tactless to Daniel, who retreats further as time goes on, and he finally resorts to avoiding Frank altogether. Even this extreme maneuver is misunderstood by Frank, who is still looking for a concrete response.

2. Neutral/Expressive (Emotion dimension)

Frank and Daniel differ on the **Emotion** dimension as well. Daniel's Expressive language and enthusiastic posture strike Frank as excessive and possibly insincere, and his displays of anger and frustration cause Frank to suspect that he is emotionally unstable. Daniel's tendency to fill silence with meaningless chatter comes off as frantic and makes Frank feel overwhelmed. Frank's Neutral style of self-expression and lack of interest in casual conversation make him seem cold and unenthusiastic to Daniel. His unwillingness to contribute personal details thwarts Daniel's attempt to get to know him and leads Daniel to suspect a hidden agenda.

3. Network/Process (Involvement dimension)

Frank and Daniel's conflicting goals for their partnership stem from differing **Involvement** tendencies. Frank's Process-oriented focus on structure seems cold and unfriendly to Daniel. Frank expects legal agreements to enforce business obligations, so he feels no strong need to know his associates personally. His goal is to move quickly through the agenda and get to the contract. Daniel's personal questions seem inappropriate and pointless to Frank. Because Frank defines the points for discussion narrowly, Daniel's attempts to introduce extraneous issues during meetings strike Frank as a waste of time.

Network-oriented Daniel bases partnership decisions on developing mutual trust. Legal agreements can't always be enforced, and in any case, suing a business partner would be distasteful and costly. For Daniel, strong personal relationships are vital; once trust has been established, business deals can proceed with very little legal formality. In fact, many of his closest friends are business associates he's known for many years. In his view, rushing into a deal without this foundation would be foolish on his part, and Frank's pressure tactics seem a bit devious. Understanding the fuller context is important to Daniel, and typical of a Network communicator, he wants to explore peripheral aspects of the business issues discussed. By trying to limit their discussions to the central topics, Frank comes across as trying to hide something.

4. Schedule/Flow (Organization dimension)

Frank and Daniel have different expectations of timeliness due to their orientations in the **Organization** dimension. Frank expects information exchange to proceed in a structured manner and is surprised at Manaus's seemingly haphazard responses. He also values punctuality and is taken aback by Daniel's multitasking and tardiness, which seem disorganized and disrespectful. Flow-oriented Daniel considers schedule changes routine and views multitasking as a natural way to operate in a fluctuating environment. It doesn't occur to him that ending a call as he enters a meeting is something he should apologize for. Daniel is also used to addressing tasks according to his preference and their degree of urgency. He doesn't rush to send the information Frank requests because he doesn't consider it important at this phase of the discussion.

5. Independent/Group (Collaboration dimension)

Differing perspectives on **Collaboration** are responsible for the confusion Frank and Daniel experience with respect to making decisions. Frank, the CEO of his company, has full decision-making authority. He values the input of his colleagues and discussed his plans with them before Daniel's visit. But as an Independent, he feels authorized to innovate and change direction during negotiations as he sees fit—and speak for all of Avesta when doing so. Once his decisions have been made, he will share them with the staff members responsible for finding ways to implement them. Frank's negotiating moves are therefore relatively quick and decisive, and he's comfortable introducing new ideas and pivoting during discussions. In Frank's mind, Daniel's inability to make decisions on the spot calls his competence into question.

Daniel's more Group-oriented approach is to discuss important decisions thoroughly with the staff members and business partners who will be affected by them and responsible for implementing them. Decisions made by the group will have the endorsement of all concerned and include plans for execution. Daniel and his associates take time to reach a consensus, but once they do so, implementation is quick and seamless. Frank's casual innovation and changes in direction seem

9

illogical to Daniel, who wonders how he can make promises on behalf of people he hasn't consulted. Furthermore, each change Frank suggests must be discussed with Daniel's colleagues back home. Frank's zigzag approach delays the negotiation, which seems inconsiderate to Daniel and possibly irresponsible. He doesn't understand how Frank can expect him to make quick decisions away from his network of colleagues—and wonders whether he is being tricked.

Coping Strategies

Frank and Daniel have little insight into one another's goals or behavior. Below are a few specific strategies for resolving the problems they're dealing with:

1. Indirectness/Directness

    Frank's failure to recognize Daniel's subtle signals is typical for a Direct communicator. Understanding Indirect approaches to conflict would help him recognize nonverbal signs of disagreement. Daniel's failure to comment on the pricing proposal is a sign that there is a problem with it, and if Frank realized this, he could have backed away instead of continuing to push and making things worse. If he had paid close attention to Daniel's first response, he might have found the clue in the contextual information. Failing that, he might pick up on Daniel's later unresponsiveness and research the issue on his own. He could also ask an intermediary to get Daniel's views to avoid pushing Daniel into full-fledged retreat. Learning to recognize and respond to Indirect cues would enhance Frank's skills in future business dealings, and Daniel could serve as a vital asset in situations where tact and diplomacy are called for.

    Daniel's Indirect style is causing a serious problem. His attempt to be tactful about the flaws in Frank's pricing proposal has created confusion and mistrust. If he had realized that Direct communicators don't take criticism of their ideas personally, Daniel could have explained his objections more overtly to avoid miscommunication. To lessen his own discomfort, he could begin by praising Frank's work on the proposal and any of its strong points, and then gently share his objections. Frank's conciseness could be an asset for Daniel when negotiating with parties that value clarity and the bottom line.

2. Neutral/Expressive

Differences in tendencies for the **Emotion** dimension also contribute to the misunderstanding in this scenario. If Frank were more familiar with Expressive tendencies, he would know that Daniel's effusiveness was intended to convey goodwill. By reciprocating a bit in style, Frank could help make Daniel more comfortable, and even if Frank couldn't match Daniel's enthusiasm, he would understand that it was just a communication style rather than an indication of emotional instability. Frank might also come to appreciate being able to read Daniel's reactions and opinions in their work together.

Daniel's lack of familiarity with Neutral behavior is making him work harder than he needs to. If he understood that brief, unemotional responses and long pauses were normal and comfortable for Frank, Daniel could relax a bit rather than trying to uphold both sides of the conversation. He could respond to silences with questions that put the conversational ball in Frank's court, knowing that despite Frank's quiet manner, he is still engaged in the discussion. Working with Frank, Daniel might come to appreciate Frank's calm and rational approach in stressful situations.

3. Network/Process

Recognizing differences in perspective on the **Involvement** dimension could relieve some suspicion on both sides. If Frank understood Daniel's desire to form a solid partnership by developing trust, he would be more comfortable with personal questions and might resist steering the conversation to business topics. Understanding the importance of strong relationships to Network partners might help Frank slow down to meet Daniel's expectations. He could design an agenda that accommodated lengthier discussions and negotiations and focus on helping Daniel feel comfortable. Frank could also learn from Daniel's expertise at creating strong relationships as Avesta expands into markets where personal contacts are vital to success.

Understanding Frank's Process-oriented desire to get down to business would help Daniel correctly interpret Frank's intentions and respond accordingly. He might explain the "logic" of relationship building as well as Manaus's working environment to help Frank predict the pace of the deal. Daniel could also benefit from Frank's clarity of purpose and his efficiency in moving business forward.

4. Schedule/Flow

Frank would be less confused by Manaus's seemingly erratic replies if he understood Flow tendencies. He might focus more on final deliverables, recognizing that much of Manaus's work would probably be done toward the end. If he recognized the creativity and problem-solving ability associated with Flow tendencies, he might be less rigid about time and learn to rely on Daniel when surprises came up.

Understanding Frank's Schedule-oriented expectations would help Daniel anticipate Frank's frustration when information and decisions were not forthcoming. By describing Manaus's Flow environment, Daniel could help Frank understand the company's working style and help set expectations. Appreciating Frank's need for structure and early notification could motivate Daniel to keep Frank informed as things progress and reassure him that Manaus is a reliable business partner. And Frank's reliability would be an asset to Daniel in joint projects.

5. Independent/Group

Daniel's difficulty making quick decisions would be less mysterious to Frank if he understood Daniel's approach to **Collaboration** and the way Group-oriented companies set policy and respond to proposals. Taking this into account would help Frank factor consensus-based decision making into the negotiating schedule, and he would understand the consequences of surprising Daniel with sudden ideas and changes. At the same time, he would know that Manaus would be ready to move forward once the decision had been made.

Daniel wouldn't be so confused by Frank's changes in direction if he understood Independent decision making. Recognizing that Frank has full authority to set policy for Avesta would give Daniel more confidence in Frank's suggestions, and he might come to appreciate Frank's creativity and willingness to pivot to get the best results. He would also be prepared for the possibility of Avesta being slow to begin implementation once a decision is made. Explaining Manaus's more laborious decision-making process would help Daniel justify his need for time and help Frank predict how long negotiations will take.

9

The ARC System
Part III: Capitalize

10

Being Persuasive

Now that you understand how cultural tendencies shape your counterpart's priorities and preferences, you can learn to state your own position in a way that will resonate with them. The formula is easy to understand: Frame your proposals in terms of your counterpart's cultural preferences. As straightforward as this may sound, it's not easy to do. This is because we naturally design our arguments around what would be most persuasive to *us*—we base them on our own cultural preferences, and unlearning this habit takes work.

Designing Arguments That Influence

To unlearn your own culturally conditioned strategies, begin by using a mechanical three-step process whenever you make a proposal, request, or explanation:

1. Identify your counterpart's cultural orientation.
2. Identify the goals and values associated with that orientation.
3. Frame your proposal in terms of those goals and values (not your own).

Although these seem like simple steps, they don't come naturally, and if you aren't careful, you'll find yourself slipping into old patterns. It's a good idea to go through the steps in a conscious way until the process becomes second nature.

Here's an example of designing a persuasive argument: Suppose you're a marketing manager assigned to oversee an important marketing campaign in an overseas subsidiary of your company. You've noticed that the team members assigned to you, while enthusiastic workers, tend to overlook financial reporting procedures—and the project's books are a mess. You've explained the process several times, but your team is still ignoring the accounting procedures. You're responsible for every aspect of the project, and you need the accounting done properly. What do you do?

1. **Identify your counterpart's cultural orientation.**

   To make the most persuasive case possible, you must consider all eight of your counterpart's cultural tendencies. For simplicity's sake, this example revolves mainly around the Authority (Rule vs. Situation) dimension. Your Situation-oriented team members know what the rules are, but they're ignoring them.

2. **Identify the goals and values associated with that orientation.**

   The goals and values associated with the Situation tendency are flexibility, adaptability, and the freedom to act based on context. Situation counterparts tend to prioritize personal relationships over rules and may be suspicious of authority. They follow rules that make sense to them when they have a good reason to do so.

3. **Frame your request in terms of those goals and values.**

   Based on the information in Step 2, it's clear that to convince a Situation counterpart to comply with rules, you should:

   - Give them the option to choose.

   - Give them a relationship-based reason to follow procedure.

   - Help them see the value of the rules.

Here are a few arguments that might work in this situation:

- *"Let me tell you why this procedure is important to the project . . ."*

  - This explains the value of the rules so counterparts can *choose* to comply.

- *"I'd like your help . . ."*
  - This is not an order. It gives the other party the option to refuse and invokes an interpersonal appeal for help. This is good for Network counterparts, especially if they're Endowment-oriented (because they'll be inclined to respect a superior).
- *"Our reputation is on the line . . ."*
  - This strategy establishes a negative outcome for failure to comply.

Easy, right? Well, not so easy if you're strongly Rule-oriented, in which case you'll be more inclined to say, "Please review the rules in the handbook. We're all required to follow them, and from now on, I expect you to comply." This strategy invokes authority (your own and the rule makers'), issues a directive (eliminating choice), and gives the rules priority over your relationship, which is anathema to Situation-oriented people. To avoid this trap, practice going through the three steps in a conscious way until the process becomes natural.

The next section highlights the goals and values for each of the eight cultural dimensions and presents strategies for appealing to different sorts of counterparts.

Strategies for the Eight Dimensions

Clarity

INFLUENCING INDIRECT COUNTERPARTS

Indirect values:

- Avoiding confrontation and demonstrating verbal sophistication
- Suggesting opinions rather than expressing them clearly
- Implying criticism so that it is never actually stated

Strategies for persuading Indirect counterparts:

- Express positive reactions to their ideas first, followed by gentle criticism.

10

- Express negative opinions through vagueness or humor.
- Withdraw ideas when you encounter negativity, and explore the objection later.
- Resolve disputes through intermediaries or private social interaction.

Indirectness is the most sensitive cultural tendency to manage because missteps can easily create awkwardness or even cause offense. The challenge is to introduce ideas in a way that gives you feedback and doesn't cause others discomfort if they disagree. Before advancing an idea in public, vet it beforehand with someone who understands the system. When introducing a proposal, if you encounter any signs of negativity, drop the matter and investigate the obstacle carefully later. (This applies if you're the boss as well. Subordinates won't cause you to lose face by disagreeing with you directly, so they may agree and then not comply.) If you encounter any resistance from juniors, say, "I'll give this more thought," change the subject, and later consult with a third party. Minimize ownership of ideas with such phrases as, "I wonder how it would be if X happened," rather than, "Well, *I* think we should do X."

INFLUENCING DIRECT COUNTERPARTS

Direct values:

- Reaching consensus through exchange and debate
- Achieving clarity regardless of personal feelings
- Getting to the point so action can be taken

Strategies for persuading Direct counterparts:

- Introduce ideas explicitly.
- Make sure your own opinions are represented. (Someone else can act as a surrogate if you are uncomfortable speaking for yourself.)
- Take ownership of your ideas to get credit for them.

- Defend or reformulate your ideas as appropriate—don't back down if you think you're right.

If you're Indirect, Direct environments may be very difficult because they require behaviors that may seem disrespectful or unsophisticated and make you feel vulnerable to attack, and the point of your well-crafted arguments may go over people's heads. Practice making statements such as, "I think we should do X, and here's why," before presenting your ideas. Likewise, practice challenging others' ideas with only minimal preliminary praise. (E.g., "That's an interesting approach, but I have some concerns.") Anticipate criticism, and be prepared to respond without engaging emotionally. If you're uncomfortable making a proposal yourself, try asking a colleague to bring it up for you.

Emotion

INFLUENCING NEUTRAL COUNTERPARTS

Neutral values:

- Seeking strategic advantage by masking emotions, opinions, and reactions
- Keeping problems to oneself to avoid burdening others
- Showing self-control and stability even in emotional situations

Strategies for persuading Neutral counterparts:

- Present proposals in a calm, unemotional manner.
- Maintain the appearance of emotional detachment from your ideas.

It's important to remain calm when presenting to Neutral contacts. Stress that you are committed to your ideas based on their merits. Avoid emotional language and demeanor, both positive and negative, during discussions.

INFLUENCING EXPRESSIVE COUNTERPARTS

Expressive values:

- Bonding through shared emotion
- Motivating through enthusiasm and preventing negative outcomes through strong objection

Strategies for persuading Expressive counterparts:

- Appeal to human values such as caregiving and mutual support.
- "Sell" your ideas—show enthusiasm, engage others emotionally, and defend your ideas energetically.

When making a proposal to Expressives, make sure they can feel the strength of your conviction. Try to engage them on an emotional level, using language that conveys intensity. (E.g., "I really think this is an exciting opportunity for us to . . ." or, "Doing this could have disastrous consequences!") Use facial expressions and gestures that support your comments. Show energy when you present and defend ideas so others will perceive your faith in them.

Status

INFLUENCING ACHIEVEMENT COUNTERPARTS

Achievement values:

- Egalitarian interaction and a lack of hierarchy
- Gaining status and reward through personal accomplishment
- Continuous improvement and "outside the box" thinking
- Winning and personal advancement

Strategies for persuading Achievement counterparts:

- Don't wait for instructions from above; if you have suggestions, present them.

- Explain how your ideas will contribute to reaching goals and gaining competitive advantage.

- Frame your proposals in terms of the credentials and skills they offer.

- Describe the steps involved and show how they advance the agenda.

Achievement counterparts want to move things forward and get results, so tie your ideas to those goals rather than to your status or connections. A prestigious title won't make your ideas more valuable, and a low position won't keep you from having a voice. Frame proposals in terms of innovation and improvement, and describe their advantages in terms of the bottom line.

INFLUENCING ENDOWMENT COUNTERPARTS

Endowment values:

- Respect for seniority and influence
- Knowing and respecting one's role within an established hierarchy
- Relationship maintenance and benefit to all concerned

Strategies for persuading Endowment counterparts:

- Introduce your ideas at the right time and in the right context based on your role and relationships.

- Begin by getting support from colleagues close to you, especially superiors, and build outward or let them advance your ideas.

- Frame your ideas in terms of their benefit to all concerned.

Achievers have difficulty operating within Endowment hierarchies and can come across as poor team players. *How* an idea is presented may be as important as the idea itself, so be sure you introduce proposals in a manner appropriate to your position. It may be best to give your ideas to your boss, who can then introduce them for you. Don't worry about losing credit—you'll earn the respect of your boss, who will support your career in ways that you could not on your own. Use a modest demeanor, which is required of juniors in Endowment environments and greatly appreciated in seniors.

Involvement

INFLUENCING NETWORK COUNTERPARTS

Network values:

- Building give-and-take relationships
- Prioritizing relationship maintenance over the "bottom line"
- Solving problems by leveraging contacts
- Special treatment based on relationships

Strategies for persuading Network counterparts:

- Introduce proposals after relationships are developed.
- Frame ideas as beneficial to both parties.
- Advocate ideas in terms of their benefit to the relationship.
- Frame concessions as special favors based on a relationship.

Rushing business discussions with Network counterparts is a mistake, so new ideas should be introduced after the relationship has had time to develop. Indicate that the relationship is your ultimate goal. ("This would be a great pilot project for future collaborations.") Emphasize mutual gain, and avoid bottom-line-oriented arguments. ("This project will give us an opportunity to get to know one another better," rather than, "This project will make a lot of money.")

INFLUENCING PROCESS COUNTERPARTS

Process values:

- Moving things forward efficiently
- Prioritizing business goals over relationships
- Fairness and equal treatment for all
- Solving problems by working through processes

Strategies for persuading Process counterparts:

- Frame ideas in terms of business goals.
- Advocate your position in terms of efficiency and the bottom line.
- Explain the "logic" of special favors and how they will contribute to results.

Process-oriented counterparts will appreciate your getting to the point quickly and basing your arguments on facts and logic. You may need to explain that cultivating or maintaining certain relationships is the most effective way of advancing a business agenda. Any suggestion should be framed in terms of the business goals it will accomplish.

Collaboration

INFLUENCING INDEPENDENT COUNTERPARTS

Independent values:

- Decision-making authority for individuals and small groups
- Expression of personal opinions and perspectives
- Contributing and being recognized for one's ideas
- Getting to the "best" decision, whether or not everyone likes it

10

Strategies for persuading Independent counterparts:

- Make your proposals to the decision maker.
- Frame your ideas and opinions as your own.
- Introduce your ideas wherever an opportunity arises.
- Argue for the value of your ideas based on their contribution to the bottom line.

To influence an Independent organization, it's helpful to identify the decision maker in the group. (In Achievement environments, you may be able to approach this person directly; in Endowment contexts, you may need to work your way up.) When you're asked questions, try to provide at least tentative answers, since hesitance may make you seem less competent. If you're unsure, hedge your answer. ("I think X may be the case. I'll confirm and let you know.") As a member of an Independent team, propose and defend your ideas directly to be recognized as a contributor. You'll get more recognition for good ideas than for modesty.

INFLUENCING GROUP COUNTERPARTS

Group values:

- Sharing decision-making authority among affected parties
- Speaking as a representative of the group, rather than as an individual
- Prioritizing team membership over receiving individual credit
- Preserving group boundaries and protecting group members

Strategies for persuading Group counterparts:

- Present fully formed proposals rather than tentative ideas.
- Avoid expressing personal impressions or opinions; always speak "for the group."
- Emphasize that your proposals are supported by your organization—use "we" more than "I."

- Determine whether it's appropriate to advance proposals on your own; if not, suggest them to the appropriate person.
- "Give away" your ideas to help your group.

To advance your agenda with Group-oriented counterparts, have their consensus-based decision-making process in mind. Consider a proposal thoroughly before presenting it, because it will be deliberated at length by multiple people. Avoid making casual suggestions or changes, which will take them back to the discussion table, and avoid presenting too many scenarios at a time, which could cause confusion. When answering questions, recognize that your answers will be seen as representing your organization's position; be very sure of them. Never criticize your team's processes or members around outsiders. Observe group protocol: Introduce your ideas subtly or allow others to propose them. You'll get more credit for being a team player than for brilliance.

Authority

INFLUENCING RULE COUNTERPARTS

Rule values:

- Prioritizing stability and universal order over personal preference
- Fulfilling commitments despite changing conditions
- Supporting others' need for stability

Strategies for persuading Rule counterparts:

- Explain why an idea supports long-term stability, even if it's disruptive in the short term.
- Apologize if an idea will cause disruption for others.
- Explain why changes are worth the inconvenience they cause.

To avoid being perceived as inconsiderate and capricious, it's important to frame new ideas as enhancing stability in the long term. ("The

10

most efficient way to keep our schedule on track in the long run is to take time now to deal with this new problem.") Even a good idea may be perceived as causing more work than it's worth if introduced at the last minute. Acknowledge inconvenient timing and, if possible, offer to help with extra work. Speak respectfully of the structures already in place. ("I respect our plan and will work to keep it intact in the face of these proposed changes.")

INFLUENCING SITUATION COUNTERPARTS

Situation values:

- Flexibility, adaptability, and the freedom to follow one's own beliefs and preferences
- The right to choose a course of action based on the situation
- Mistrust of authority and dislike of arbitrariness
- Priority of personal relationships over rules

Strategies for persuading Situation counterparts:

- Explain the value of your proposal.
- Offer them the choice to adopt your suggestion.
- Frame ideas in terms of how they will support relationship goals.

Frame suggestions in terms of their benefit to people rather than systems. ("Alima must work extra hard to correct these defects, and following this procedure will really help her out," rather than, "Compliance with process controls for this production line is mandatory.") Give counterparts (even subordinates) a choice—if you've done a good job explaining the value of a rule, they will support it. In extreme cases, "Follow this rule, or lose your job," may be the kind of value proposition that gets results, but it should only be a last resort.

Action

INFLUENCING OPPORTUNITY COUNTERPARTS

Opportunity values:

- Seizing the moment
- Flexibility in the face of changing conditions
- Promoting innovation and progress
- Showing results

Strategies for persuading Opportunity counterparts:

- Frame proposals in terms of near-term gain.
- Relate outcomes to forward motion and improvement.
- Express your willingness to change direction as needed.

Opportunity counterparts respond best to arguments that emphasize short-term benefits. Convey the value of caution by explaining the context you operate in, and advocate your ideas in terms of progress and results. ("In four years, these innovations will have improved our competitive position and increased market share X percent. But we can review the plan each year to be sure we're on track to reach this goal.")

INFLUENCING THOROUGHNESS COUNTERPARTS

Thoroughness values:

- Maintaining tradition and preserving reputation
- Recreating past success
- Showing caution when contemplating new directions
- Thorough analysis and investigation of potential consequences

10

Strategies for persuading Thoroughness counterparts:

- Frame suggestions in terms of long-term benefits.
- Demonstrate thoroughness in researching new ideas and possible consequences.
- Identify opportunities to build on short-term projects you propose in the future.
- Describe new ideas as recreations of past successes or precedents.

Make sure that your position is thoroughly considered when presenting to Thoroughness counterparts, and avoid introducing casual ideas or brainstorming. Discuss proposals in terms of their value in the long run. Describe ways that your ideas could be further developed. Research past initiatives of long-term partners, and frame your proposals as a way to recreate past success. ("When your founder, Mr. X, introduced product Y in 1937, he used a similar strategy. We think it can work again.")

Organization

INFLUENCING SCHEDULE COUNTERPARTS

Schedule values:

- Advance planning to avoid surprises in work flow
- Discomfort with last-minute urgency
- Respect for others' time

Strategies for persuading Schedule counterparts:

- Describe ways that your ideas support existing schedules.
- Acknowledge any disruption of work plans caused by new proposals.
- Provide advance warning and an apology if schedules will be disrupted.

If possible, new ideas or requests should be framed in terms of how they will help keep projects on track and meet deadlines in the long run. Always alert Schedule-oriented colleagues of changes in plans as early as possible; if they have time to reschedule, they will experience less disruption. If you develop a reputation for reliability, requests for greater flexibility will be taken seriously, particularly if you acknowledge the inconvenience and describe its benefits to preserving the schedule in the long run.

INFLUENCING FLOW COUNTERPARTS

Flow values:

- Flexibility and adaptability in scheduling
- Having a choice in planning work flow based on urgency and personal inclination
- Preference for working harder closer to deadlines

Strategies for persuading Flow counterparts:

- Describe ways you've tried to build flexibility and freedom into plans.
- Acknowledge the inconvenience of restrictiveness.
- Build in internal deadlines that create urgency.
- Create incentives for meeting internal deadlines—and, failing this, penalties for missing them.

Flow-oriented counterparts will resent structures that limit their self-determinism, and these will also undermine their creativity. When introducing restrictive suggestions, acknowledge the inconvenience and describe ways you've tried to build in flexibility. For longer projects, internal deadlines can be used to create the sense of urgency that motivates Flow-oriented counterparts.

10

To practice developing persuasive strategies for complete cultural pro-files, rather than a single cultural tendency at a time, see the examples on my website.[1]

---

[1] www.deirdremendez.com/persuasive-strategies

11

Anticipating and Solving Problems

In addition to accommodating your counterparts' preferences, there will be times when your goal is specifically to gain concessions from others. Understanding cultural factors will help you figure out what your contacts value, predict areas of relative flexibility, and develop appropriate persuasive strategies. But regardless of your ultimate goal, it's a good idea to adapt *stylistically* to adversaries as well as partners. Both will be more accommodating if you do. And when it's your turn to make concessions, you can avoid giving in on points that really matter.

Your relative status compared to your counterpart plays an important role in deciding who will accommodate whom in a negotiation. Employees make concessions to their superiors, suppliers make concessions to customers, and so on. But even if you're the low-status person in a relationship, the nature of your concessions is up to you to some degree. Understanding cultural dimensions will help you predict how international counterparts want to be treated and how to create a rapport. Accommodating them in style will make them more willing to accommodate you in substance.

Of course, there are times when you can and should expect others to accommodate you. If you're a supervisor or customer at the top of the hierarchy, you can expect concessions from counterparts lower down. But you will gain by stylistically accommodating them even in these situations. For example, if you're a customer, a Flow- and Situation-oriented supplier must fully understand the binding nature of your contracts and expect to be held accountable to their terms. Taking time to go over this issue before a contract is signed might eliminate the need to explain late deliveries to your own customers or take action against the supplier later on. One of the most valuable principles in intercultural interaction is:

If you accommodate people in style, they will be much more likely to accommodate you in substance.

In negotiations, your goal is to ensure that your concessions are relatively painless for you but valued by your counterpart. Understanding your negotiating partner's cultural orientation will help you avoid conflict, meet their stylistic expectations, frame requests in agreeable terms, and identify concessions you can offer at minimum cost.

The following pages identify intercultural challenges associated with each dimension and suggest strategies for managing them. You can refine these general recommendations to suit your own situation.

Communication

INDIRECT AND DIRECT APPROACHES TO CLARITY

Challenges for Indirect communicators dealing with Direct counterparts:

1. Convey your ideas and advance your agenda when working with people who cannot understand your level of subtlety in communication.

2. Make your knowledge, skills, and abilities known in an environment where self-acknowledgment and self-promotion are expected.

3. Defend your position in the face of disagreement and criticism.

4. Recognize that your contacts' frank assessment of your ideas is not designed to humiliate you; avoid taking disagreement personally.

5. Benefit from Direct colleagues' ability to move the business agenda forward rapidly.

Challenges for Direct communicators dealing with Indirect counterparts:

1. Offer opinions and feedback without offending people who consider direct criticism insulting or clumsy.

2. Create an environment in which highly diplomatic people are comfortable providing honest feedback.

3. Promote new ideas through private channels considered appropriate by your colleagues.

4. Develop strategies for getting frank communication from juniors.

5. Benefit from Indirect colleagues' ability to solve problems tactfully and maintain good working relationships.

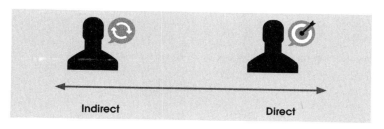

Indirect   Direct

Strategies for Indirect Participants	Strategies for Direct Participants
Prepare for brief, factually oriented encounters that place little emphasis on interpersonal relations.	Prepare for lengthy, rambling interactions that are slow to get to the point.
Deliver information in a straightforward manner, using chronological order and lists. Stick to the main point as much as possible.	Provide as much contextual information as possible, and use stories and examples to illustrate points.
Try to speak up and ask questions during presentations. It's efficient and demonstrates your interest and knowledge.	Provide contextual information beforehand. If there are few questions during presentations, offer to answer them afterwards.
Structure opinions with the "punch line" first and then follow with reasons. ("I recommend X because A, B, and C happened.")	Tell the story first and end with your conclusion and recommendations. ("A, B, and C happened, so I recommend X.")

Strategies for Indirect Participants	Strategies for Direct Participants
Avoid being too subtle. For your counterparts, the goal of verbal interaction is to accomplish business goals. State your opinions directly to move the conversation forward.	Avoid causing offense by stating opinions too directly. For your counterparts, conversations are as much about preserving face for all participants as they are about accomplishing business goals.
Don't take criticism of your ideas as a personal attack—it doesn't reflect others' opinion of you. People and their ideas are considered separate. Criticism helps new ideas develop fully.	Avoid negativity about others' statements and ideas, especially in public. When it's unavoidable, begin responses with a positive statement and mention negatives briefly and gently. Consider discussing serious negatives privately.
Direct speakers respect and reward people who promote their ideas directly and challenge others to move the agenda forward. Try to learn to do this.	Indirect speakers respect and reward people who use appropriate subtlety. Avoid correcting others, even if they are wrong.
If you're uncomfortable introducing your own ideas in a meeting, ask a colleague to mention them for you.	Introducing ideas in public causes embarrassment if others disagree. Test ideas casually on a colleague beforehand and introduce them carefully.
Give negative feedback as directly as possible; polite agreement may be interpreted as a strong "yes," which will lead to problems later.	Don't take "yes" for an answer. Pay attention to body language and tone of voice. Interpret vagueness, avoidance, sarcasm, and humor as a "no."
When feedback is requested, do your best to give your true opinion. Begin with praise if you need to, but state your criticisms clearly.	When discussions stall or feedback is confusing, request a private meeting to get an honest, off-the-record explanation.

Strategies for Indirect Participants	Strategies for Direct Participants
Don't look too hard for subtext; doing so can lead to false conclusions. Assume people are being forthright.	Learn to look "between the lines" for subtle cues and ask colleagues for context. Use personal contacts to get the full story.
There may be few opportunities outside of work to discuss your concerns with colleagues. You may need to address problems overtly and publicly.	Meals, cocktails, and other social events are often used to relieve social pressure and resolve disputes. Try to participate in these bonding opportunities.
Speaking to a third party about a problem with a colleague may be perceived as "going behind their back." It's best to discuss problems with the colleague yourself.	Challenging a colleague's behavior may be perceived as aggressive. It may be best to look for an intermediary—someone both of you know but who isn't involved directly in the dispute.
If you try to indicate a problem by altering your behavior from what is normal, you will likely not be understood. Others won't grasp the meaning if you, say, skip a social event you usually attend. Try to voice problems directly.	When someone does something out of character or different from their habit, consider this a possible indication of problems in your relationship and inquire tactfully.
Cultivate friendships and convey problems privately to friends who will pass them along.	Cultivate friendships to gain information about problems that won't be shared in public.
Be prepared for partners to raise difficult points early. You are expected to handle possible deal breakers head-on.	Be prepared for partners to raise difficult points last, assuming they'll be easier to manage once agreement has been reached on other points.

11

NEUTRAL AND EXPRESSIVE APPROACHES TO DISPLAYING EMOTION

Challenges for Neutral communicators dealing with Expressive counterparts:

1. Get the job done while demonstrating enthusiasm and sensitivity.
2. Provide regular feedback to indicate engagement and interest.
3. Benefit from Expressive colleagues' enthusiasm and ability to get discussions going.

Challenges for Expressive communicators dealing with Neutral counterparts:

1. Enjoy interaction with others while demonstrating the competence and rationality they rely on.
2. Recognize subtle signs of approval or disagreement so you can change direction as needed.
3. Benefit from Neutral colleagues' reflective tendencies to arrive at the best solution.

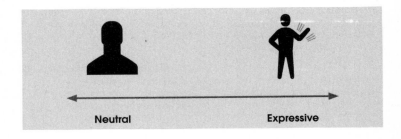

Strategies for Neutral Participants	Strategies for Expressive Participants
Physical contact indicates friendliness. Take it as a sign that things are going well.	Restrict physical contact, especially during greetings. Allow counterparts to make the first "move" and follow their example.

Strategies for Neutral Participants	Strategies for Expressive Participants
Try to express interest through your voice, facial expression, and gestures.	Restrict your body language and tone of voice to avoid overwhelming your counterparts.
Recognize that interruption may be used to show engagement and move the discussion along.	Avoid interrupting, which may be perceived as impolite. Allow a pause after others speak.
Don't be intimidated by displays of annoyance or frustration; these may not indicate serious problems.	Avoid showing anger or frustration, which can be perceived as unprofessional or even alarming.
Provide both positive and negative feedback so others can assess what you are thinking and adapt accordingly.	Avoid excessive praise or criticism to avoid embarrassing your counterparts.
Don't interpret "excessive" emotion as an indication of instability or frivolousness; it's just a cultural style.	Don't interpret a lack of expression as an indication of a lack of personality; it's just a cultural style.
Avoid hiding your reactions, which may imply secrecy or duplicity.	Avoid giving away too much information about your reactions.
Don't interpret positive feedback as agreement. It may just be politeness.	Don't interpret a lack of feedback as a lack of interest. Reactions may just not be expressed.
Try to avoid long silences, which others may consider uncomfortable. If you need time to think, say so.	Avoid filling in silences—you'll end up doing all the talking. If you can't stand the silence, ask a question.
Use others' digression from the agenda to understand their priorities and gather contextual information.	Digressions from an agenda may confuse your counterparts. Explain why you're bringing up tangential topics.
Illustrate points with stories to hold your counterparts' interest. If they tell confusing stories, ask questions to confirm their meaning.	Follow talking points closely; long stories may confuse your counterparts. If you do tell a story, explain how it relates to the subject under discussion.

11

Strategies for Neutral Participants	Strategies for Expressive Participants
Accept social invitations to avoid causing offense, and use the opportunity to get to know your counterparts.	Don't be insulted if your colleagues focus on work. Seek social opportunities through outside outlets.
Allow others to engage you in social interaction at work to strengthen relationships.	Avoid discussing personal matters at work, which may be perceived as unprofessional.
After a group social encounter, be prepared for discussions of "what we did last night" among your colleagues.	After a social encounter, expect behavior at work to resume as before; work and social interaction are separate. Don't bring up "what we did last night" at work.

Cooperation

ACHIEVEMENT AND ENDOWMENT ORIENTATIONS TO STATUS

Challenges for Achievement collaborators or negotiators dealing with Endowment counterparts:

1. Use your talent and drive to get things done while conveying respect for status derived from seniority and connections.

2. Operate effectively without going outside the hierarchy to show respect for the existing structure.

3. Make junior Endowment employees feel comfortable taking initiative and expressing their opinions.

4. Benefit from Endowment seniors' institutional knowledge, experience, and influence.

Challenges for Endowment collaborators or negotiators dealing with Achievement counterparts:

1. Use your influence and seniority to get things done while harnessing others' talent and subject matter expertise.

2. Show the initiative necessary to satisfy Achievement superiors' expectations.

3. Give Achievement-oriented employees enough responsibility and reward to motivate them.

4. Benefit from Achievers' ambition and can-do attitude to overcome obstacles.

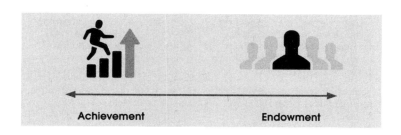

Strategies for Achievement Participants	Strategies for Endowment Participants
Intelligence is perceived as having limited value without experience, and drive can seem like aggression. Avoid pairing "whiz kids" with Endowment leaders.	A person who did not "earn" his or her status may be suspect. Avoid pairing people with little subject knowledge with Achievement leaders.
Expect Endowment leaders to be older men. If your leader is young or female, have an older executive from your side introduce him or her.	Expect young leaders of both genders who are subject matter experts. Include subject experts on your team to answer their questions.
"Borrow" prestige by having a senior person describe the company's regard for a younger leader.	Have a subject expert explain an older leader's position in the company to establish their value.
Learn counterparts' titles and find out how they use them (e.g., "Assistant Director Wu").	Expect to use first names soon after introductions. Choose a nickname for yourself if this makes you uncomfortable.

Strategies for Achievement Participants	Strategies for Endowment Participants
Review titles to understand the relative seniority of your counterparts. Try to match their rank with rank on your side.	If you're paired with counterparts who are not your equals, don't take it personally. Use the opportunity to learn about people you wouldn't normally talk with.
As a senior, you should delay making decisions or answering questions until you have the answers. Indecision and acknowledging ignorance are perceived as weakness.	As a senior, it's better to admit that you don't know something than to hide it. Being wrong is all right as long as you correct mistakes and learn from them.
Treat senior members with formality and respect. Don't correct or interrupt them; listen more than you talk.	An informal, egalitarian attitude doesn't imply disrespect for senior members. Don't take offense at young people's "forwardness."
Capitalize on your colleagues' knowledge of their system, and ask them to help you navigate their hierarchy.	Use your colleagues' creativity and energy to advance your joint agenda.
Create relationships by expressing interest in your Endowment counterparts' background and connections.	Create relationships by helping Achievement counterparts navigate your system and become effective quickly.
Refer to mutual friends, educational institutions, organizations, and associates to establish a connection.	Refer to common goals, experience, expertise, and opportunities to establish a connection.
Expect extended interpersonal interaction and a focus on building personal rapport.	Expect emphasis on accomplishing goals and maximizing business results.
Focus on understanding and supporting others' personal feelings.	Focus on building a strong business case and executing effectively.
Don't praise or reward junior members individually—seniors take responsibility for success.	Give credit where it is due; today's project leader may be tomorrow's vice president.

Strategies for Achievement Participants	Strategies for Endowment Participants
Some people's principal role is to leverage their personal connections or give prestige through their high titles. Look to others for task-related output.	Explain the role and importance of well-connected employees who lack other credentials; they may otherwise be resented by Achievement counterparts.
Promotions and compensation are based on seniority and relationships in addition to performance. Failing to consider these human factors may cause resentment.	Promotions and compensation are based on performance. Using subjective measures or showing favoritism may cause resentment.

NETWORK AND PROCESS ATTITUDES TOWARD INVOLVEMENT

Challenges for Network collaborators or negotiators dealing with Process counterparts:

1. Spend enough time to assess contractually oriented counterparts as partners, given the short time they are willing to spare.

2. Establish plans and structures that satisfy Process partners' desire for formalism.

3. Move quickly enough to convey the efficiency, competence, and professionalism valued by Process counterparts.

4. Benefit from Process partners' ability to efficiently advance a business agenda.

Challenges for Process collaborators or negotiators dealing with Network counterparts:

1. Develop agreements in a timely manner with relationship-oriented partners accustomed to extended social interaction.

2. Spend the time necessary to satisfy Network partners' desire for trust, while justifying the expense to management.

3. Be sensitive to Network partners' desire for personal connections; convey an interest in a long-term association.

4. Benefit from Network partners' ability to manage problems by leveraging contacts and creating relationships.

Strategies for Network Participants	Strategies for Process Participants
Expect them to want a quick settlement. Process companies see themselves as groups of individuals paid to produce value. Partnerships are contractual.	Expect business to take time. Network companies see themselves as organic social entities, and it takes time for them to integrate a new partner.
Process partnerships are based on business opportunity. Expect colleagues to discuss business from the first meeting.	Network partnerships are based on trust and friendship. Expect colleagues to avoid discussing business until these have been established.
Prepare for brief, factually oriented encounters with little emphasis on interpersonal relations.	Prepare for lengthy social interactions that seem to ignore the business goals of the relationship.
Recognize that an impersonal, logical style is not a sign of coldness or a lack of interest. Engage colleagues on the basis of common goals rather than through personal questions.	Recognize that personal questions are crucial to establishing a relationship. Explore common interests, and get to know your colleagues personally.

Strategies for Network Participants	Strategies for Process Participants
Lengthy contracts are standard and may be required by your counterpart's legal system, so be prepared to spend a lot of time on contract negotiations.	Lengthy getting-to-know-you activities are considered an essential basis for trusting partners, so be prepared to spend a lot of time on social interaction.
Contracts will describe specific, detailed obligations and penalties, so expect to be held to a tight standard.	Contracts will be short and general, so be flexible regarding the interpretation of wording.
If you're not prepared to honor the terms of a detailed contract, explain your position and add contingencies to protect yourself.	Explain the importance of honoring the specific terms of a detailed contract and suggest that Network partners add contingencies to prevent surprises.
Work colleagues will focus on accomplishing business tasks and may not interact socially with you. Don't take this personally.	Work colleagues may expect to interact socially with you, even if it disrupts your work. Recognize this as an opportunity to develop relationships.
Develop personal relationships with neighbors or club members rather than coworkers. Be professional at work.	Participate in social activities with coworkers outside work to cultivate friendly and useful relationships.
Relationships outside the workplace are more relaxed, and hierarchy is lessened. Don't interpret a casual attitude toward seniors as a sign of disrespect.	Relationships outside the workplace remain formal, and the hierarchy is still observed. Don't become overly casual with seniors or expect juniors to interact as your equal.
Employees have no obligation to managers away from work. Avoid asking for personal favors, which could be perceived as insulting or inappropriate.	Employees feel an obligation to their managers even away from work. Helping a manager with a personal project is a good way to build a relationship.

Strategies for Network Participants	Strategies for Process Participants
Process colleagues will be surprised at company policies that don't directly address business goals (e.g., hiring relatives of colleagues). Explain why these are important to relationships.	Recognize that company policies that don't directly support business goals may be important to sustaining partnerships.
You will be recognized more for the quality of your work than for your personality. Focus on the task to gain prestige.	You will be recognized as much for your interaction with others as for the quality of your work. Focus on building relationships.
Prepare for complex, explicit rules that everyone is expected to follow. Respect these.	Prepare for a lack of explicit rules and a tendency to prioritize relationships over policies.

Cooperation

INDEPENDENT AND GROUP APPROACHES TO COLLABORATION

Challenges for Independent collaborators or negotiators dealing with Group-oriented counterparts:

1. Convey your authority and competence as decision maker to Group-oriented colleagues.

2. Assess correctly the progress of deals and projects with little feedback from Group-oriented partners.

3. Keep your team's problems private to maintain the appearance of unity and professionalism.

4. Identify undisclosed internal problems in Group-oriented partners in time to react effectively.

5. Benefit from Group-oriented teams' internal cohesion and commitment.

Challenges for Group-oriented collaborators or negotiators dealing with Independent counterparts:

11

1. Explain your decision-making process and time frame to Independent colleagues to avoid surprises and confusion.

2. Assess whether Independent counterparts have the internal support needed for efficient implementation.

3. Provide sufficient internal information to satisfy Independent partners.

4. Distinguish between individual speculation and internal discord when members of a partner team convey conflicting information.

5. Benefit from Independent teams' subject expertise, openness, and willingness to share information.

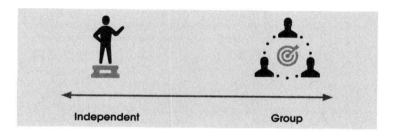

Strategies for Independent Participants	Strategies for Group Participants
Group-oriented negotiating teams tend to be large. Including technical experts in negotiations and social events will strengthen your position and avoid awkwardness.	Independent teams may be quite small. Don't expect your team members to be matched with counterparts in negotiations or at social events.
They will expect you to have knowledge equal to that of their experts. If you're on your own, plan to call home for supporting information.	The negotiators may not have detailed information, but you can request that they obtain it for you.

Strategies for Independent Participants	Strategies for Group Participants
They will ask detailed questions from the beginning. Be prepared to obtain information as needed.	They will expect to address general matters first and deal with details later. You may have to request detailed information.
Allow two or three times as much time as you would expect for their consensus-based decision-making process.	Expect quick decisions from their side, as only one or two people must agree to the deal.
Expect quick implementation once you have a deal, since everyone on their side has discussed the decision in detail.	Watch for slow implementation while the negotiator briefs the rest of the company on the plan and works out details.
A response of, "I don't know," or "I'll check," reflects the preference for an official answer. Give them time to clarify with colleagues—you'll get a more useful answer.	Differing responses to the same question by different people may indicate individual opinions rather than an official position.
Avoid guessing at questions you are unsure of. Confer to guarantee everyone responds the same way. Answers will be taken as official statements.	To be sure you're getting an official response, ask whether people are "speaking for the company" or just estimating. Asking the leader is safest.
Group-oriented teams will protect nonperforming members. Don't suggest replacing weak members or criticize them to their colleagues.	Independent groups may speak openly about technical and personnel problems. Don't interpret this as a sign of incompetence or low morale.
Don't expect a Group-oriented team to let down its boundaries because you're working on a joint project. Avoid asking group-internal questions, which may be considered intrusive.	Expect an Independent team to be casual about group boundaries. Hiding internal problems may be perceived as a lack of commitment to the partnership.
Avoid sharing inside information, especially problems; this could be perceived as a sign of disloyalty or low morale.	Share as much inside information as you can; notify partners of problems that will affect them as early as possible.

Strategies for Independent Participants	Strategies for Group Participants
Team member attrition may be perceived as a sign of low morale or incompetence. Explain turnover immediately and prepare to answer questions.	Team member attrition is common and not necessarily a sign of problems. Don't assume the worst. Ask questions to assess team morale.
Building relationships may take time, as external boundaries are strong. Keep up the effort.	Shutting out your partner may make them suspicious. Try to get to know them as individuals.
Cultivate a friendship with a team member and ask about internal problems or perspectives in a casual setting.	Ask team members directly to gain insight into internal problems or perspectives.
Social interactions such as meals, athletic events, or drinking are good opportunities to ask for context on business interaction.	Ask directly for context on business interaction.

Structure

RULE AND SITUATION ATTITUDES TOWARD AUTHORITY

Challenges for Rule-oriented collaborators or negotiators dealing with Situation-oriented counterparts:

1. Meet deadlines and fulfill contractual obligations when working with counterparts who give them less value.

2. Explain policies and procedures to help counterparts see their importance.

3. Accommodate counterparts' need for flexibility; demonstrate adaptability when circumstances change.

4. Recognize the importance of relationships and accommodate procedural irregularities and preferential treatment where possible.

5. Benefit from partners' creativity and ability to overcome obstacles.

Challenges for Situation-oriented collaborators or negotiators dealing with Rule-oriented counterparts:

1. Solve problems and develop creative solutions when working with counterparts who prefer highly structured policies.

2. Explain your need for flexibility to help partners accept your lack of structure.

3. Accommodate counterpart's need for clarity and detail in agreements and schedules.

4. Recognize the importance of consistency to partners and minimize procedural irregularities and preferential treatment.

5. Benefit from partners' reliability and stability.

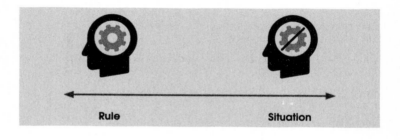

Strategies for Rule Participants	Strategies for Situation Participants
Gain access through a mutual contact or intermediary if possible.	Initiate business on the basis of mutual opportunity; personal connections are unnecessary.
Plan for business to take a long time and involve changes and surprises.	Expect counterparts to make decisions quickly and according to set guidelines.
Research potential partners carefully; pay attention to their reputation.	Focus on the terms of the deal and don't expect a long-term partnership.

Strategies for Rule Participants	Strategies for Situation Participants
Develop a strong relationship. Don't assume that contracts will keep you safe.	Expect a detailed contract. Don't expect partners to modify terms after it's signed.
People may come off as idiosyncratic. If someone seems very odd to you, confirm reliability with an intermediary.	Company representatives may demonstrate little individual personality. It may take time to get to know them as individuals.
Simplify contracts as much as possible and give legal matters a low profile, especially in the early stages of a relationship.	Don't take a preference for contracts or the presence of lawyers as a sign that you're considered untrustworthy; this is standard.
Be prepared to take time to walk partners through contracts, explaining meanings and penalties.	Get the legal support to understand detailed contracts and make sure what you're agreeing to.
Be very clear regarding your expectations of contracts' binding nature in all their detail.	Include provisions describing any changes you foresee in the business environment and how they will be managed.
Try to be flexible regarding agreements if conditions change, regardless of the terms of a contract.	Expect an inflexible attitude toward changes to a signed contract.
Minimize arbitrary rules—they will create discord. Simplify policies and procedures as much as possible.	Prepare for more forms, rules, and procedures; more-frequent audits; and tighter control than usual.
Explain the importance of your policies and procedures to justify them to partners.	Speak up when policies and procedures are counterproductive.
Use interpersonal relationships rather than rules to gain leverage.	Emphasize facts and structures rather than personal relationships to gain leverage.
Introduce sensitive changes privately and gently; notify key personnel in advance, anticipating personal reactions.	Expect changes to be made publicly and to be based on principles rather than personal factors.

11

Strategies for Rule Participants	Strategies for Situation Participants
Anticipate complex internal relationships that prevent uniform behavior.	Anticipate uniform reactions and unwillingness to make exceptions based on relationships.
Recognize the value of personal and political connections that facilitate business.	Be aware that emphasis on personal and political connections may be interpreted as a sign of unethical activity.
Expect managers to be good motivators rather than technical experts.	Expect managers to be technical specialists rather than interpersonal motivators.
Partners may respect people with personal connections although they have few skills. Recognize that connections are a kind of expertise, and look to others for execution.	Partners respect those with expertise and competence. Explain the importance of influence and connections to them.

Action

OPPORTUNITY AND THOROUGHNESS ATTITUDES TOWARD ACTION

Goal for Opportunity collaborators or negotiators dealing with Thoroughness counterparts:

1. Move initiatives forward while accommodating counterparts' preference for caution and thoroughness.

2. Promote decisive action to partners by linking initiatives to priorities of stability, continuity, and past success.

3. Benefit from partners' analytical tendencies and long-term relationships to create resilient collaborations.

Goal for Thoroughness collaborators or negotiators dealing with Opportunity counterparts:

1. Maintain consistency and reputation while accommodating counterparts' priorities of innovation and opportunity seizing.

2. Promote thoroughness and caution in partners by explaining the constraints of your environment.

3. Benefit from partners' sensitivity to change to enhance your responsiveness and maintain currency.

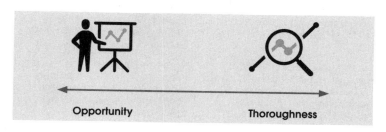

Strategies for Opportunity Participants	Strategies for Thoroughness Participants
Emphasize your proposal's good fit with your partner's history and values.	Emphasize that your caution is intended to protect the joint endeavor and explain the consequences of failure for your company.
Emphasize history and stability when describing your company. For a young company, draw on founders' prior experience or other sources of credibility.	Emphasize recent initiatives and performance. Refer to projects that demonstrate innovation and vigor.
Discuss current opportunities in terms of how they fit with your partner's tradition.	When making decisions, emphasize the value your longer-term considerations bring to both sides.
Describe your company's need to be proactive in seizing opportunity, given its business environment.	Describe your company's need for stability and long-term relationships, given its business environment, policies, and philosophy.

Strategies for Opportunity Participants	Strategies for Thoroughness Participants
Begin presentations with historical background and relate the present and future to that history.	Begin presentations with recent performance and goals and relate your strategy to those factors.
Recognize that business initiatives are expected to maintain continuity. Radical shifts will be resisted.	Recognize that business initiatives are expected to capture new opportunity. Lengthy decision making will be resisted.
Frame new ideas in terms of recreating past successes based on similar strategies; emphasize long-term goals that will be served by the current project.	Frame your process in terms of the protection offered by long-term thinking. Accommodate your partner where possible by taking quick action.
Emphasize experiences that tie the current project to the past, such as a visit you've made to the partner's country.	Emphasize examples of innovation that demonstrate your ability to take advantage of opportunity when the situation is right.
Without a strong relationship, you have no right to expect honorable dealings, so be cautious with new partners.	One collaboration does not guarantee that the relationship will continue. Partners will consider future projects based on their immediate value.
Expect business dealings to take a long time and involve significant discussion and interaction.	Expect business dealings to proceed quickly with less interaction than you are used to.
Prepare for lengthy meals and cultural events. Don't make concessions under deadline pressure just to get a deal.	Very lengthy negotiations may cause your partner to give up. Move forward as quickly as possible.
Moving very slowly doesn't mean they don't want to deal. Don't give up on the relationship. Ask for information about their internal process.	They expect to make constant progress and will interpret long waits as a lack of interest, so try to keep things moving and provide updates.

Strategies for Opportunity Participants	Strategies for Thoroughness Participants
Don't rely on rules or contracts to get compliance. Develop a strong relationship to gain leverage.	Don't expect partners to accommodate you based on your relationship. Insert contingencies into contracts as needed.
Consider proposing some long-term projects that will make the most of their tendencies.	Try to move on short-term opportunities that will accommodate partners' need to show results.

Organization

SCHEDULE AND FLOW APPROACHES TO ORGANIZATION

Challenges for Schedule-oriented collaborators or negotiators dealing with Flow-oriented counterparts:

1. Manage projects and meet deadlines while working with colleagues operating under fluid conditions.

2. Demonstrate flexibility and adaptability when schedules are disrupted.

3. Anticipate and prepare for last-minute requests to prevent surprises.

4. Benefit from colleagues' creativity and ingenuity.

Challenges for Flow-oriented collaborators or negotiators dealing with Schedule-oriented counterparts:

1. Manage change effectively while working with colleagues accustomed to stability and predictability.

2. Demonstrate respect for internal milestones and deadlines while responding to changes.

3. Explain areas of unpredictability to prepare partners for changing conditions.

4. Benefit from colleagues' stability and accountability.

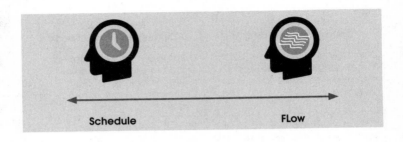

Strategies for Schedule Participants	**Strategies for Flow Participants**
Expect people to arrive somewhat late to meetings. Learn to estimate the wait time and plan to arrive when they do.	Recognize that people expect you to arrive on time for meetings, and organize your schedule to do so.
Plan to make phone calls or do other work while waiting for meetings to start.	Get peripheral work done outside of meeting time so you can focus.
Consider scheduling meetings earlier than you'd prefer. Be prepared for cancellations and have a backup plan for getting other things done.	Don't make appointments that you can't attend. If you must be late or absent, notify counterparts immediately.
Expect meetings to go overtime if a matter isn't concluded; avoid scheduling appointments close together.	Expect meetings to begin and end as scheduled; additional meetings will be added as needed to conclude business.
Recognize that multitasking during meetings—such as taking phone calls or checking e-mail—is normal. Don't worry or take offense at this behavior.	Focus on the agenda during meetings. Avoid taking calls or other activities to convey competence and respect for others.
Be aware that frequent schedule changes may be necessary to accommodate a fluid environment. Don't assume final deadlines won't be met.	Be aware that schedule changes are considered disruptive and will be resisted. Attempt to meet intermediate as well as final deadlines.

Strategies for Schedule Participants	Strategies for Flow Participants
Recognize that last-minute changes are common, and prepare to be flexible. Sometimes they are for the better.	Recognize that last-minute changes are considered disruptive; suggest new directions as early as possible.
Build relationships so counterparts will accommodate your need for greater stability.	Demonstrate reliability so counterparts will accommodate your need for flexibility. Notify them early if you expect delays.
Find ways to concentrate in a noisy or busy work environment, or explain your need to focus to avoid alienating others.	Don't take offense if others show a preference for working alone. Many will resent interruptions.
Explain your preferences and request help to maintain your personal sense of order.	Explain your need for flexibility and request help to maintain your freedom.
Show flexibility in dealing with spontaneity and social interaction to avoid seeming unfriendly.	Limit social and spontaneous discussions at work, which may be considered unprofessional.
Recognize the preference for face-to-face interaction and use it to gauge reactions and build relationships.	Recognize the preference for indirect communication and save time by communicating via phone or e-mail.
Take advantage of colleagues' flexibility when you need extra time or are running late.	Call on your colleagues' efficiency when you have a deadline to meet.

11

12

Culture-Based Strategies for Hiring, Job Seeking, and Management

Intercultural Strategies for Employers and Job Seekers

Intercultural hiring is complicated by the fact that employers and job candidates may not share expectations about communication and interaction. Differences in conventions for talking with strangers may cause confusion at career fairs and networking meetings. Candidates may describe their skills and abilities in ways that make it hard for employers to evaluate their true potential. And different norms for self-promotion and showing respect may make it difficult to tell whether a candidate will integrate successfully into an organization. At a deeper level, there may be differences in employer and candidate expectations about relationships with colleagues and superiors, what constitutes a useful contribution, and how and when employees are rewarded and promoted.

Cultural analysis can enhance the preparatory research conducted by both employers and job candidates. Employers can use it to identify the tendencies that mold candidates' answers about their skills, experience, and motivation, and job seekers can use it to assess an employer's expectations and preferences. Understanding cultural orientations can also help minimize surprises about financial reward and advancement.

In addition to the other types of research, it's helpful to do a preliminary cultural assessment to evaluate the cultural characteristics of a candidate's previous employers. Once you have a preliminary profile, you can modify it when you communicate or interact in person.

If you're a job seeker, you can use a *Quick Reference Profile*[1] to assess the country where an employer is headquartered. (Keep in mind that this will be less accurate if you're hiring into an overseas branch). From there, assess the corporate culture by reviewing sources such as articles and annual reports. You can modify your preliminary profile later based on personal observation.

The sections below describe the behavior and expectations of employers and job candidates for each cultural dimension and make recommendations to each.[2] To understand the perspectives associated with each cultural tendency, review Chapters 4–6. For persuasive strategies, review Chapter 11, and for strategies for negotiating a contract, read Chapter 15.

Strategies for Employers: Cultural Tendencies in Job Seekers

The Clarity Dimension: Indirect and Direct Tendencies

INDIRECT CANDIDATES

Common strengths: Tact, willingness to give in to preserve harmony

Possible weaknesses: Difficulty defending good ideas in the face of opposition

What to expect during social events and interviews: Candidates from Indirect social environments have been taught that self-promotion is rude and unsophisticated, so they tend to express humility and gratitude rather than self-confidence. They may describe their accomplishments indirectly. ("The

---

[1] www.deirdremendez.com/quick-reference-profiles.
[2] To practice preparing for an interview based on multiple cultural characteristics (rather than a single dimension at a time), see employer and candidate scenarios at www.deirdremendez.com/interview-preparation

project finished under budget," or "We were able to complete the project early.") They are likely to take a responsive posture.

Strategies for Direct employers:

Refer to résumés to assess skills and avoid mistaking modesty for a lack of ability. Be prepared to take the lead in the discussion and work harder than usual to identify accomplishments. Ask probing questions to clarify skills, experience, and personal contributions in previous positions. Prompt them to ask questions about the company or position.

Note: Candidates who are both Indirect and Neutral are unlikely to maintain eye contact and may have very weak handshakes. Keep in mind that these are culturally determined behaviors and not necessarily indicators of personality.

DIRECT CANDIDATES

Common strengths: Succinctness in getting to the bottom line

Possible weaknesses: Lack of interpersonal sensitivity, difficulty managing relationships

What to expect during social events and interviews: Candidates from Direct environments have been taught that clear, thorough communication is the most honest approach, so they will be forthright about their skills and experience. They will express self-confidence through their comments and body language. They may ask directly about sensitive topics (salary or promotion opportunities, for example) or express negativity overtly ("No, that's wrong—I was actually the team leader," or, "Your sales have been low this year") without meaning to offend. Some may miss unspoken signals or fail to recognize when the meeting is concluding. They may feel they should speak as much as you do.

Strategies for Indirect employers: Be prepared for self-confident behavior, and avoid confusing it with arrogance or disrespect. Ask questions clearly and fully. Describe your working environment, and ask candidates how they would adapt their behavior to fit in.

Note: Direct candidates will probably shake hands firmly and make eye contact. Keep in mind that these are culturally determined behaviors and not necessarily indicators of personality.

The Emotion Dimension: Neutral and Expressive Tendencies

NEUTRAL CANDIDATES

Common strengths: Calm and steady work, meeting objective goals

Possible weaknesses: Difficulty engaging others to develop relationships

What to expect during social events and interviews: Candidates with Neutral backgrounds believe that it's polite and dignified to have a controlled demeanor at all times. They will give little information about their emotional state and answer questions briefly, without much elaboration. If they are also Direct, they will state their answers firmly, possibly conveying their opinions as fact. If they are Indirect, they may say very little about their accomplishments out of modesty. Neutral candidates will expect you to lead the conversation and take a responsive posture themselves. You may need to work harder than usual to get information.

Strategies for Expressive employers: Be prepared for quiet interactions and little overt enthusiasm, regardless of a candidate's level of interest. If you have trouble gauging their eagerness, ask them to explain why they're interested. Be prepared to lead the conversation, and ask multiple, brief questions, especially if the candidate is also Indirect.

EXPRESSIVE CANDIDATES

Common strengths: Enhancing social dynamics through enthusiasm

Possible weaknesses: Difficulty working in environments that don't encourage self-expression

What to expect during social events and interviews: Candidates from Expressive environments have been taught that it's polite and friendly to convey warmth and enthusiasm, so they will greet you with a smile and possibly effusive thanks for the meeting. They will illustrate points with facial expressions and gestures. If they are also Direct, they may seem very assertive and perhaps overconfident. If they are Indirect, they may appear excessively grateful for the opportunity. Expect long, elaborate statements or rambling answers that use up time. They may interrupt your comments as a "helpful" way to express agreement or correct a mistaken impression, and they may feel the need to talk whenever you are silent to fill in "uncomfortable" pauses.

Strategies for Neutral employers: Be prepared for energetic body language and wordy answers. Remind candidates of time constraints at the beginning of a meeting. Avoid mistaking a show of enthusiasm for a lack of self-control, desperation, or overconfidence. Don't confuse collaborative interjections or interruptions with impatience or disrespect. Help candidates focus their answers with precise questions that specify what you want to know.

The Status Dimension: Achievement and Endowment Orientations

ACHIEVEMENT CANDIDATES

Common strengths: Using their drive and determination to enhance the bottom line

Possible weaknesses to probe for: Difficulty performing within a hierarchy and impatience to be rewarded for personal accomplishment

What to expect during social events and interviews: Candidates from Achievement environments overtly display confidence and optimism and will arrive prepared to showcase their skills. They will greet you energetically, probably with a strong handshake, and make and maintain eye contact. Their demeanor may be informal by your standards, and they may not show the respect for seniority you expect. Their interactions with people from different genders, for example, might be more casual. They may speak early and often and describe their experience, qualifications, and goals in positive terms. They are likely to take credit for past success without mentioning former colleagues or superiors. Due to their rather transactional view of exchanging their work for a salary, they may be more interested in learning new skills than creating close or lasting workplace relationships. Based on their expectations of performance-based promotion, they may ask questions about leadership opportunities in early meetings.

Strategies for Endowment employers: Be prepared for candidates who are informal and forthright. They may tend to dominate the conversation, even if they are young. Avoid confusing a candidate's self-confidence with arrogance or dishonesty, and ask specific questions about their expertise and past work to make an accurate assessment. Achievement candidates may expect to advance quickly based on their individual performance, so explain your company's hierarchy as well as your criteria and timeline for advancement.

ENDOWMENT CANDIDATES

Common strengths: Respect for colleagues, loyalty to superiors and the company

Possible weaknesses: Difficulty driving change, challenging the status quo

What to expect during social events and interviews: Candidates with Endowment backgrounds have been taught to behave formally and show respect for their superiors. Younger candidates may not sustain eye contact. They will expect you to take the lead. Candidates with extreme Endowment tendencies may give special deference to older and male representatives regardless of their positions, possibly directing their attention and responses to the person they believe is senior. They will describe their skills and experience modestly and may emphasize teamwork and relationships with their managers. Because they expect working relationships to be important, they may prioritize positive working conditions, opportunities for mentorship, and close relationships with colleagues. Young or female candidates, especially if interacting with an older male, may need encouragement to answer questions in detail.

Strategies for Achievement employers: You can expect courteous, respectful behavior and an emphasis on creating a warm personal impression. Be prepared for greater apparent shyness (deference) from young or female candidates. Take the lead by asking detailed questions if necessary, and let interviewees know you expect them to treat all company representatives equally regardless of age or gender. Emphasize the importance of taking personal initiative in your organization.

12

The Involvement Dimension: Network and Process Tendencies

NETWORK CANDIDATES

Common strengths: Creating and enhancing internal and external relationships

Possible weaknesses: Difficulty working alone or in highly work-focused contexts

What to expect during social events and interviews: Candidates from Network backgrounds usually rely on personal connections to find job opportunities, and they work hard at finding common ground and establishing rapport. They may prolong social conversation with detailed answers to personal questions. They will emphasize emotion over facts and may focus more on relationships and their feelings about previous employers than on skills or results. Their answers will be long and possibly digressive, and they may be vague about objective measurements. They may rely more on intuition than on research, possibly preparing less than other candidates for meetings. Their questions may focus on the working environment, and they may be surprised by specific, "mechanistic" criteria for performance reviews and promotions.

Strategies for Process-oriented employers: Be prepared to spend some time getting to know candidates and connecting with them personally, identifying common ground if possible. Don't mistake an emphasis on social discussion for a lack of ability or commitment. Remind candidates of time limits at the beginning of a meeting. Avoid vague or open-ended questions; keep candidates on topic with specific questions. Confirm a good fit by discussing the working environment in your company. Follow up afterwards if you don't get the level of detail you need during an interview.

PROCESS CANDIDATES

Common strengths: Logical approach, skill at performing to specification

Possible weaknesses: Difficulty developing and leveraging personal relationships to accomplish business goals

What to expect during social events and interviews: Candidates with Process tendencies will prepare thoroughly for meetings. They will be more concerned about showing their relevance to the job description than on developing a relationship during meetings and interviews. They will answer personal questions briefly and may be surprised at prolonged social discussion. They will be ready to summarize their skills and past experience succinctly and describe their goals and interests briefly. Their comments will probably be fairly scripted, and they may be unprepared for off-topic questions. They will focus on measurements and outcomes, and provide specific and detailed information about technical matters. They will expect an explicit description of job duties and criteria for performance reviews and promotions.

Strategies for Network-oriented employers: Be prepared for a facts-based, concise interaction. If you want to focus on developing a rapport, signal this by designating a "getting to know you" phase. Don't mistake candidates' to-the-point approach for coldness or a lack of personality; they will be happy to relax into social interaction when business is concluded. If flexibility and creativity are important to you, test for these with off-topic questions.

The Collaboration Dimension: Independent and Group Tendencies

INDEPENDENT CANDIDATES

Common strengths: Strong individual performance, acceptance of personal responsibility and accountability

Possible weaknesses: Unwillingness to relinquish personal opinions and ideas to preserve working relationships, difficulty forgoing reward for personal performance

What to expect during social events and interviews: Candidates from Independent environments take personal responsibility for their work and careers, expecting credit for success and accepting blame for failures. Their demeanor will be self-confident, and they will describe their work experience in terms of personal skills and accomplishments. They may give little credit for past results to teammates or superiors. They are accustomed to autonomy in decision making and recognition for their personal contributions. They may have questions about how their performance will be evaluated on group projects.

Strategies for Group-oriented employers: Avoid mistaking self-confidence for arrogance. If you have concerns about a candidate's potential for close-knit teamwork and self-sacrifice, describe your working environment and expectations of collaboration. Clarify the way your company rewards individual contributions. Behavioral questions and scenarios may be helpful in determining how a candidate would adapt to a Group environment.

GROUP CANDIDATES

Common strengths: Prioritizing group dynamics and goals over personal preferences

Possible weaknesses to probe for: Discomfort with autonomy and defending creative ideas in the face of opposition

What to expect during social events and interviews: In Group environments, people work together closely to produce a joint product and do not regard their own contributions as stand-alone "bodies of work." Group-oriented interviewees may appear excessively modest and unable to describe their personal accomplishments. They may use "we" more than "I" and only reluctantly take credit for successful outcomes. Since they're accustomed to working through personal connections and interacting with people they know well, candidates with extreme Group tendencies may be uncomfortable introducing themselves to strangers and making "small talk." They will present themselves in a very conventional manner without distinguishing characteristics. They may ask few questions and seem hesitant to talk about themselves.

Strategies for Independent employers: Avoid confusing modesty and conformity with a lack of qualifications or personality. To identify skills and experience, ask questions designed to pinpoint their individual contributions. Be clear about your expectations regarding personal initiative and responsibility and your criteria for assessing individual performance. Behavioral questions and scenarios may be helpful in determining how a candidate would adapt to an Independent environment.

The Authority Dimension: Rule and Situation Orientations

RULE-ORIENTED CANDIDATES

Common strengths: Stability, respect for policies and procedures

Possible weaknesses: Developing creative solutions, managing change

What to expect during social events and interviews: Rule-oriented candidates will dress and behave in a conventional manner, arrive promptly and well prepared, and answer questions in a straightforward manner. They are likely to have a scripted delivery and describe their strengths and experience without much exaggeration. Questions that require unusual problem-solving skills may throw them off guard. They are likely to accept a reasonable offer without much negotiation.

Strategies for Situation-oriented employers: Don't try to "read between the lines" for strategy or exaggeration—Rule-oriented candidates are unlikely to embellish. Check for problem-solving ability with behavioral questions or scenarios.

12

SITUATION CANDIDATES

Common strengths: Flexibility, adaptability, and skills at problem solving

Possible weaknesses to probe for: Unwillingness to follow procedures they don't understand or that seem arbitrary

What to expect during social events and interviews: Situation candidates will take a strategic, creative approach to interaction with employers and may seem idiosyncratic in their dress and behavior. They may redirect the conversation to emphasize strengths or avoid discussing weaknesses. They may exaggerate their skills or personal connections and represent impressions or opinions as fact. They are creative negotiators and may try to gain concessions of some kind.

Strategies for Rule-oriented employers: Separate fact from marketing language on résumés and in interviews. Request objective measures of past performance. Check references and confirm influential connections. Be prepared to be drawn into negotiations if you make an offer.

The Action Dimension: Opportunity and Thoroughness Tendencies

OPPORTUNITY CANDIDATES

Common strengths: Creative, entrepreneurial approach, adaptability to change

Possible weaknesses: Impatience with the status quo, lack of respect for existing structure and direction

What to expect during social events and interviews: Candidates with an Opportunity background expect to have many jobs during their careers and look at each one as a chance to gain skills that will enhance their marketability. They may seem self-promoting and a bit flashy. They will emphasize skills and subject expertise over diligence or experience when answering questions. Short periods of prior employment are not necessarily a sign of a poor work ethic or skills, but they may indicate a lack of long-term commitment to a single position. Candidates will probably ask about short-term advancement and skills development.

Strategies for Thoroughness-oriented employers: If you're looking for a long-term commitment, emphasize opportunities your company offers for continuous skills development and promotion over time. Ask whether a candidate can commit to a certain period of employment. Check references if the appearance of "job hopping" worries you.

THOROUGHNESS CANDIDATES

Common strengths: Thorough analysis, ability to work within existing structures

Possible weaknesses: Difficulty responding to opportunity and threat in dynamic environments

What to expect during social events and interviews: Candidates with Thoroughness tendencies will present themselves as diligent, serious employees and emphasize consistent effort over the years. They will stress their experience and stability and point to prior positions as evidence of long-term employer satisfaction.

Strategies for Opportunity-oriented employers: If you're looking for innovation and rapid decision making, use behavioral questions and scenarios that elicit examples of these traits. Clarify the fact that your reward structure emphasizes creativity and short-term performance.

The Organization Dimension: Schedule and Flow Orientations

SCHEDULE CANDIDATES

12

Common strengths: Reliability, organizational skills, attention to deadlines

Possible weaknesses: Lack of troubleshooting ability, difficulty adapting to change

What to expect during social events and interviews: Candidates with Schedule tendencies will arrive promptly and be well prepared and organized. They will have prepared a concise summary of their skills and experience and will ask scripted questions. They may respond poorly to changes in schedule or agenda.

Strategies for Flow-oriented employers: If your environment requires flexibility or adaptability to shifting conditions, test for these traits by changing the schedule or agenda shortly before a meeting. Use behavioral questions and scenarios to assess a candidate's ability to multitask or perform in unstable environments.

FLOW CANDIDATES

Common strengths: Creativity, adaptability to changing conditions, crisis management

Possible weaknesses to probe for: Poor time-management skills, difficulty contributing in a steady, timely manner

What to expect during social events and interviews: Flow-oriented candidates may be less punctual or prepared than you expect. They may improvise during meetings. They may answer questions in a rambling manner, and their own questions may depart from the agenda you've prepared. They may fidget or seem distracted.

Strategies for Schedule-oriented employers: If your environment requires strong skills at organization, planning, and meeting deadlines, probe for these with behavioral questions. Ask for details about prior projects the candidate has worked on.

Strategies for Job Seekers: Cultural Tendencies in Employers[3]

The Clarity Dimension: Indirect and Direct Orientations

INDIRECT EMPLOYERS

Are more likely to reward employees who: Introduce ideas tactfully to preserve relationships

Are less likely to reward employees who: Introduce ideas in a way that damages relationships, no matter how they affect the bottom line

Preparing for interaction: Employers from Indirect environments appreciate candidates who express themselves humbly and allow their résumés to speak for them. They dislike assertiveness and self-promotion and prefer a listening, responsive demeanor. They prefer restrained body language. If shaking hands is appropriate, Expressive representatives will prefer warm, but not powerful handshakes, and Neutral ones will prefer brief, weak handshakes.

Strategies for Direct candidates: Express humility, gratitude, and commitment in written communication, cover letters, and face-to-face meetings. Maintain a modest tone of voice and body language. Rather than promote your abilities, refer employers to your résumé regarding your skills and achievements. Take a responsive posture, allowing the interviewer to lead, and save questions for the end. Avoid asking questions that reflect

---

[3] I am grateful to Susan Masson for sharing her expertise with intercultural strategies for interviewing.

self-interest (such as salary and promotion opportunities), especially in early interviews.

DIRECT EMPLOYERS

Are more likely to reward employees who: Express themselves clearly to move projects forward and achieve company goals

Are less likely to reward employees who: Use hints and back-channel discussions to convey their opinions and ideas

Preparing for interaction: Employers from Direct environments appreciate explicit and accurate descriptions of experience and skills. They may interpret modesty as insecurity or insincerity and prefer candidates who respond fully to questions and are comfortable describing their skills and experience. They favor confident body language and eye contact. If shaking hands is appropriate, Expressive employers will prefer enthusiastic handshakes; Neutral ones will prefer handshakes that are firm but not lengthy.

Strategies for Indirect candidates: Convey self-assuredness in written communication, cover letters, and face-to-face meetings. Use a confident tone of voice and physical posture, and express confidence in your ability to do the job in question. Shake hands firmly, and make and maintain eye contact. Describe your skills and achievements clearly. Ask questions directly.

The Emotion Dimension: Neutral and Expressive Tendencies

NEUTRAL EMPLOYERS

Are more likely to reward employees who: Seem mature and self-controlled

Are less likely to reward employees who: Seem dramatic or waste time with displays of emotion

Preparing for interaction: Employer representatives with Neutral tendencies tend to be calm and contained. They prefer candidates with a still demeanor who listen quietly while others are talking. They may perceive extreme enthusiasm as desperation and interpret a very expressive demeanor as a lack of self-control or strategic ability. They expect succinct answers to questions and ask for elaboration if they want it. They may perceive candidates who give long answers as arrogant or immature. They will perceive overlapping talk as rude interruption and may be silent for long periods while making notes or deliberating. If shaking hands is appropriate, employers will prefer brief handshakes.

Strategies for Expressive candidates: Maintain a calm tone in written communication, cover letters, and face-to-face meetings. Greet employers in a reserved manner. Express interest in the company in terms of its relevance to your skills, experience, and goals rather than your personal feelings. Keep answers brief, and allow employers to redirect you if answers are not on target. Avoid interrupting, and allow pauses after others speak. Sit quietly during silences.

EXPRESSIVE EMPLOYERS

Are more likely to reward employees who: Seem enthusiastic and contribute energy to the workplace

Are less likely to reward employees who: Seem withdrawn or unenthusiastic about their work and interaction with colleagues

Preparing for interaction: Employers with Expressive tendencies tend to be energetic and interactive. They prefer candidates who smile, use gestures to illustrate points, and provide verbal and physical feedback. They may interpret a very quiet demeanor as a lack of interest in the job or poor rapport with them. They expect enthusiastic and fairly elaborate answers to questions, and may perceive candidates who give brief answers as having little to say for themselves. If shaking hands is appropriate, employers may prefer more prolonged handshakes.

Strategies for Neutral candidates: Express enthusiasm in written communication, cover letters, and face-to-face meetings. Greet employers energetically with a friendly demeanor, and express gratitude for the opportunity. Communicate enthusiasm about the company and position in terms of your interests and preferences as well as the work involved. If you have difficulty conveying enthusiasm with body language, express it verbally. Provide detail and context in your comments and answers. Make eye contact. A two-handed handshake may be appropriate.

The Status Dimension: Achievement and Endowment Orientations

ACHIEVEMENT EMPLOYERS

Are more likely to reward employees who: Take personal initiative and "speak truth to power"

Are less likely to reward employees who: Rely on instruction from above and are unwilling to challenge their superiors or the status quo

Preparing for interaction: Representatives of Achievement companies are looking for employees who will overcome obstacles and drive them forward to success. They prefer displays of confidence and optimism. They react favorably to candidates who articulate their skills and experience in terms of their value to the employer and are less interested in expressions of loyalty or team spirit. They may have a more relaxed, informal demeanor than you're used to. They will be interested in personal initiative, leadership positions, obstacles overcome, and other indications of energy and drive. Their reward structures are typically based on performance and results.

Strategies for Endowment-oriented candidates: Communicate an energetic presence in written communication, cover letters, and face-to-face meetings. Prepare a brief summary of your qualifications that demonstrates self-confidence and showcases your knowledge and achievements. Make and maintain eye contact. If there are multiple interviewers present, treat all of them with equal respect regardless of age or gender. Describe the way your skills and experience relate to the employer's goals. Prepare examples of prior initiative and leadership. Ask about opportunities for leadership experience and skills development.

ENDOWMENT EMPLOYERS

Are more likely to reward employees who: Respect the company hierarchy, demonstrate loyalty to their superiors, and "wait their turn" for advancement

Are less likely to reward employees who: Disregard the hierarchy, promote ideas aggressively, or expect to rise more rapidly than their peers

Preparing for interaction: Representatives of Endowment-oriented companies are looking for employees who will fit well in their corporate culture and develop over time through mentoring. Shared educational or social affiliations can be a basis for making a connection. Endowment employers dislike aggressiveness and "me-first" attitudes. They may be quite formal in their dress and demeanor and prefer candidates who show respect for their superiors. Their reward structure will factor in loyalty and team spirit.

Strategies for Achievement candidates: Research the academic and social backgrounds of relevant company contacts to see if you have any connections in common. Use a respectful tone in written communication, cover letters, and face-to-face meetings. Work to create a personal connection. Maintain a respectful demeanor throughout interactions—as the lowest-ranking person in the interaction, you should be the most formal. If you meet with a team or group, acknowledge the leader in particular. If the hierarchy is unclear, introduce yourself first to the oldest male and show him special respect. Let company representatives lead the discussion, and wait to see whether they have a particular seating order. Express a commitment to supporting your colleagues. Take a responsive posture and hold your questions until the end. Your contribution to the bottom line may matter less than your work ethic and loyalty, so be sure you understand the promotion timeline and reward structure.

The Involvement Dimension: Network and Process Tendencies

NETWORK EMPLOYERS

Are more likely to reward employees who: Are good at creating and leveraging relationships with influential partners, clients, and customers

Are less likely to reward employees who: Ignore the importance of personal relationships in business

Preparing for interaction: Employers with a Network orientation want to know candidates thoroughly before making a decision. Provide some personal information in written communication, cover letters, and face-to-face meetings. Your qualifications may be less important than your fit with the corporate culture, and they may spend a lot of time asking you about yourself. Meetings may be long and unscripted, with lengthy explanations and vague, open-ended questions. There may be multiple meetings with different interviewers.

Strategies for Process candidates: Focus on creating a warm, trusting personal relationship in your written communication, cover letters, and face-to-face meetings. Be prepared to go into more detail than usual about personal topics such as your family, background, interests, and hobbies. Provide context when you ask questions, and illustrate your answers with examples. Be responsive to all questions, and ask for clarification if you're unsure what they're designed to find out.

PROCESS EMPLOYERS

Are more likely to reward employees who: Focus on meeting and exceeding expectations of job performance

Are less likely to reward employees who: "Waste time" on social activities or do not fully address the specifics of their job description

Preparing for interaction: Employers with a Process orientation want to assess your ability to make a professional contribution. They prefer candidates with appropriate credentials and will be less interested in personal details. They will get down to business quickly after brief social preliminaries. They will ask brief, succinct questions and expect concise answers. Skills, experience, and objective measures will be prioritized. They will have a detailed agenda for the meeting and will not appreciate being diverted from it.

Strategies for Network candidates: Take a businesslike approach in written communication, cover letters, and face-to-face meetings. Be prepared for detailed questions about your credentials and experience. Answer social questions briefly and focus on your competencies and results. Avoid rambling and moving off topic—give concise answers and add detail if prompted. If you have questions about peripheral topics, hold them until the end.

The Collaboration Dimension: Independent and Group Tendencies

INDEPENDENT EMPLOYERS

Are more likely to reward employees who: Demonstrate personal initiative and accountability and contribute individually to organizational goals

Are less likely to reward employees who: Are uncomfortable with autonomy or unwilling to advance or defend useful ideas

Preparing for interaction: Employers from Independent backgrounds are looking for employees whose specific skills and expertise will benefit the company's bottom line. They prefer candidates who demonstrate self-confidence and are willing to argue forcefully for their ideas if they feel they are right—even if others disagree. They are looking for self-starters who show personal initiative, accept individual responsibility, and work with some degree of autonomy. Reward systems are often based on individual performance. They will ask questions about leadership experience and achieved results, and may interpret an emphasis on group accomplishments as a lack of skills or self-confidence.

Strategies for Group-oriented candidates: To prepare, separate prior responsibilities and accomplishments from the work of other teammates. Practice describing your individual achievements. Take a confident tone in written communication, cover letters, and face-to-face meetings. Use "I" rather than "we," and express confidence in your ability to get results. Communicate willingness to assume responsibility, solve problems on your own, and take credit for results. Ask questions about an employer's approach to group work to determine whether the environment will be suitable for you.

GROUP-ORIENTED EMPLOYERS

Are more likely to reward employees who: Prioritize the team and are willing to sacrifice personal time, autonomy, and rapid advancement

Are less likely to reward employees who: Advance their own ideas in the face of opposition, require autonomy, and expect credit for individual work

Preparing for interaction: Employers from Group-oriented companies are looking for people who will bond closely with their colleagues and put the team's interests before their own. They prefer candidates who speak modestly about their own accomplishments and talk more about group results. Reward systems are typically based on group performance, and individual ability and contributions may not be acknowledged or rewarded for some time.

Strategies for Independent candidates: Prepare by reflecting on the accomplishments of the teams and projects you've worked with. Use a humble tone in written communication, cover letters, and face-to-face meetings. Emphasize "we" rather than "I," and only discuss your personal contribution if prompted. Communicate your willingness to prioritize group unity and sacrifice your own preferences. Understand that your advancement will derive from performance of the groups you are assigned to. Ask questions about their approach to group work and advancement to confirm that the environment will be suitable for you.

The Authority Dimension: Rule and Situation Orientations

RULE EMPLOYERS

Are more likely to reward employees who: Conform to expectations and follow guidelines

Are less likely to reward employees who: Follow policies selectively

Preparing for interaction: Employers are looking for stable, reliable employees who will uphold company policies and work within guidelines. They will expect punctuality and advance preparation, favoring candidates with conventional self-presentations. They will ask straightforward questions and expect clear, complete answers. They may perceive digressions as evasive. Rule-oriented interviewers often view exaggeration or "creative marketing" of accomplishments as dishonest. They may react negatively to candidates who negotiate at length or request special deals.

Strategies for candidates: Avoid flowery or emphatic language in written communication, cover letters, and face-to-face meetings. Dress conventionally and present yourself as steady and trustworthy. Be prepared to answer questions in a candid manner and avoid exaggeration. Accept fair offers and avoid elaborate negotiation for small gains.

SITUATION EMPLOYERS

Are more likely to reward employees who: Are able to think for themselves and improvise in situations where policies are unclear or inadequate

Are less likely to reward employees who: Are uncomfortable making decisions without guidance and have difficulty devising a course of action in new or unusual situations

Preparing for interaction: Employers from Situation environments are looking for creative employees who are good at overcoming obstacles and solving problems. They may equate very conventional self-presentation with a lack of creativity. Interviewers may ask unusual questions or require unusual types of problem solving. They may begin with a low salary offer and expect some negotiation.

Strategies for candidates: Express your individuality in written communication, cover letters, and face-to-face meetings. Present yourself as an adaptable employee capable of thinking on your feet. Allow your personality to come through, and emphasize experience troubleshooting problems or developing creative solutions. Be prepared for tests of your problem-solving ability. Attempt to negotiate more favorable employment terms if they seem low to begin with.

The Action Dimension: Opportunity and Thoroughness Tendencies

OPPORTUNITY EMPLOYERS

Are more likely to reward employees who: Are able to anticipate near-term opportunities and threats and suggest resourceful strategies for redirection

Are less likely to reward employees who: Have difficulty making decisions in stressful situations and prefer a cautious, incremental approach to change

Preparing for interaction: Employers from Opportunity-oriented business environments value creative employees with skills at assessing risk and reward, innovating, and adapting to changing conditions. They may ask questions about your experience proposing innovative solutions. They are more likely to offer skills development in a dynamic environment than steady advancement over time. They may interpret lengthy periods with a single employer as showing a lack of ambition unless you moved up rapidly.

Strategies for candidates: Take an energetic tone in written communication, cover letters, and face-to-face meetings. Present yourself as a quick thinker able to synthesize information efficiently and respond to change as needed. Provide examples of innovative solutions you've developed to adapt to changing conditions.

THOROUGHNESS EMPLOYERS

Are more likely to reward employees who: Develop long-term solutions that take all relevant factors into consideration

Are less likely to reward employees who: Focus on the near term, advocate frequent changes in direction, or expect rapid advancement

Preparing for interaction: Thoroughness employers value diligent employees who are good at long-term planning and in-depth analysis. They will favor candidates who can contribute strategies for making incremental changes without diverging drastically from the current direction. Their reward structure is likely to be based on length of service and seniority. They may interpret multiple short-term positions in your work history as a sign of a poor work ethic or team spirit.

Strategies for candidates: Use a sober tone in written communication, cover letters, and face-to-face meetings. Present yourself as serious, conscientious, and thorough, with a focus on the long term and the big picture. Provide examples of analysis you have conducted and modifications you have introduced that improved business strategies or systems without disruption.

The Organization Dimension: Schedule and Flow Orientations

SCHEDULE EMPLOYERS

Are more likely to reward employees who: Are punctual, well prepared, and focused, and who meet deadlines consistently

Are less likely to reward employees who: Are often late to meetings, multitask, improvise rather than preparing, and miss deadlines

Preparing for interaction: Schedule-oriented employers value punctuality, stability, and good organizational skills. They will have a scripted agenda and maintain their focus during meetings. They may ask about your project management skills, experience meeting difficult deadlines, and history of on-time delivery to clients and customers. They may interpret distracted behavior as a lack of interest or immaturity.

Strategies for Flow-oriented candidates: Use a respectful tone in written communication, cover letters, and face-to-face meetings. Provide advance notice if you need to reschedule. Arrive a few minutes early, and eliminate sources of distraction such as cell phones. Stay focused during interviews. Communicate reliability and steadiness. Highlight your experience managing complex projects, and provide examples of successfully meeting deadlines.

FLOW EMPLOYERS

Are more likely to reward employees who: Are adaptable troubleshooters who are good at responding to change

Are less likely to reward employees who: Are inflexible and unnerved by dynamic conditions or have difficulty modifying existing schedules

Preparing for interaction: Flow-oriented employers value creativity and adaptability to changing conditions. Interviewers may seem to improvise, jumping from one topic to the next. They may probe for your ability to effectively circumvent obstacles. They may interpret scripted answers as a lack of flexibility or originality.

Strategies for Schedule-oriented candidates: Present yourself as relaxed and adaptable in written communication, cover letters, and face-to-face meetings. Provide examples in which you have overcome obstacles and developed creative solutions.

Integrating and Managing International Employees

Integrating new international employees can be a formidable task. Managing expectation from the outset and providing early guidance when problems arise are key to helping employees transition to your corporate culture. You can avoid a great deal of confusion by pairing new international hires with mentors who will help them navigate new processes and protocols. Mentors trained in culture-based problem solving will be especially effective.

Do your best to motivate and reward employees according to their cultural tendencies. Refer to the information in Chapters 4–6 to identify the perspectives and preferences related to each one. The persuasive strategies in Chapter 10 will help you tailor arguments to cultural preferences, and the discussion of teamwork dynamics in Chapter 13 will help you manage culture-based problems within groups.

Organizational Structures

If you have flexibility in creating organizational and reporting structures, consider your employees' preferences in the Status (Achievement/Endowment), Involvement (Network/Process), and Collaboration (Independent/Group) dimensions. Keep in mind that Endowment members expect seniority-related privileges and that Achievers expect to benefit from their own initiative. Network employees expect to advance based on their relationships with coworkers, while Process members expect detailed performance-based criteria. Independents expect to be rewarded for their personal contribution of ideas and solutions, and Group-oriented employees expect their team's performance to be closely monitored and rewarded.

Culture-Based Coaching

12

If you find that an employee's experience and expectations are poorly suited to your company's systems or policies, you can help them make the transition. Giving them verbal input and encouragement that address their cultural tendencies while providing tools and strategies that work in your environment will help them acclimate.

The section below describes challenges employees with each cultural tendency may have working in unfamiliar environments and makes recommendations for coaching if problems arise.

Indirect employees working in Direct environments may hint at their proposals so tentatively that their ideas don't receive full consideration, and they may back away in the face of even mild objections. They may feel attacked when their ideas are criticized and retreat from group discussions to avoid conflict. They may express disagreement so subtly that colleagues don't recognize their concerns or take them seriously. If they fail to participate fully in discussions, coworkers may see them as disengaged or as having little to contribute. If they complain privately to a friend or ask someone else to speak for them, they may be perceived as secretive or devious.

Coach employees by encouraging them to:

- See that Direct colleagues distinguish criticism of ideas from personal attacks and don't mean to hurt their feelings
- Recognize challenge and debate as a collaborative mechanism that helps identify problems and move quickly towards solutions
- Make suggestions with confidence and plan to defend or revise good ideas
- Express criticism clearly enough to be heard, beginning with thanks and praise first if necessary

- Express problems directly to other parties in a conflict rather than to third parties

Direct employees working in Indirect environments may cause unintentional offense. They may present new ideas abruptly without going through proper channels, creating confusion and embarrassment. They may miss signs that their ideas are unpopular or push inappropriately upon meeting resistance. They may criticize others' ideas overtly, causing insult without meaning to. Their Indirect counterparts may respond by refusing to interact with them or excluding them from discussions. They may feel isolated and misunderstood.

Coach employees by encouraging them to:

- Identify mentors who can assess the value of their proposals and suggest appropriate contexts for making them public
- Watch their colleagues for unspoken signs of discomfort or disagreement
- Withdraw ideas that meet with resistance and get off-record advice on reformulating them
- Soften their criticism by expressing thanks and praise first, then following with gentle objections
- Observe their Indirect colleagues' behavior to identify appropriate ways of interacting

Neutral employees working in Expressive environments may perceive their colleagues' emotional behavior as childish or undisciplined. They may in turn be perceived as standoffish, disengaged, or disapproving. They may be excluded from social groups and have trouble gaining support for their ideas.

Coach employees by helping them:

- Recognize that emotional behavior is used to strengthen relationships and does not mean that people are out of control
- Create interpersonal connections by engaging more enthusiastically

Expressive employees working in Neutral environments may feel emotionally isolated when their colleagues fail to match their exuberant behavior. They may feel that their Neutral colleagues are unfriendly or uninteresting. Their colleagues may see their extreme changes in mood as a sign of immaturity, and if they communicate anger or frustration, they may be perceived as unstable.

12

Coach employees by helping them:

- Recognize that Neutral behavior demonstrates stability and control in your company culture and does not imply unfriendliness
- Create personal relationships with Neutral colleagues
- Manage their expressiveness in the workplace to better meet expectations and gain respect

Achievement employees may find it difficult to work within the strict hierarchies of Endowment environments. They may propose ideas out of turn and ignore the chain of command. They may be frustrated when promotions take time and worry that they are not being recognized for their efforts.

Coach employees by encouraging them to:

- Recognize the benefits of mentorship and guidance
- Appreciate the importance of their relationships with their colleagues and superiors to their career advancement
- Become familiar with appropriate procedures for navigating your hierarchy
- Feel reassured that their skills and abilities are noticed

Endowment employees working in Achievement environments may fail to take initiative as expected, waiting for instructions from superiors or defining their own responsibilities very narrowly. ("That's not in my job description.") If they are also Indirect, they may hesitate to criticize their superiors' ideas and stall or make excuses instead, or wait to give them bad news until it's unavoidable.

Coach employees by encouraging them to:

- Understand your lack of hierarchy and expectations of personal initiative
- Work autonomously and make decisions as appropriate
- Express their reservations about ideas—even their superiors'
- Deliver bad news without fear of negative consequences

Network employees working in Process environments may feel socially isolated or that their colleagues are unresponsive and unfriendly. Their tendency to socialize in the workplace may be perceived by others as a sign of laziness or immaturity. They may give special favors to people they know and like, causing them to appear unfair or even dishonest to their colleagues.

Coach employees by encouraging them to:

- Understand the way socializing is perceived in your environment and the importance of focus while at work
- Identify potential outlets for social interaction outside the workplace to help them make personal connections
- Appreciate the importance of maintaining a work focus in order to advance
- Recognize the importance of fair and equal treatment in your corporate culture

Process employees working in Network environments may have difficulty engaging colleagues and partners on a personal level, ignoring social relationships and focusing on tasks and outcomes. They may skip workplace parties and other social activities. They may object to relationship-based privileges and resent being asked to prioritize projects for influential people. If they insist on fairness and unbiased treatment for all, they may be perceived as cold and inflexible.

Coach employees by encouraging them to:

- Recognize the importance of personal relationships with colleagues in your environment

- Identify contexts for social interaction and create a plan for engagement
- Appreciate the role of strong working relationships in their advancement
- Recognize the value of "social currency" in your business environment and the benefits of using it to strengthen crucial relationships

12

Independent employees may feel suffocated by the lack of autonomy in Group environments and the need to work intimately with teammates. They may resist after-hours social interaction and gain a reputation for unfriendliness. They may have trouble backing away when their ideas are resisted and may be perceived as selfish or as poor team players. They may be frustrated by the lack of recognition they receive.

Coach employees by encouraging them to:

- See that their contribution is recognized, even if not overtly acknowledged
- Recognize the importance of team relationships in maximizing their integration and productivity
- Appreciate the importance of effective teamwork to their own advancement
- Dedicate their energy to the team's success, rather than to their own, to advance their career

Group-oriented employees may feel unsupported and rudderless in Independent environments. They may feel emotionally isolated from their teammates. If they have difficulty advancing their own ideas without group support, their colleagues may think they lack originality or creativity.

Coach employees by encouraging them to:

- Understand that more distant working relationships are a way of preserving individual strengths and getting diverse perspectives
- Articulate and advocate innovative ideas and solutions
- Appreciate the importance of showing initiative to their advancement

- Identify outlets for creating interpersonal relationships outside the workplace

Rule-oriented employees working in Situation-oriented environments may be dismayed by a lack of explicit guidance in rapidly evolving circumstances. They may wait for others to make decisions or rely excessively on policies and guidelines. They may feel unnerved by a lack of structure.

Coach employees by encouraging them to:

- Recognize the level and limits of their autonomy and take action appropriately
- Appreciate the importance of effective problem solving to their advancement
- Develop confidence in their ability to develop solutions without guidance

Situation-oriented employees may feel frustrated by the bureaucratic structures and elaborate procedures of Rule-oriented environments. They may ignore policies they feel are arbitrary, criticize existing structures, and question authority.

Coach employees by encouraging them to:

- Understand the general value of standardized policies, even if some are arbitrary or seem unnecessary
- Appreciate the importance of compliance to their advancement
- Recognize the basis of important policies by explaining the rationale behind them

Opportunity employees working in Thoroughness environments may feel stifled by slow-moving bureaucracy and negative reactions to their bold proposals. They may be frustrated if promotions come slowly. If they press for change, they may be perceived as immature and thoughtless.

Coach employees by encouraging them to:

- Understand that your business model requires steadiness and care for your reputation
- Appreciate the importance of diligence and big-picture thinking to their advancement
- Recognize that they will be more successful proposing modest modifications to existing policies than extreme changes in direction
- Feel reassured that their skills and abilities are being noticed and that their advancement is on track, given company policies

Thoroughness employees working in Opportunity environments may be unnerved by rapid change and feel that they aren't given time for the detailed analysis necessary to make good decisions. Their careful deliberation before contributing their ideas may cause them to be left out of decisions.

Coach employees by encouraging them to:

- Understand that your rapidly changing business environment doesn't always allow for extensive analysis
- Appreciate the importance of innovative thinking to their advancement
- Describe their perceptions and impressions earlier, even if their ideas aren't fully formed

Schedule-oriented employees working in Flow-oriented environments may feel blindsided by frequent change and disruption to their plans. They may spend inordinate time creating detailed strategies and revising them as circumstances evolve. They may be surprised if they are asked to help in areas outside their normal duties and feel threatened by unpredictable environments.

Coach employees by encouraging them to:

- Understand that change is a fundamental part of your work environment
- Appreciate the importance of flexibility to their advancement

- Develop strategies such as scenario planning to avoid investing too heavily in a single direction
- Create flexible plans that don't need to be reworked each time conditions change

Flow-oriented employees working in Schedule environments may feel constrained by detailed schedules and timelines. They may earn a reputation for unreliability if they miss, postpone, or arrive late for appointments or multitask during meetings. They may miss project deadlines, especially internal ones.

Coach employees by encouraging them to:

- Understand the role of punctuality and focus in conveying respect and trustworthiness in your company culture
- Appreciate the importance of reliability to their advancement in the company
- Use tools for scheduling and organization to keep track of appointments, cycles, and deadlines
- Articulate their need for flexibility in order to contribute their most creative work
- Schedule a greater contribution towards the end of projects when they have more energy and focus

To practice managing an employee based on multiple cultural characteristics (rather than a single dimension at a time), see the scenario on my website.[4]

---

[4] www.deirdremendez.com/managing-employees

13

Strategies for Intercultural Team Management

The way people collaborate is strongly influenced by culture-based learning and preferences. To enhance morale, unity, or productivity, start by creating a *Group Profile*—a single chart with each member's Personal Profile indicated by a unique color or symbol. Group Profiles provide a lot of information about areas of potential confusion and conflict, as well as opportunities for synergy. Below is a discussion of possible configurations and their implications.

Assessing Group Profiles

TEAMS WITH LITTLE DIVERSITY IN THE CULTURAL DIMENSIONS

Advantages: Intercultural teams whose members are similar for most or all of the cultural dimensions come to agreement relatively easily. Team members get along well and make decisions quickly. There is relatively little internal stress.

Disadvantages: These teams have less diversity and creativity. Too much agreement may lead to groupthink and a limited number of options considered. When all members have the same strong tendency for a dimension, the team will lack the advantages of the opposing one. For example, a team whose members are all Thoroughness-oriented will be highly ana-lytical and conscientious, but "analysis paralysis" may lead to difficulty making timely or innovative decisions.

TEAMS WITH SIGNIFICANT DIVERSITY IN THE CULTURAL DIMENSIONS

Advantages: Teams whose members are far apart in the cultural dimen-sions will bring multiple perspectives and solutions to every task. These teams have the potential to be the most creative and dynamic.

Disadvantages: There is potential for confusion and conflict if cultural dif-ferences aren't integrated. For diverse teams, it is vital to quickly develop common goals and policies and proceed in an organized way, making sure all team members contribute and are heard. Otherwise, disunity and gridlock will result in low morale, discord, and disengagement.

TEAM MEMBERS WITH EXTREME TENDENCIES

Team members with an extreme tendency in any dimension will have more difficulty understanding the opposing tendency. It's important to recognize extreme tendencies early and work to explain each perspec-tive. Note that it's not necessarily bad to be extreme—strong tendencies carry extreme gifts as well—and there is great learning potential as people learn to rely on those with opposing tendencies. Members with strong tendencies should explain their own perspective and work to "get inside" the opposing tendencies by asking their teammates how they *feel* about relevant circumstances. For example, a strongly Schedule-oriented mem-ber might describe their feelings when projects fail to move forward as planned. Saying, "I feel anxious and worried, and I don't sleep well at night. I wonder if I should take on extra work to get things back on track," provides information a Flow colleague can empathize with. By the same token, hearing that tight schedules make a Flow-oriented teammates feel like she's "in a straitjacket and can't breathe," let alone do her most creative work, can help motivate Schedule-oriented colleagues to accommodate them. Note that it's very important for participants to talk about their *own* emotions rather than expressing judgments of others. ("I feel that my Flow colleagues are being lazy.")

Team Members with Weak Tendencies

Members who have a weak tendency for a dimension (their mark is in the middle of the continuum) will find it easy to accommodate both perspectives. They can serve their team by explaining the perspective of people at the extremes to each other. People in the middle for *all* the dimensions may be cultural "chameleons" with natural adaptability, or they may have learned flexibility through intercultural experience. They can use this talent to assist team members who cannot understand one another.

Note: In spite of their ability to go in multiple directions, adaptable people aren't always good at explaining and coaching—sometimes it comes so naturally that they're not analytical about it. In such cases, they should use their experience to learn what is difficult for people at the extremes and develop ways to explain each tendency.

Contributions, Typical Problems, and Potential Synergies for Opposing Tendencies

The section below describes common teamwork problems for people with strong opposing cultural tendencies. It identifies what each tendency brings to the table and suggests opportunities for creating synergies to maximize effectiveness.

CLARITY: INDIRECT/DIRECT

Indirect   Direct

POTENTIAL PROBLEMS

Direct team members' overt criticism may seem pushy and overbearing to Indirect members. Indirect team members' cautiousness may suggest to Direct colleagues that they have little to contribute or are excessively shy. Indirect members whose ideas are challenged directly may disengage and become silent and resentful. Direct team members may perceive Indirect nuances and back-channel machinations as manipulative or passive-aggressive. If Indirect members withdraw, Direct colleagues may find themselves doing a disproportionate share of the work, leading them to perceive Indirect colleagues as uncommitted or incompetent.

- **Contribution of Indirect members:** Tact, team harmony, awareness of others' emotional reactions, and relationship preservation
- **Contribution of Direct members:** Incisiveness, clarity, and quick resolution of problems
- **Synergistic outcome:** Direct members rely on Indirect colleagues' skill at "reading between the lines" and handling politically sensitive situations, while Indirect members look to Direct teammates to represent them when forcefulness is required. Members discuss ideas tactfully and openly to reach the best solution without intrigue or offense.
- **Integrative goal:** Develop a communication protocol that acknowledges all ideas in a positive manner while choosing the best one efficiently; one that preserves interpersonal relationships, and that actively seeks and supports the contribution of all members. Leverage both Indirect tact and Direct bluntness when dealing with third parties.

EMOTION: NEUTRAL/EXPRESSIVE

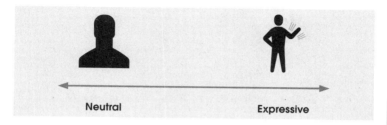

Neutral   **Expressive**

POTENTIAL PROBLEMS

Expressive team members' talkative approach and energetic "brainstorming" may overwhelm their Neutral colleagues, who may find it difficult to process information or "get the floor" and contribute. Expressives' tendency to interrupt may also insult Neutral members and cause them to withdraw. Expressives may miss Neutrals' subtle indications of disagreement, unintentionally ignoring their objections and dominating discussions. Neutrals may feel frustrated and ignored, especially if they're also Indirect, and may contribute less to the team. If Neutral members withdraw, Expressive colleagues may be left to do most of the work and perceive Neutrals as being unengaged or ineffective.

- **Contribution of Neutral members:** Calm demeanor, ability to focus, good listening skills, and clear thinking under stress
- **Contribution of Expressive members:** Enthusiasm, ease of expression, and responsiveness to input from others
- **Synergistic outcome:** Neutral colleagues look to Expressives to get discussions going and facilitate an energetic team dynamic. Expressive members rely on Neutral teammates to listen closely, capture detail, and synthesize solutions. Team members check in frequently while giving everyone time to provide input without interruption. Teams are dynamic and enthusiastic while retaining focus and making well-considered decisions.
- **Integrative goal:** Create a communication protocol that invites and facilitates contribution by all members and that provides opportunities for brainstorming as well as quiet contemplation.

STATUS: ACHIEVEMENT/ENDOWMENT

POTENTIAL PROBLEMS

Conflicts can arise between the formality and hierarchical tendencies of Endowment-oriented members and the egalitarian ambition and boldness of Achievement members. Endowment members may feel that the team structure should be based on seniority and may resent a young or female leader or one from a disfavored ethnic or social group. Achievement members may be frustrated by Endowment members' attempts to impose a hierarchy they don't respect or limit their freedom or autonomy.

- **Contribution of Achievement members:** Creative energy, bold aspirations, innovative thinking, and subject matter expertise
- **Contribution of Endowment members:** Well-placed connections, big-picture knowledge, experience, and personal influence
- **Synergistic outcome:** Achievement members seek the experience of senior Endowment colleagues to vet new ideas in light of the broader picture. Endowment members rely on Achievement colleagues to maintain focus on the bottom line, devise creative solutions, and overcome obstacles. Junior team members have opportunities for advancement, while being conscientiously mentored. Endowment members leverage connections and influence to meet team goals, while Achievement members "ask forgiveness rather than permission" to drive projects through to completion. Integrating Achievement and Endowment tendencies can yield great benefits when it comes to strategy.
- **Integrative goal:** Create a team dynamic that respects all members' offerings and leverages their complementary abilities to influence others and

solve problems. Create an organizational structure that acknowledges seniority while providing opportunity for personal initiative.

INVOLVEMENT: NETWORK/PROCESS

Network   Process

13

POTENTIAL PROBLEMS

Network-oriented team members will want to begin meetings with social interaction, and may perceive Process colleagues' lack of interest in personal relationships as unfriendly and antisocial. Process-oriented members, who prefer to get down to business right away, may see socializing as a waste of time. Due to their preference for preset agendas, Process members may perceive Networkers' digressions as irrelevant. Network members may feel that the highly focused Process approach prevents the team from considering all related issues during discussions. They may view Process colleagues as rigid and distant, while Process members may perceive them as immature. Network members may feel isolated and unappreciated.

- **Contribution of Network members:** Developing a positive team dynamic and working relationship, seeing the bigger picture, managing internal disputes, and presenting the team's ideas in an appealing way to third parties

- **Contribution of Process members:** Developing equitable policies, using rational approaches to problem analysis and decision making, maintaining project focus, and ensuring that deliverables meet specifications

- **Synergistic outcome:** Network members look to Process colleagues to stay organized and use objective criteria to develop rational solutions.

Process members rely on Network counterparts to keep meetings positive, manage conflict, and develop creative and insightful solutions. Teams maintain focus while considering broader issues. Teams are both cohesive and efficient and recognize the value of social interaction while maintaining focus on objectives.

- **Integrative goal:** Develop policies and procedures that accomplish tasks efficiently while making time for team-building activities (formal or informal) that develop member relationships and a positive team dynamic.

COLLABORATION: INDEPENDENT/GROUP

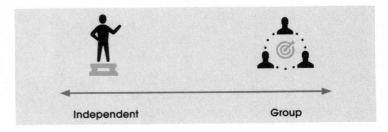

Independent   Group

POTENTIAL PROBLEMS

Single Team Interactions

Group-oriented members may expect almost constant collaboration and enjoy working in the same location—or even the same room. Independent members may feel stifled by this and prefer to work alone on specific tasks, coming together periodically to integrate contributions. Group-oriented members may perceive the need to integrate multiple approaches as inefficient. Time-consuming Group consensus building methods may exhaust Independent members, while Independent processes of majority rule or tiebreaking may seem unfair and arbitrary to their counterparts. Independent members may be frustrated if they aren't acknowledged and rewarded for their personal contribution, and Group-oriented members may perceive such expectations as selfish. If conflict arises, Group-oriented members may form oppositional factions, while Independents may isolate themselves and refuse to participate in group activities.

- **Contribution of Independent members:** Highly focused work, creative ideas and innovation, efficiency, and willingness to fight for controversial ideas

- **Contribution of Group members:** Thoroughness, ability to foster unity, a focus on ensuring that all members' perspectives are considered, and willingness to sacrifice their preferences for the good of the team

- **Synergistic outcome:** Independent members look to Group colleagues to make sure that all members' perspectives on an issue are considered. Group members rely on Independents for raw creativity and fresh ideas. Team policies combine freedom for individual reflection and strategic thinking with close collaboration to produce creative, well-considered strategies. Team members introduce and defend ideas they believe in while respecting others' preferences. Both personal contributions and team spirit are acknowledged and rewarded.

- **Integrative goal:** Develop work plans and decision-making procedures that consider all perspectives and promote group cohesion while accomplishing goals efficiently and allowing personal freedom. Create reward structures that acknowledge both individual contribution and sacrifice.

Multiteam Interactions

Independent teams may find it difficult to blend with Group-oriented teams to form a larger integrated group. Receiving less information than they provide, particularly about internal problems on their partner team, may cause to them to feel they are not true partners. Group-oriented teams may interpret their Independent partners' tendency to discuss internal problems openly as an indication of low team morale or incompetence, and they may be surprised when their attempts to preserve team boundaries are resented. Independent teams may be frustrated by their inability to create trusting relationships with Group partners, who may perceive their lack of boundaries as sloppy and inappropriate. If Group members refuse to answer casual questions before getting an "official" answer, Independent teams may suspect that they are uninformed or have hidden motives. Group teams may perceive Independent members' willingness to speculate as a sign that the team lacks cohesion or competence.

- **Contribution of Independent teams:** Transparency with their partners, a desire to collaborate, diverse and innovative solutions, and a focus on the larger goals of the collaboration

- **Contribution of Group teams:** Professional demeanor, unity and clarity in their position, thoroughly considered decisions, and willingness to solve internal problems on their own

- **Synergistic outcome:** Independent teams rely on Group-oriented partners for well-coordinated contributions and unity of voice. Group-oriented teams count on Independent partners to propose creative solutions and maintain focus on the dynamic of the partnership. Protocols for mutual information sharing ensure that both teams notify one another of problems as needed. Members of individual teams speak in one voice rather than expressing multiple opinions, and the joint team exhibits professionalism, unity, and competence.

- **Integrative goal:** Develop a trusting, integrated relationship and establish policies that facilitate information sharing and collaboration while respecting the internal integrity and boundaries of each team.

AUTHORITY: RULE/SITUATION

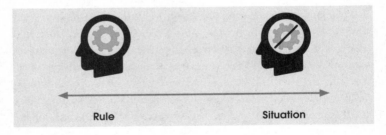

Rule   Situation

POTENTIAL PROBLEMS

Rule-oriented members may impose strict policies and detailed procedures that make Situation members feel stifled. Colleagues with Situation tendencies may question or ignore policies they consider arbitrary or excessive. Rule members may see Situation colleagues' lack of respect for policies as indications of dishonesty or a lack of commitment. Situation members may perceive Rule-oriented counterparts as petty and inflexible and may find it difficult to act creatively within their constraints.

- **Contribution of Rule members:** Reliability, trustworthiness, and structure
- **Contribution of Situation members:** Flexibility, creativity, and trouble-shooting skills
- **Synergistic outcome:** Team policies and processes are relevant to team goals and are clear to everyone. Situation members understand and value the team's policies and follow them willingly. Situation members rely on Rule-oriented colleagues to supervise policy implementation and interface with bureaucracies. Rule members turn to Situation-oriented colleagues for creative solutions and responses to problems and surprises.
- **Integrative goal:** Create structures that give Rule members security while allowing Situation members enough freedom. Establish the value of policies and minimize their arbitrariness so Situation members will conform.

ACTION: OPPORTUNITY/THOROUGHNESS

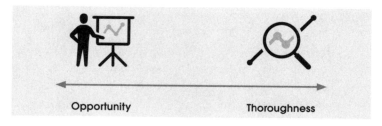

Opportunity   Thoroughness

POTENTIAL PROBLEMS

Opportunity-oriented members will want to move quickly. They may worry about missing favorable conditions due to Thoroughness-oriented colleagues' caution and desire for analysis. Their "nothing ventured, nothing gained" approach may seem excessively risky to their counterparts, who may fear that the team is making decisions without adequate analysis.

Thoroughness members, who tend to deliberate before expressing their thoughts, may not have enough time to articulate their ideas during meetings and may be perceived as unwilling or unable to contribute. They may perceive Opportunity members' brainstorming and "tossing out" incomplete ideas as immature. If Thoroughness members offer criticism late in the discussion process, Opportunity colleagues may resent the late notice as disruptive to an "agreed-upon" direction.

- **Contribution of Opportunity members:** Recognizing possibility, intuition, strategic risk-taking skills, quick implementation, and adaptation to change

- **Contribution of Thoroughness members:** Strategies for building on existing systems, caution, meticulous analysis, big-picture thinking, and long-term strategy development

- **Synergistic outcome:** Thoroughness members look to Opportunity colleagues to identify opportunities and suggest innovative directions. Opportunity members rely on Thoroughness colleagues to research and analyze various options. Opportunity members actively solicit Thoroughness counterparts' input throughout decision making, and Thoroughness members practice sharing their thoughts as early as possible. The team explores both opportunity and risk and makes decisions that balance near-term benefit with long-term positioning.

- **Integrative goal:** Develop flexible decision-making policies while relating decisions to long-term goals. Manage communication so that all members' opinions are integrated to develop decisions that balance caution and bold action.

ORGANIZATION: SCHEDULE/FLOW

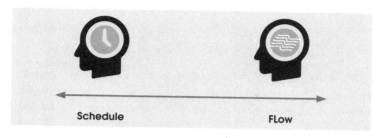

Schedule   FLow

POTENTIAL PROBLEMS

Schedule members may interpret Flow members' fluid arrival times and multitasking during meetings as a lack of commitment. Concern about reliability may cause them to suggest stricter schedules or penalties for late deliverables. Flow members may feel constricted and frustrated by excessive structure. If criticized, they may feel unappreciated and lose motivation and creativity.

- **Contribution of Schedule members:** Organization, schedule maintenance, and consistency

- **Contribution of Flow members:** Creativity, flexibility, and performance under stressful conditions

- **Synergistic outcome:** Flow-oriented members become more productive and reliable as a result of structures that help them stay on schedule. Schedule-oriented members appreciate Flow colleagues' ability to respond to change and handle crises and are willing to accommodate their need for flexibility. Projects are internally structured but not inflexible, and delivery commitments are met.

- **Integrative goal:** Create structures that respect Schedule members' desire for predictability and efficiency while allowing Flow members the freedom they need for maximum creativity. Openly discuss concerns about reliability and accountability to reassure Schedule members that Flow colleagues are committed to the team.

To practice managing diverse teams of various configurations, see the examples and analysis on my website.[1]

Leading Diversity: Creating Cohesion

Now that you understand the potential conflicts and synergies associated with each cultural dimension, you may want to develop a strategy for integrating opposing tendencies and minimizing conflict. You may be wondering how to show respect for everyone while juggling all these diverse tendencies. To develop a set of structures and processes that all members will respect, it's important to create a "team culture."

Developing a team culture involves introducing new policies and procedures, and you may encounter some resistance. People will need to unlearn old behaviors and acquire new ones, and uncomfortable changes will be accepted only if everyone recognizes their importance. The first step in designing a team culture is to create a sense of urgency. You can use that urgency to justify the changes you are about to impose. Your driver might be something such as an important new project, a poor sales quarter, or the arrival of new members on the team.

Once you have established that things need to change, implement the following:

1. **Identify team or project goals.** It's important for team members to agree, so gain consensus on what they are and articulate them clearly. Begin by asking each member to identify what they believe are the top three goals to get a sense of how they think. Work together to agree on the top three to five goals; if your style is more hierarchical, identify them yourself and explain why they are the top priorities. At the end of this process, everyone must be aware of the primary goals and accept their importance.

2. **Design clear structures and processes** that will facilitate meeting your goals. Everyone, including you, will follow these processes, and any

---

[1] www.deirdremendez.com/managing-employees

conflicts will be resolved according to them. Regardless of how people operated in their home country or previous job, this is the way you will do things from now on. Linking each policy to its importance in achieving goals helps you justify asking people to change their habits.

3. **Explain that conflicts will be resolved according to the team goals and policies** rather than any individual's cultural preferences. Make sure this rule is enforced.

4. **Explain the basis of accountability.** Describe your own commitment to the team's goals and the consequences of failure for you. Discuss how the team's performance will be assessed and the metrics of success for its members. Tie your reward structure to your goals and policies as much as possible.

5. **Complete a Team Profile** to identify your team's strengths and weaknesses, likely areas of confusion and conflict, and potential synergies. Combining your Team Profile with other frameworks such as the Myers-Briggs Type Indicator or DISC Assessment can give you additional insights. Be sure to:

   - Encourage team members to acknowledge their tendencies, reminding them that each has strengths and weaknesses and that none is better than another. Denying difference is dangerous and causes people to internalize conflict more deeply.

   - Acknowledge that the cultural tendencies of any region are interpreted by each member in a unique way, and emphasize that your goal is not to stereotype. The Team Profile will help everyone see each other as individuals and understand how they interact on the team.

   - Explain that culture-based confusion and conflict are to be expected and should not reflect negatively on anyone. The goal is for each person to recognize their own tendencies; identify signs of discomfort, confusion, and disagreement in others; and develop skills for resolving misunderstandings.

   - Explain that the benefits of synergy will outweigh any inconveniences and result in a dynamic, highly productive team everyone can be proud of.

13

- Point out your own cultural tendencies and reactions and learn to laugh at them to help people relax.

6. **Establish communication policies** that help everyone communicate clearly and fully as appropriate to your established hierarchy, while respecting one another's feelings and ideas. Clear and constant communication is vitally important to intercultural teams, and people must learn to explain themselves and ask questions. Indirect members may need to make a special effort, so be sensitive to this fact. Discuss ways of integrating communication styles on the team.

7. **Establish interactive norms** that help people with opposing tendencies deal with each other. These should promote inclusion and mutual respect while taking individual profiles into account.

8. **Define or develop consensus on a philosophy and processes** for:
   - Building the team dynamic (achieving cultural integration, enhancing interpersonal connections, etc.)
   - Accomplishing teamwork (sharing information, integrating work, etc.)
   - Conducting productive meetings (formality, punctuality, efficiency, directness, inclusion, etc.)
   - Decision-making (consensual, majority rule, top-down, etc.)
   - Information sharing among team members (frequency and level of formality) and with external constituencies (whether these are treated like "full" partners or not)
   - Conflict resolution (see Chapter 16)

It can be helpful for team members to have some role in designing your new policies, but it's not mandatory. (Not asking for contributions is better than asking and then ignoring them.) People will respect clear policies that encourage their growth and development, tie reward to accomplishing the team goals, and are enforced consistently and fairly by whatever metrics you identify.

14

Strategies for Intercultural Sales

For business functions such as sales, where understanding a counterpart's perspective is vitally important, recognizing cultural tendencies can help you separate culturally based behavior from personal idiosyncrasies and anticipate people's priorities, expectations, and reactions.

People with strong preferences for one cultural tendency will respond poorly to strategies based on the opposing tendency. As with persuasion in general, the goal is to orient your arguments in the right direction. Below is a list of common objections, along with strategies that will better appeal to your counterpart's preferences.[1]

Clarity

INDIRECT CLIENT OR CUSTOMER

- Preference: To purchase from someone who acknowledges my standing, intuits my needs, and communicates with delicacy and sophistication.

- Reaction to a Direct strategy: "You're moving too fast. Rather than focusing on what you offer, you should work harder to find out what I really

---

[1] I am grateful to Bryan Turnbough for sharing his expertise in culturally based sales strategies.

want and need. You need to read between the lines and get the context behind my objections. Your expectation of a "yes or no" is crude."

- Your strategy: Take time to discover a client or customer's underlying attitudes and preferences to fully anticipate their needs.
- Sales message: "Our goal is to really understand your needs. We've been studying your business model. What do you like or dislike about the product you're currently using?"

DIRECT CLIENT OR CUSTOMER

- Preference: To purchase from someone who states the product's benefits clearly and moves forward briskly.
- Reaction to an Indirect strategy: "What are your product's advantages over your competitors'? I expect clear answers to my questions. We've met twice already, and you haven't asked for my business. Where's your pricing sheet? You're wasting my time."
- Your strategy: Communicate your product's advantages and your "ask" clearly and succinctly.
- Sales message: "Our product has the following advantages, and we'd like your business."

Emotion

NEUTRAL CLIENT OR CUSTOMER

- Preference: To purchase from someone who is serious and reliable.
- Reaction to an Expressive strategy: "Your claims seem a bit exaggerated, and your behavior is over the top. I don't care about how *you* feel about your product—I want the facts and figures. I'm going to buy from someone more stable."

- Your strategy: Project an earnest and responsible image.
- Sales message: "This product is receiving very good reviews. I'd like to show it to you."

EXPRESSIVE CLIENT OR CUSTOMER

- Preference: To purchase from someone who appears lively and enthusiastic.
- Reaction to a Neutral strategy: "You don't seem very engaged—do you really believe in this product? And you're putting so little energy into this transaction. I'd rather buy from someone who really wants my business."
- Your strategy: Convey energy and enthusiasm for the interaction.
- Sales message: "We're really excited about the fabulous reviews for this product. I can't wait to show it to you!"

Status

ACHIEVEMENT-ORIENTED CLIENT OR CUSTOMER

- Preference: To do business with someone who can persuade me that a product's performance will get results and make me look good to my superiors.
- Reaction to an Endowment strategy: "I'm not interested in who you're related to or what university you went to. My reputation is on the line with this purchase. I need to know what your product will do for my company and my career, and I want a good deal."
- Your strategy: Focus on the customer's bottom line. Provide supporting materials that demonstrate performance, value, and results.
- Sales message: "Buying this product at this price will improve your results and reflect favorably on you. You've negotiated a great deal for your employer."

ENDOWMENT-ORIENTED CLIENT OR CUSTOMER

- Preference: To purchase from a social peer who acknowledges and respects my senior position.
- Reaction to an Achievement strategy: "You weren't referred by someone I trust. How did you get my phone number? And you're just a kid. Send your boss to talk to me."
- Your strategy: Avoid cold calls. Find an intermediary affiliated with your customer. If you're young or from a low-status background, gain status by having your manager introduce you. Present a senior person's business card, and speak as their agent. Emphasize the status, seniority, and experience of your product's designers. Leverage any prestige your product offers.
- Sales message: "I'm grateful to Mr. X for introducing us. The top two companies in your industry use our brand. With your experience, you're in a position to know quality when you see it."

Involvement

NETWORK-ORIENTED CLIENT OR CUSTOMER

- Preference: To purchase from someone I know and trust and who will repay the favor.
- Reaction to a Process strategy: "You're moving too fast. I prefer to do business by referral. How do I know I can trust you? Besides, I can get this from my brother-in-law, which is good for me in multiple ways. Why would I buy from a stranger, even if your price is better?"
- Your strategy: Avoid cold calls. Find an intermediary affiliated with your customer. Take time to get to know them and establish a personal relationship before talking business. Identify and leverage common interests and experience. Find ways to add value beyond the transaction.
- Sales message: "I'm so glad you enjoyed those tickets to the game—I had a great time, too. I was thinking that one of my contacts might be interested in your services. Oh, and by the way, I want to tell you about our product."

PROCESS-ORIENTED CLIENT OR CUSTOMER

- Preference: To purchase from someone who will guarantee the quality and performance of their products, whose processes are transparent, and who won't expect or promise special treatment.

- Reaction to a Network strategy: "Don't come by to 'visit' or try to bribe me with free tickets or meals. You'll have to go through our supplier qualification process like everyone else. I'm not looking for another best friend or some shady 'special' deal. Be honest about what you want and what you can do for me."

- Your strategy: Focus on the bottom line. State your business case quickly and succinctly. Prepare supporting materials that answer technical questions. Save relationship building for the end of the meeting if there is time.

- Sales message: "Here are the statistics showing how our product outperforms the competition. Let me know if I can answer other questions for you."

14

Collaboration

INDEPENDENT CLIENT OR CUSTOMER

- Preference: To purchase from someone who recognizes my authority and makes quick decisions.

- Reaction to a Group strategy: "Why are you requesting a meeting with other people? I'm the only one you need to talk to. Why do you take so long to respond to my counterproposals? Do you really want my business?"

- Your strategy: Be prepared to deal with a single decision maker. Expect quick decisions, and respond quickly to questions and counterproposals. Include relevant team members in customer meetings to answer questions.

- Sales message: "Here's the information you requested. We'll be ready to ship as soon as we have your decision."

GROUP-ORIENTED CLIENT OR CUSTOMER

- Preference: To purchase from someone who understands our consensus-based decision-making processes.

- Reaction to an Independent strategy: "Why are you so impatient, and why are you asking for the 'decision maker'? Your product will be considered by the appropriate committee when they meet again."

- Your strategy: Expect a long approval process, and be prepared to present to multiple groups of people. Provide detailed supporting materials that answer all possible questions.

- Sales message: "I'll make myself available to anyone who would like a demo. Please let me know a convenient time."

Authority

RULE-ORIENTED CLIENT OR CUSTOMER

- Preference: Engage in a straightforward transaction with a trustworthy supplier.

- Reaction to a Situation strategy: "Your price is too high for my budget, so there's no point in further discussion. What—now you're changing your price? That means your product wasn't worth your original quote."

- Your strategy: Prepare a variety of pricing options or action-based special deals to build in price flexibility without changes in direction.

- Sales message: "Our company is the most reliable source. We'll give you an option that fits your budget, and there will be no surprises."

SITUATION-ORIENTED CLIENT OR CUSTOMER

- Preference: To purchase from someone who will give me the best possible deal and make sure I gain special concessions in the process.

- Reaction to a Rule strategy: "You need to come down on your price. Everything's negotiable. To close this deal, you'll have to offer me a special incentive or a volume discount . . . What if I pay in full?"

- Your strategy: Be prepared for creative bargaining and prepare a variety of deal configurations. Keep your best offering as a last concession, and identify smaller incentives and concessions to use as you go.

- Sales message: "You drive a hard bargain, but on a one-time basis we can offer this special price—and maybe even include some extras."

Action

OPPORTUNITY-ORIENTED CLIENT OR CUSTOMER

14

- Preference: To purchase from someone with strategic, innovative offerings that provide benefit as quickly as possible.

- Reaction to a Thoroughness strategy: "We need a purchasing contract through the third quarter, not for the next ten years. Dealing with your detailed explanations is a lot of work. Just make your business case, and let's move on."

- Strategy: Prepare for a series of one-off sales. Identify a first-time attractant and be prepared to implement it quickly. Offer follow-up opportunities to develop an ongoing relationship.

- Sales message: "Take advantage of this one-time pricing deal. We'll get the paperwork done right away, and you can start saving next week. And we'll have a new product to show you next month."

THOROUGHNESS-ORIENTED CLIENT OR CUSTOMER

- Preference: To purchase from someone I trust—a stable, reliable source that can supply us for years to come with products that evolve with our needs.

- Reaction to an Opportunity strategy: "Why are you rushing this deal? Are you hiding something? I can't tell if your company will even be in business three years from now. I don't do business with fly-by-night operations."

- Strategy: Develop a relationship first and wait to introduce business discussions. Expect sales to take a long time and involve many—possibly social—meetings. Identify long-term benefits of the sale for your customer. Make preparations to provide support for a longer period than normal.

- Sales message: "We'll offer you a long-term service contract to make sure your customers are taken care of. We'll work with you as new needs arise and support you for years to come."

Organization

SCHEDULE-ORIENTED CLIENT OR CUSTOMER

- Preference: To purchase from someone who is conscientious about deliverables and deadlines.

- Reaction to a Flow strategy: "Don't just drop in when you're in the neighborhood. Call me to set an appointment, and be here on time with all the relevant information."

- Strategy: Be punctual and organized in meetings. Prepare in advance to meet both internal and final deadlines. Provide materials or testimonials that support your claims of reliability.

- Sales message: "You can count on us to keep your projects on track. We pride ourselves on our reputation for on-time delivery."

FLOW-ORIENTED CLIENT OR CUSTOMER

- Preference: To purchase from someone who is flexible and responsive.

- Reaction to a Schedule strategy: "I don't know what I'll be doing Tuesday at 3:00 p.m. Why are you trying to tie me down? It's your job to come by and see if I'm available."

- Strategy: Make multiple sales calls if necessary for a casual visit. Expect customers to be less available toward the end of large projects, and request their attention during quiet times.

- Sales message: "We'll put our creativity to work and adjust as needed to give you the best results possible."

To practice developing sales strategies for complete cultural profiles (rather than a single dimension at a time), see the examples on my website.[2]

14

15

Strategies for Intercultural Negotiation

Intercultural negotiation introduces unknowns that can add confusion to an already complex process. These include the way parties view their history, role, and relationships with others; their attitudes towards fairness and ownership; and their approaches to partnership and collaboration—to name just a few. Structural unknowns may include internal policies and processes, methods of decision making and problem solving, expectations regarding meetings, and the amount and type of information people expect to share. Behavioral unknowns include expectations regarding verbal and nonverbal cues as well as negotiating strategies and tactics. Cultural analysis will help you identify these factors, and understanding the cultural tendencies of a group and its representatives will help you design persuasive proposals, deflect bad offers without causing offense, and make as few concessions as possible.

Negotiations are conducted between collaborators as well as between hostile parties. In collaborative negotiations, although each side is angling for the best deal, neither wants to lose the other as a partner, so good will—and even friendship—is often a key goal for both sides. In adversarial negotiations, a winner-take-all approach is more likely, and it's possible that one or both parties are willing to walk away from the table. Even so, there are many cases where personal friendships have greatly assisted diplomacy between highly adversarial parties. In either case, establishing a mutually respectful and trusting relationship with your counterpart will be an advantage.

In addition to understanding the history and context of a negotiation, cultural analysis can help you recognize the agenda and perspective of your counterpart and the group they represent. You can then develop strategies to gain good will and respect; make successful arguments and counterarguments; understand reactions to your proposals; and distinguish between real problems, culturally based behavior, and negotiating tactics.

If you deal with Situation-oriented partners, who may have low regard for legal enforcement, you should develop a strong relationship to make sure they fulfill their commitments on the basis of their connection with you. And Network partners are more likely to give you favorable treatment if you establish a personal bond first. At the same time, it is a mistake to approach every relationship with a collegial attitude. A strong Group orientation may create a barrier to friendship—you will always be an outsider in the eyes of Group counterparts, even in the context of partnerships. Strong Opportunity tendencies can yield a "take the money and run" attitude. A negotiator with strong Rules and Process preferences will have a transactional "this is just business" approach and may be uninterested in friendship. When dealing with these tendencies, focus on being effective rather than friendly, adapting your communicative style to theirs and demonstrating strength and competence as they define it.

To develop negotiating strategies for counterparts with each of the cultural tendencies, it may help to begin with a *Quick Reference Profile* of the appropriate country from my website.[1] To begin your analysis, first review the general strategies from Chapters 10 and 11. Some of the sales strategies from Chapter 14 may also be useful. Below are additional points to be aware of and strategies to use in negotiation.

---

[1] www.deirdremendez.com/quick-reference-profiles

Clarity

NEGOTIATING WITH INDIRECT COUNTERPARTS

Because so much is left unsaid by people with Indirect tendencies, you may find it very difficult to recognize your counterpart's agenda. Indirect negotiators indicate their opinions and reaction subtly, and it is easy to miss the early stages of problems. Indirect negotiators are good at uncovering their counterparts' bottom line while hiding their own. They are more likely to give concessions to those able to accommodate their communicative style.

Strategies:

- Start by intensively researching your counterpart and the organization they represent as well as the context of the negotiation. Indirect communicators won't tell you much about themselves or their preferences, so it's up to you to find out all you can.

- Expect discussions to take much longer than what is normal for you, twice as long or more. Between the time you spend gathering information, your counterpart's careful deliberation over what to say and how to say it, and miscommunications and clarification, things will proceed slowly.

- You will get useful information through tactful diligence. Cultivate a friendly relationship with your counterpart and suggest social interactions to relieve pressure and talk about issues casually.

- Ask for context rather than making direct requests for information. This includes background information, history, and descriptions of relevant players.

- Make new proposals carefully. Hint at a possibility or pose hypotheticals and check for the response. It's better to keep a bad idea to yourself than to retract it later.

- When you advance a proposal, provide context first and end with the content. ("Due to these factors, we had these ideas, and due to these considerations, we would like to suggest solution X.")

15

- If you get the sense that a counterpart's words and attitude don't quite match, give priority to nonverbal cues such as tone of voice and eye contact.

- When you encounter even subtle negativity, stop and ask for more context to uncover the problem. Avoid asking about the problem itself.

- Avoid yes/no questions—ask open-ended questions that allow your counterpart to choose what to tell you. Pay close attention to how their comments relate to the question. Ask for clarification if you don't understand the connection.

- If you find yourself at an impasse, you may have missed subtle signs of disagreement in previous discussions. Try going back to the last item you're sure you agreed on and moving forward from there.

- If discussions break down, consult an intermediary—someone who knows both parties but is not personally involved—to address sensitive topics without causing offense.

- When you disagree with a proposal, begin by expressing appreciation for it, followed by praise for any mutual goals it may address. Then explain why you're unable to adopt it. Praise, even if not entirely sincere, shows good form.

- Always show respect for your counterpart. Never express anger or frustration—style is everything, and you gain points for showing grace under fire. The most stressful situations are the best opportunities to earn—or lose—your counterpart's respect.

- Confirm mutual understanding of points you've covered frequently, and in writing if possible. Have someone take notes and review them with your counterpart.

- Create a relationship by showing patience and interest.

- Gain concessions by showing grace and subtlety.

- Exert pressure by making forceful demands.

NEGOTIATING WITH DIRECT COUNTERPARTS

Direct counterparts will express their requirements overtly, which may make them seem unsophisticated, but don't confuse blunt language with a lack of intelligence or experience. Your counterpart may miss subtle expressions of disagreement, even when you think the context makes it clear. Direct contacts who are also Expressive may use loudness and shows of anger to dominate and intimidate.

Strategies:

- Provide as much information about your situation as you can while remaining strategic. Understanding your priorities and perspective will help your counterpart make more realistic proposals.

- Speak as frankly as possible to avoid confusion. Your counterpart may not recognize the meaning of your tone of voice or facial expression—they may only hear the words you use.

- Answer questions as directly as possible. If their question asks "how many," your answer should include a number, rather than just background information.

- Structure your arguments and proposals with the outcome or bottom line first, followed by supporting points and context. ("We would like to propose Solution X. We chose this approach for Reason Y. This strategy will accomplish Goal Z.")

- Express disagreement as clearly as possible to avoid confusion. If you find this difficult, begin with praise for their position and follow with criticism.

- Keep in mind that Direct speakers separate people from their ideas. Don't take negative responses personally. Try to remember that Direct speakers see criticism as a helpful step toward finding a workable solution.

- Create a relationship by identifying common ground.

- Gain concessions by stating clearly what you want.

- Exert pressure by keeping your goals hidden.

15

Emotion

NEGOTIATING WITH NEUTRAL COUNTERPARTS

Neutral communicators tend to provide very little feedback and are difficult to read, especially if they are also Indirect. Since they talk less than Expressive counterparts, they can easily give less information than they get. Using silence to create pressure is a natural tactic for Neutral negotiators. They are also good at reading reactions while hiding their own. Neutral negotiators are more likely to make concessions to people who seem stable and controlled.

Strategies:

- Start by doing as much research as possible on your counterpart and the organization they represent as well as the context of the negotiation. Neutral communicators will give little feedback regarding their goals or preferences, so you'll need all the help you can get when interpreting their behavior.

- Negotiating with Neutrals is like playing poker. Look for subtle clues in your counterpart's reactions.

- Ask for clarification when your counterpart's position is not clear.

- If the pace of speech seems slow, try to relax and avoid rushing or talking excessively.

- Avoid interrupting. Allow enough time for your counterpart to finish speaking, then pause a moment before contributing.

- Neutral speakers consider extreme behavior immature. Maintain a grave manner and avoid showing emotion. Use controlled facial expressions and gestures. Signs of anger or fatigue may be exploited.

- Avoid touching Neutral counterparts until you know their preferences for greetings. Be wary of excessive handshaking, let alone hugging or kissing.

- Use social opportunities to develop a rapport and get a sense of how your counterpart responds in various situations. Some people who are very Neutral at the start may become more Expressive as they get to know you.

- Keep in mind that silence or a failure to respond may just mean that your counterpart is deliberating. Avoid providing additional information or concessions to fill in the gaps. Ask a question to put the ball back in your counterpart's court.

- Create a relationship and gain concessions by projecting a mature, serious demeanor during negotiations.

- Exert pressure with displays of anger or emotion.

NEGOTIATING WITH EXPRESSIVE COUNTERPARTS

Expressive people may talk a great deal and expect to carry on a lively conversation, while reacting strongly when they disagree. Be prepared to show enthusiasm. Expressive negotiators may use meaningless chatter to distract or theatrical shows of anger as a tactic. They are more likely to make concessions to people who return their enthusiasm.

Strategies:

- Show as much vigor as possible to convey that you are friendly and engaged. Smile to indicate warmth and good will.

- Expressive counterparts may greet each other with a hug or kiss. If they touch one another occasionally, don't mistake this behavior for an expression of intimacy. Try to match it at least partially as the relationship progresses.

- Provide feedback as often as possible while counterparts are speaking.

- Expressive counterparts may not recognize your reactions to their proposals from your body language. You may need to express yourself verbally.

- People who are both Expressive and Indirect may overplay their positive responses and minimize negative ones. A pleasant, smiling demeanor doesn't always indicate agreement—watch for subtle negativity.

- People who are both Expressive and Direct may express negative responses forcefully. Assertive criticism doesn't always indicate a crisis—note the way your counterparts respond to large and small problems so you can tell when they are truly upset.

- Foster relationships by showing enthusiasm and engagement.
- Exert pressure with long periods of silence.

Status

NEGOTIATING WITH ACHIEVEMENT-ORIENTED COUNTERPARTS

Achievement negotiators are likely to be informal and focus on the bottom line. They value winning and are more likely to make concessions when they feel they have gained some from their counterpart.

Strategies:

- Achievement negotiators are chosen on the basis of subject expertise and recent accomplishments. They may seem young and aggressive. Don't take this as an insult; you may be able to use it to your advantage.
- Achievement counterparts prefer to behave informally. They may expect to remove their jackets or use a relaxed posture during meetings. Create rapport by accommodating informality; exert pressure by insisting on formality.
- In Achievement environments, people emphasize equality by using first names and disregarding rank. Create rapport by accommodating this egalitarian preference or exert pressure by insisting on hierarchy.
- Create a relationship by establishing an informal camaraderie.
- When advancing proposals, get to the point quickly and focus on outcomes.
- Make small concessions to allow Achievement counterparts to "win."

NEGOTIATING WITH ENDOWMENT-ORIENTED COUNTERPARTS

Endowment representatives tend to be relatively formal and want to be treated with respect. They are more likely to make concessions to people who acknowledge their rank and influence.

Strategies:

- Endowment negotiators tend to be senior people, usually older males, who may be insulted if paired with a younger counterpart. If you are young, female, or from a lower-status background, get a higher-status person to introduce you. Treat your counterpart as a respected senior—you may be able to use flattery to your advantage.

- Endowment counterparts prefer to behave formally and interact in formal settings. Create rapport by being equally formal or exert pressure by creating an informal context.

- In many Endowment environments, people emphasize hierarchy by using titles and last names. Expect there to be a rank-based seating order. People may speak more or less depending on their rank, and low-ranking people may not speak at all unless called upon by a senior. Create rapport by acknowledging your counterparts' hierarchy or exert pressure by ignoring it.

- Develop relationships by showing courtesy and respect.

- When advancing proposals, acknowledge your counterpart's seniority, experience, and influence.

- Show graciousness and respect when making or requesting concessions.

15

Involvement

NEGOTIATING WITH NETWORK-ORIENTED COUNTERPARTS

Network communicators value personal relationships highly and trust relationships over legal agreements. They tend to begin negotiations with social interactions to establish a common ground of trust, saving business until later. Negotiations may include lengthy meals and social events where business is not discussed. Network negotiators are more likely to make concessions to people with whom they feel a connection.

Strategies:

- Plan for negotiations with Network counterparts to take longer than usual and schedule accordingly.

- Be prepared for personal questions designed to establish a trusting relationship.

- Expect Network hosts to schedule cultural and social activities unrelated to the negotiation. Use these to establish a bond.

- Entertain Network guests during evenings and weekends. Schedule cultural and social activities to establish a relationship.

- Expect meetings to begin with social interaction. Avoid rushing business discussions.

- Nondisclosure agreements and other limiting legal instruments may be resented as evidence of mistrust. Begin with nonproprietary information so you can avoid them.

- Prepare for digressions during discussions and ask how they relate to major points if you are unsure.

- Frame your proposals in terms of their benefit to your mutual relationship.

- Create a relationship by taking time to get to know your counterparts personally and sharing personal information about yourself.

- Make concessions in the spirit of friendship and reciprocity.

- Exert pressure by threatening to end the relationship.

NEGOTIATING WITH PROCESS-ORIENTED COUNTERPARTS

Process negotiators expect to get down to business quickly. They tend to have detailed, linear agendas and prefer to hold discussions to a predetermined path. They expect detailed formal agreements and expect negotiations to be focused on the value proposition. They tend to consider personal relationships irrelevant and even potentially harmful, as they could lead to inappropriate decisions or concessions.

Strategies:

- Plan for negotiations with Process counterparts to focus on goals and outcomes.

- If you are traveling to meet with them, prepare for Process hosts to focus on the negotiation itself. Don't expect many social activities.

- If you are the host, expect Process guests to schedule a short time to complete negotiations and entertain themselves during their free time. Schedule one or two dinners with them and expect them to want to talk business. Plan social activities (a contract signing party, for example) after negotiations have concluded.

- Process negotiators tend to arrive well prepared and eager to work. Don't expect to postpone discussions with social preliminaries.

- Frame your proposals as being logical and sensible. Don't propose relationship-based "special" deals.

- Create a good working relationship by focusing on the task first and introducing social topics later.

- Make concessions in the spirit of what is reasonable under the circumstances.

- Exert pressure by prolonging social activities or diverging from the agenda with tangential discussions.

15

Collaboration

NEGOTIATING WITH INDEPENDENT COUNTERPARTS

Independent negotiators tend to make quick decisions on their own authority and expect equally quick responses. They may not consult others during negotiation; as a result, implementation may be delayed until after they've briefed relevant parties and developed a plan for moving forward.

Strategies:

- Only one or two people may be sent to represent their party's interests. The chief negotiator is likely to have full authority for making decisions.

- Independent negotiators often make very quick decisions and may suggest changes in direction as they occur to them. Prepare to convene relevant parties as needed to respond.

- Independent negotiators may be unaware of consensus-based processes, and may perceive them as evidence of stalling or lack of interest. Explain your procedures to help them anticipate how you make decisions and avoid surprising you with frequent changes.

- Although Independent representatives will probably be experts on the topic under discussion, they may not have all relevant information at hand. Be prepared to give them time to contact others about peripheral details.

- Create a relationship by honoring the negotiator's prestige in being chosen for the assignment.

- Make concessions that show respect for the special skill and knowledge of the negotiator.

- Create pressure through detailed questions and drawn-out analysis.

NEGOTIATING WITH GROUP-ORIENTED COUNTERPARTS

Group-oriented negotiating teams tend to include multiple subject matter experts who ask detailed questions and expect to be paired with counterparts of similar status. Negotiations can be quite drawn out, as members need to confer often to arrive at consensus or get approval from superiors for each decision. Sudden changes in direction by counterparts can cause confusion and delays.

Strategies:

- Prepare for negotiations to take much longer than usual, with long waits for responses from your counterparts.

- A large group may be sent to represent their party's interests. The chief negotiator, however senior, is probably a facilitator who does not have decision-making authority.

- If possible, match members of their team with representatives of your organization, even if they are not formal negotiators, at social events to facilitate the relationship and ask questions. If your counterparts have Endowment tendencies, try to match the rank of their members with people of equal rank from your side.

- Group-oriented teams may make decisions slowly. Consensus-based processes require input and agreement from multiple parties. Each proposal or idea you make may initiate this process, so avoid changing direction casually.

- Group-oriented negotiators may be unnerved by the appearance of casual decision making. They may see quick decisions as evidence of poor judgment. Pausing before you introduce or respond to proposals can help you avoid this suspicion.

- They may be concerned that a "lone wolf" negotiator does not have the support of the organization. To reassure them, explain your process and structure, your relationship with your superiors, and the basis of your authority.

- Group-oriented negotiating teams will include experts from related fields who have extensive historical, contextual, and technical knowledge. They will ask detailed questions. Have resources for answering them close at hand, and ask experts on your side to be available in case there are questions.

- Create a relationship by honoring the chief negotiator's organizational knowledge and experience gaining consensus from large teams.

- Make concessions that show respect for the extensive knowledge of the team.

- Create pressure by throwing out multiple ideas and scenarios and changing direction frequently.

Authority

NEGOTIATING WITH RULE-ORIENTED COUNTERPARTS

Rule-oriented negotiators expect to follow a set procedure and place relatively little value on social interaction. They dislike sudden changes in direction and consider relationship-based special deals or other exceptions inappropriate. They tend to prefer detailed, specific contracts and enforce them to the letter.

Strategies:

- Highly Rule-oriented people may dislike the idea of "haggling" and the uncertainty of negotiating in general. Help them feel at ease by approaching the process as a way of establishing mutual benefit.
- Because they value fairness so highly, they may perceive personal relationships as possibly leading to favoritism. Try to develop equally open, cordial relationships with all members of their group to avoid the appearance of side dealing.
- Rule-oriented negotiators may perceive schedule changes, new directions, and casual ideas as disruptive, especially if they come late in the negotiation process. Give early warning of changes you propose.
- They may perceive extreme high- and low-balling as dishonest. Begin relatively close to your target.
- Rule-oriented contracts tend to be explicit, detailed, and lengthy, and they expect to enforce them without exception. Be sure you understand all the provisions you agree to. To protect against surprises, insert provisions for any potential problems and clarify how they will be dealt with.
- Describe your requests and concessions as being reasonable and equitable. Avoid appearing to ask for or make exceptions.
- Create a relationship by showing respect for rules and orderly processes.
- Create pressure by introducing sudden or late changes or requests.

NEGOTIATING WITH SITUATION-ORIENTED COUNTERPARTS

Situation negotiators tend to enjoy negotiation and are generally good at finding creative ways to gain concessions. Because they value relationships over legal systems, they tend to place high importance on establishing trust and are unlikely to come to agreement until it is established.

Strategies:

- Be prepared for lengthy social activities and detailed questions designed to confirm your reliability.

- Situation-oriented negotiators may not believe that legal structures will protect them, so they prefer to enter into agreements with people they like and trust. Cultivate a personal relationship.

- They are creative, flexible, and willing to negotiate down to the last minute. They often see negotiating as a game and are good at innovative maneuvers. Be prepared for energetic negotiations.

- They like the idea of getting the best deal possible and may not stop if they feel they can get more. You may need to insist when your bottom line is reached.

- Situation-oriented negotiators are prone to changing direction suddenly or introducing unexpected ideas late in the process. Keep a final request and concession in reserve in case they reopen negotiations at the last minute.

- Be prepared for high- and low-balling and leave yourself room for moving incrementally toward your target.

- Nondisclosure agreements and other limiting legal instruments may be resented as a sign of mistrust.

- Situation-oriented contracts tend to be relatively brief and vague, allowing room for adaptation to changing conditions. There may be an expectation that signed contracts are renegotiable. Be sure both parties agree on expectations of enforceability.

- Request and offer concessions based on commonalities and relationships rather than rules, laws, or abstract definitions of "right," "wrong," and "fairness."

- Counter changes in direction with patient reiteration of your position.

- Develop a personal connection and demonstrate your willingness to deal.

- Gain concessions in one area by offering concessions in another.

- Exert pressure by sticking to a narrow agenda that forbids creative alternatives.

15

Action

NEGOTIATING WITH OPPORTUNITY-ORIENTED COUNTERPARTS

Opportunity representatives feel a sense of urgency about coming to a conclusion. They limit risk by establishing short-term, deal-based relationships. They may become frustrated and abandon a deal that takes too long or make concessions to end a lengthy process.

Strategies:

- Opportunity goals generally center on the near term. Partnerships tend to end when a deal ends. If your goal is an extended relationship, justify it in terms of continued opportunity after the initial agreement.

- Opportunity counterparts tend to limit social interaction and get down to business quickly. Plan for negotiations to focus on outcomes and to move rapidly.

- Proposals may involve significant risk and make provisions for changes of direction. Explain your concerns about rapid changes so your counterparts can accommodate them in their proposals.

- Opportunity negotiators value innovation and creative thinking. Emphasize the novelty of your arguments and describe how they differ from the norm or the present course.

- The past may seem largely irrelevant to Opportunity negotiators, who see the future in terms of the present moment and action. Take a results-oriented approach, and include some near-term benefits in your proposals.

- Opportunity negotiators tend to make decisions quickly. If it takes you longer to deliberate, they may think you are stalling or uninterested. Clarify your process to reassure them.

- Create a relationship by expressing enthusiasm for making progress and getting results.

- Gain concessions by agreeing to close the deal if they accept your terms.

- Exert pressure by prolonging analysis and deliberation.

NEGOTIATING WITH THOROUGHNESS COUNTERPARTS

Thoroughness counterparts want to vet their partners, demonstrate conscientiousness to their superiors, and consider every possible outcome of decisions. They proceed cautiously and resist attempts to hurry discussions. They may withdraw from a negotiation if rushed.

Strategies:

- Thoroughness goals generally focus on the long term, possibly decades or more from now. Partnerships tend to be long lasting and are developed over time. If your goal is a brief, deal-based relationship, emphasize that it may be renewed if opportunity continues.

- Thoroughness counterparts agree to partnerships once friendship and trust have been established. Expect negotiations to involve lengthy discussions and to move slowly.

- Thoroughness proposals may focus on consistency with history or past direction and avoid significant change. Explain your need for a rapid response so they can accommodate it in their proposals.

- Thoroughness negotiators value steadiness and respect for tradition. Research their history and emphasize how your proposals will reflect tradition or recreate past success.

- Include the past in your discussions. Introduce ideas and proposals by beginning with historical context and moving forward to the present.

- Thoroughness negotiators tend to conduct deep analysis and reflect at length when making decisions. Justify moving quickly by citing past examples of bold action on their part that turned out well.

- Spend time getting to know your counterparts, and create an impression of thoughtfulness and steadiness.

- Exert pressure by insisting on quick action.

15

Organization

NEGOTIATING WITH SCHEDULE-ORIENTED COUNTERPARTS

Schedule-oriented negotiators want discussions to proceed according to a predetermined plan and may resist scheduling changes during negotiations. They may resist even good ideas or make concessions to avoid changes or delays.

Strategies:

- Be prepared for negotiators with Schedule tendencies to be punctual or even early for meetings. They may interpret late arrival as a sign of unreliability. They dislike rescheduling meetings and may perceive postponements as indicating a lack of commitment.

- Schedule-oriented counterparts will focus intently during meetings. Activities such as checking cell phones, making calls, or leaving and reentering meetings may be considered impolite. Let them know in advance if you need to attend to other business during a discussion.

- They will expect to receive information in a timely manner. If you're unable to provide requested answers or documents quickly, explain the nature of the delay and give them a workable delivery estimate.

- They prefer to proceed through predetermined schedules in an orderly manner. They will revise their plans as needed when changes occur. Avoid repeated rewriting by grouping multiple changes together into a single proposal or request.

- They will resist tangential discussions that divert negotiations from the established path. Notify them formally if new agenda items are required.

- Avoid making changes to the schedule late in the process. Let them know as early as possible when a change is unavoidable.

- Create a relationship by demonstrating commitment to a timely, orderly process.

- Exert pressure by straying from the established schedule, going off-topic, or reopening negotiations near closing.

NEGOTIATING WITH FLOW-ORIENTED COUNTERPARTS

Representatives with Flow tendencies are flexible, creative negotiators who do not tire easily. They expect to revise schedules as needed to accommodate emergencies.

Strategies:

- Be prepared for negotiations with Flow-oriented counterparts to take longer than usual. Anticipate postponements and allow additional time to avoid deadline pressure.

- Negotiators will be casual about meeting times and structures. They may arrive late and multitask by taking calls, leaving and returning, or holding side conversations in the meeting room. If these activities disturb you, suggest a break to allow them to complete their other business.

- Information you request may arrive incomplete or late. Be patient and explain its importance to your continued discussions.

- Flow-oriented negotiators move fluidly from one topic to another in an unstructured manner. They tend to create lists of items for discussion rather than detailed plans. Avoid rigid schedules that discourage flexibility.

- Counterparts may introduce tangential topics or additions to the agenda that divert negotiations from the path you anticipate. Ask for clarification on their relevance to assess whether they should be accommodated.

- Flow-oriented negotiators may need incentives to move in a timely, orderly direction. Offer incentives for timely decisions and deliverables or penalties for hesitating or missing deadlines.

- Create a relationship by demonstrating flexibility and willingness to deal.

- Exert pressure by insisting on a detailed schedule and narrow list of topics.

15

Two factors in particular are advantages in intercultural negotiation: (1) the flexibility to accommodate changes in agenda and direction; and (2) willingness to spend time developing relationships, gathering and providing contextual information, and allowing deliberations on both sides.

To practice developing negotiating strategies for complete cultural profiles, rather than a single cultural tendency, see the example on my website.[2]

16

Managing Intercultural Conflict and Achieving Synergies

In conflicts that require intercultural mediation and diplomacy, groups may be competing for status, power, or resources. Cultural differences probably aren't the sole cause of a dispute[1] in this type of conflict, but they can greatly complicate the process of conflict resolution or attempts at conflict transformation if fundamental concepts such as rights, reciprocity, contractual obligation, and sovereignty are understood differently. To address such disputes effectively, it's crucial to identify the cultural underpinnings of the grievances claimed by each side. How do parties interpret the central concepts of the dispute and frame their arguments? Include culture along with historical, political, and other contextual factors when looking for an answer.

Many diplomatic conflicts, and most business disagreements, involve friction between two parties trying to collaborate despite having different culturally based interests, goals, or processes. Conflict between well-intentioned collaborators can occur for many reasons. When they have different concepts of terminology related to outcomes—"prosperity," "partnership," or "success," for example—partners may believe that they share goals but in fact have tangential or even conflicting goals. They

---

[1] For a discussion of the role of cultural difference in this sort of dispute, see Kevin Avruch's book *Context and Pretext in conflict Resolution:Culture, Identity, Power and Practice* (Paradigm Publishers, 2012)

may also have different expectations of negotiation, information sharing, decision making, and contract development and enforcement. At an interpersonal level, conflict can occur when one party's actions or communication style conveys disrespect or malice, or when an unintentional slight is perceived as deliberate. Often, all of these are combined.

A party that feels it has been wronged may respond in deliberately harmful ways, which compounds the offense and increases animosity. Recognizing and immediately working through misunderstandings helps avoid these cycles of retribution, so identifying the early signs of confusion and conflict is a valuable skill. Even where there is a history of disagreement between two groups, if individual negotiators can communicate without reinforcing stereotypes or creating new animosity, it is possible to make headway.

In situations where a cultural misunderstanding has led to prolonged back-and-forth retaliations, parties show signs of stress, animosity, and disengagement. Even so, I am often surprised at how willing people are to give each other a second chance once they realize that the initial "offense" was unintentional. Deconstructing misunderstandings can help you integrate cultural differences and promote synergies.

Common Sources of Culture-Based Conflict

Differences in the way goals are expressed and processes are implemented are a common source of confusion and conflict. Although the same terms and concepts are used in business throughout the world, the way they are understood can be quite different. Consider this example: A multinational company assigned software design teams from its U.S. and Japanese branches to develop a product for a Japanese customer. Midway through, the customer changed its requirements, necessitating additional work to complete the project. The Japanese team added personnel to do the extra work, but the U.S. team did not, which endangered the delivery schedule for their portion of the work. The Japanese team was astonished that the American team failed to respond "appropriately" by adding people. The U.S. side was equally astonished. The customer had signed a contract for specific deliverables, and the U.S. team had staffed accordingly. These changes weren't in the contract. Why didn't the Japanese team just tell the customer to pay for them?

This misunderstanding was based on different approaches to "customer relations" and "staffing" as defined by the two groups. In Japan, where strong Endowment tendencies place customers at the top of a steep hierarchy, postcontract changes in specifications are not uncommon. Well aware of this, the Japanese team made provisions to deploy additional personnel as needed. For the U.S. team, which was both Achievement- and Rule-oriented with regard to contracts, staffing involved calculating the number of people needed to accomplish the work outlined in the contract on the date it specified. They expected any changes to be paid for by the customer. Their superiors would have perceived requesting more money to add staff as mismanagement.

This sort of misunderstanding is quite common in international business, and the later it is detected, the more difficult it is to manage. In addition to sorting out the difference in expectations of each side, it may be necessary to revisit prior decisions.

Avoiding Conflict

16

Needless to say, it would be best if you could avoid misunderstandings that lead to conflict altogether. In intercultural collaborations, at least, this is possible if you begin talking about cultural variation before conflict arises. Intercultural conflict can be greatly reduced when participants are:

1. Aware of their own cultural tendencies
2. Aware of how those tendencies are perceived by people who don't share them
3. Skilled at recognizing cultural tendencies in others
4. Skilled in explaining themselves and asking questions to prevent conflict
5. Skilled at perceiving subtle signs of discomfort, frustration, or disagreement
6. Skilled at deconstructing early-stage misunderstandings
7. Skilled at adapting their style and strategies to address others' preferences

For example, explaining and asking for clarification can greatly reduce confusion. I recommend variations on the following script:

1. "I notice that you just said/did X, and I want to be sure I understand."
2. "In my country/company, we would say/do/propose Y. "
3. "We would choose Y because . . . (give your reason)."
4. "Can you tell me why X seemed like the thing to say/do/propose? How does it fit with your priorities or processes?"

You can learn a great deal and avoid conflict in the process by explaining your system and asking counterparts about theirs. You may not always have time to go through the above steps, of course, and sometimes you won't catch a miscommunication until it's too late to ask. And people aren't always willing or able to explain their behavior. But developing a practice of explaining and clarifying can be extremely helpful, and although it's time-consuming on the front end, it's much less so than repairing a conflict.

Deconstructing Misunderstandings

Whether you're a participant in the conflict or a third party, to get to the bottom of a culture-based miscommunication, you must identify the areas where meanings of underlying concepts were different for the parties involved. (These can include different conceptions of rights and obligations, partnerships, goals and priorities, strategies, processes, appropriate behavior, and communication.) This is done through a process of deconstruction:

1. Ask each side to tell you what happened and how they felt about it. Hearing their *judgments* of each other's actions will help you intuit what they expected from each other and why they reacted the way they did.
2. Have them retell the story a second time, as a series of actions on either side—just the *facts*—and separate these from any speculation about others' actions or motives.
3. Try to identify the action that caused the **initial** confusion or offense.

4. Establish how the party that committed this action perceived it and what they hoped to achieve. Identify differences in the way each side viewed the action and the underlying perceptions or definitions that led to different interpretations.

5. Explain these differences in expectations and interpretation to both sides.

6. Deconstruct the rest of the conflict. Once the basis of the misunderstanding is clear, look for a path forward that meets both parties' needs, carefully defining and explaining terms as you go.

Of course, this process can be quite complex. Getting people to give you the facts can be difficult. My conversations with clients often go something like this:

Team 1: Our partner's morale is very low. Eric just left to work on another project, and Joachim, his manager, didn't even know he was going.

DM: So you're concerned that having an employee leave means there's a morale problem?

Team 1: Of course. And he didn't trust his manager enough to talk to him about it. What a disaster—and if they fire Joachim, that will mean even more destabilization.

DM: You think Joachim might be fired because Eric left the team?

Team 1: Yes! It's his job to make sure his employees are satisfied, and losing someone this way is shocking. We don't know how to deal with Anne, his replacement. We can hardly look her in the eye.

Followed by:

Team 2: They really hate Anne, our new team member. They won't even talk to her.

DM: I heard Eric left. What was going on?

Team 2: He wasn't that good at what we're doing, and another project requested him. It was a better fit for him, and we're much happier with Anne. But it turns out they don't like working with women, so things aren't going so well.

DM: You think the problem is her gender?

Team 2:   What else could it be? She's more competent than Eric and is doing a great job for us, but they treat her like a pariah. And they're giving Joachim, our manager, the cold shoulder for hiring her.

The facts in this misunderstanding are straightforward: A member from Team 2 has left and has been replaced. But the two sides' interpretations of the situation are vastly different. Team 2 has an Achievement, Independent, Process orientation, according to which employee movement between projects is considered unremarkable and potentially even beneficial. Team members are valued primarily for their abilities, and managers seek employees who are the best fit in terms of skills and knowledge. In Team 2's view, replacing a mediocre performer with an expert is an improvement, and it doesn't occur to them that they have anything to justify.

Team 1, on the other hand, views employee attrition from an Endowment, Group, and Network perspective. Employees are expected to bond with their teams and have strong personal relationships with their managers, whose job it is to help them integrate with the team. Unhappy employees are expected first to speak with their manager, and a departure without doing so indicates that the manager was not even trusted to try to reintegrate them successfully. In the face of such disruption, the departed employee's replacement would be an uncomfortable reminder of the team's dysfunction.

In examples like this one, I use the deconstruction process to identify the source of the conflict. Explaining Team 2's approach to staffing and management/employee relations will help relieve Team 1's anxiety so that they can work harmoniously with Anne. Whether you're an interested party or an impartial mediator, it is vital to take the position of investigator and suspend judgments or interpretations of your own. It's equally important to share the knowledge you gain from this fact-finding process so that all parties become partners in recognizing and deconstructing culture-based conflict.

Resolving Conflict with a Synergistic Approach

Resolving intercultural conflict can do more than just get things back on track. It can help people understand themselves better, anticipate and avoid future misunderstanding, develop empathy for one another, and create interpersonal synergies. Like brawlers who pound on each other and then go home best friends, working through conflict can lead to much stronger relationships. An example is an intercultural team I worked with that was having difficulty establishing a rhythm and getting an equal contribution from all members.

For this team, meetings began with lively brainstorming. Most members contributed, throwing out and debating a series of ideas. But one, whom I'll call Xueling, was not contributing much. When a tentative decision was made, the team leader asked whether everyone agreed with the direction. Each time, Xueling indicated that she agreed, but with little conviction. Once, she made an online recommendation after a meeting for a significant change in direction. Her teammates felt that she should have contributed her opinions during the meetings, because the team wasted time making the first round of decisions, only to change direction afterwards. They also felt that using the online posting was a sneaky, "behind-the-back" way to contribute.

For her part, Xueling reported feeling that meetings were so chaotic she could hardly think. When she did have a point to make, she would have to interrupt someone else to do so, which she considered rude and unprofessional. Her teammates' tendency to toss out half-baked ideas and criticize each other's suggestions struck her as immature and combative. And given the fact that she said very little, it seemed to her that other members should notice and more actively give her the floor.

It became clear that Xueling had Indirect, Neutral, Group, and Thoroughness tendencies, whereas the other members of the team were Direct, Expressive, Independent, and Opportunity-oriented. While other

16

members expected to throw out ideas and develop solutions via debate, Xueling expected to think deeply and propose solutions only after they were fully developed. She had been taught that expressing incomplete ideas was a sign of poor discipline and would lead to embarrassment, and criticizing others' ideas felt confrontational, so she ended up with almost nothing to say during meetings. Her vague agreement with proposed solutions was intended to signal her unhappiness with them, but her Direct colleagues didn't notice. Once Xueling had had adequate time to process the discussion and develop a clear opinion, posting her objections online seemed to her a polite way to avoid a personal confrontation.

After some discussion, the group realized that there had been no deliberate offense on either side and moved toward a solution. The team's Direct, Expressive members decided to stop their discussions periodically to give Xueling time to think, ask for her input, and give her time to respond without interruption. Once her colleagues began to actively solicit her ideas, Xueling felt more comfortable providing input, and as she understood their decision-making process, she became more willing to contribute less-than-finished ideas. Although the pause-then-contribute process seemed artificial and mechanical at first, she needed less time to think as time went on. The team's communication became more natural with time, and its morale and productivity improved.

This synergistic solution acknowledged the cultural preferences of both parties to achieve greater collaboration and productivity. Synergistic solutions are different from compromises—rather than give up something they value, both sides' cultural priorities are addressed so that both gain from the solution. The integrated team's results are more creative and holistic than those either group could have achieved alone.

17

Developing Cultural Intelligence

When I began consulting, my goal was to help my clients embrace cultural diversity and enjoy the adventure of intercultural collaboration. It quickly became clear to me that most of them just wanted to be more effective in their work, and some were alienated by "touchy-feely" approaches to cultural training. So while I'm always pleased when my work helps people appreciate other ways of thinking and living, I focus first on helping them accomplish their business goals. Interestingly, once they've learned to create cultural synergies in teamwork and partnerships, even highly goal-oriented clients and students often become interested in understanding cultural variation in greater depth. So whether you're passionate about the topic or are just getting interested, this chapter discusses ways to increase your cultural intelligence. My website offers readings and other resources for continuing your exploration.[1]

For our purposes, developing cultural intelligence is a process of gradually becoming more accepting of, comfortable with, and proficient in other approaches to business. Some attributes to cultivate as you work toward cultural intelligence are:

- Openness to other ways of thinking and doing
- Flexibility and adaptability in new situations

---

[1] www.deirdremendez.com/suggested-reading

- The ability to deal with uncertainty and a lack of control
- Sensitivity to others' moods and reactions
- Respect and empathy for others
- Willingness to modify your attitudes and methods

Some people are born with these characteristics, but most of us have to work at them. Don't be discouraged. Thinking of yourself as a cultural researcher will lessen the feeling that you should know everything from the beginning, and your international colleagues will appreciate your efforts.

Identify the Game

Remember the analogy from Chapter 1, where I compared cultural systems to different types of ball games? They are similar in many ways but have their own equipment and rules, and using our own cultural rules in a new environment is like bringing a baseball bat to a basketball game. Acquiring cultural intelligence is like realizing that baseball is only one of many games you can play with a ball. You might recognize that the bat you're holding isn't the right piece of equipment for your new environment. By putting down the bat, learning to use new equipment, and following the rules of a new game, you'll learn new skills and improve your overall athleticism. An important first step in the process is to recognize signs that you're "playing the wrong game." These signs can take many forms, such as a feeling that someone's behavior doesn't make sense, that there's something you're missing in a conversation, or that people aren't really on board with a plan despite verbal agreement. When you first see these signs, it's important to explain yourself and ask for clarification from your counterparts—without jumping to any conclusions. To avoid a mistaken conclusion based on your own cultural orientation, you must go to the source and deconstruct misunderstandings.

Don't Blame the People

No matter how open-minded you are, dealing with cultural difference on a daily basis can be frustrating and exhausting. Remind yourself that each cultural system is a group response to certain environmental conditions. Consider, for example, that many people conduct business in places with frequent changes in government, where policies favor the current group in power and laws change with political shifts. Where legal systems provide no stability, support, or protection, companies may be unable to prosecute or litigate against an unscrupulous partner, so they will naturally choose business associates they know and trust. If a problem arises, they can rely on social pressure to ensure that partners fulfill their promises. Maintaining these relationships will naturally be more important to people than following externally imposed rules, and working with existing partners will be favored.

Imagine how these factors would affect, say, sales culture. In this sort of environment, factors such as product price and quality may not be the strongest selling points to purchasing managers. A sales representative in such an environment would do well to get an introduction from someone who knew the purchasing manager and drop by for a social visit. By finding ways to create a connection, demonstrate trustworthiness, and deliver value as defined in local terms—playing the game according to local rules—they would have a greater chance of winning.

Once you understand the game, you must decide how much to accommodate a new cultural system. Working within the legal and procedural structures of your corporate headquarters while addressing new cultural priorities can be a difficult balancing act. But even if you have little freedom to change policies, adopting the local interpersonal style can greatly improve your ability to get things done.

All this said, people sometimes have serious difficulty with the cultural values of a particular country or group of people. It may help to remember that cultural values are externally imposed. Culturally based behavior reflects what a counterpart has been taught, and it is possible to forge personal relationships across even vast cultural difference if you can connect with them on a human level. If all else fails, as a professional

17

with a job to do, simply focus on developing effective strategies by using your cultural knowledge, and forgo philosophical discussions.

Maintain Perspective

Even in situations where beliefs and values are not an issue, culture-based frustration is natural. There may be situations where you think, "I'm doing my best to be open-minded, but this is just too much!" At times like these, it can be helpful to step back and reorient. I recommend the following:

- Experience the emotional reaction. Don't think that open-mindedness means not getting frustrated or that being angry or overwhelmed is wrong. Allow yourself to feel what you feel.
- Then get analytical. Remind yourself that intercultural frustration arises when people are playing different games. The behavior you're seeing would make more sense if you better understood the game being played.
- Try to explain yourself and request clarification from others about the cultural context of the behavior you're observing.
- Remind yourself that adapting stylistically to others' preferences is the best way to gain influence, and develop a culturally based strategy for moving things forward. Beginning to play by new rules is often a turning point in acclimating to a new cultural system. Success using the new rules will boost your confidence, people will respond to you more favorably, and your insights and successes will increase as you go.
- Learn as much about the "other" cultural environment as you can. Cultural resources—readings, local friends, colleagues, or experts—can help you understand the historical, social, and political context of the system. Your interest and knowledge will be appreciated.

Focus on Synergy

There are hundreds of books on difficulties caused by intercultural difference. Although this is changing, most writers, as well as most managers, view cultural difference as a negative—as a source of endless problems and conflict with few benefits. But as I've tried to show, integrating cultural difference offers specific, identifiable benefits. Intercultural synergy is the brass ring you're reaching for. Having it as a goal will help you stay on the path toward cultural intelligence, and its rewards will make your hard work worthwhile.

An example of this process is a program I teach in that brings together students from top business schools around the world. Intercultural teams form and manage companies in a demanding online business simulation. The students are highly motivated and the schedule is punishing. They attack their work, often without much thought to the team dynamic. Some teams work well together, but for others problems quickly surface, resulting in conflict and dysfunction. In my meetings with these teams, we deconstruct culturally based misunderstandings and conflicts, referring to their team profiles, and look for synergistic solutions to the problems. As new challenges arise, different members demonstrate their value. The overly cautious person who can't make snap decisions becomes a vital resource when deep analysis is called for. The exuberant risk taker whose wild ideas must constantly be reined in takes center stage when a bold move is needed. As the teams see the value of each approach, they begin to trust and rely on one another. The experience of moving from conflict to synergy is powerful, and the results are clear in the teams' performance.

Taking Intercultural Strategy to the Next Level

17

Understanding a counterpart's cultural tendencies will help you anticipate their behavior in any type of interaction. And understanding the contextual factors that shape your counterpart's tendencies will add to this predictive ability. This is because people from different backgrounds express each cultural tendency in various ways. Take Indirectness, for example. In China, avoiding overt disagreement through subtle hints at negativity helps prevent open confrontation and preserves relationships. In other parts of the world—France, for example—Indirect strategies may take the form of humor or sarcasm that conveys a stinging insult everyone recognizes, and Indirect barbs may be traded back and forth in a social game of one-upmanship. So your experience of Indirectness with Chinese and French counterparts would be quite different, and you would want to modify your strategy accordingly. Knowing how a cultural tendency shows up in a particular group of people will help you plan and execute more effective strategies.

Any information you gather on a counterpart can help deepen your cultural analysis. Learning about a negotiating partner's regional history, political background, and social context will give you insight into their tendencies for the Status, Involvement, Collaboration, and Action dimensions. Research on the current political, social, and economic issues will help you know what to expect regarding the Authority and Organization dimensions. Novels by native authors and locally produced films provide valuable insight into the way representatives will express themselves in terms of the Clarity and Emotion dimensions. Talking with natives will help you predict how participants in a dispute will describe and explain the issues they are dealing with. The more you know about the context and perspective surrounding an intercultural interaction, as well as symbols and terminology used by your counterparts, the easier it will be to develop strategies based on their goals, expectations, and preferences.

18

Cultural Analysis in Training and Consulting

Intercultural Training

The ARC system provides a useful framework for cultural training. Below is a sample design for a workshop that prioritizes the Achievement, Process, and Opportunity tendencies of a North American business audience.

1. Introduce the ARC system, identifying the cultural tendencies associated with each of the eight cultural dimensions.

2. Have participants review scenarios, cases, or examples illustrating culture-based problems in relevant contexts. Help them identify the cultural tendencies of each character and discuss how they led to the conflict.

3. Ask participants to review the self-assessment questions in Chapter 2 and complete Personal Profiles. Discuss their implications.

4. Have participants practice recognizing cultural tendencies in a scenario, case, or film (the scenarios in Chapter 10, for example), creating profiles of each character. Participants might also complete Counterpart Profiles (p. 35) for other participants or groups they work with.

5. Discuss common problems caused by cultural difference in functional areas such as sales and management and the benefits of integrating diversity.

6. Guide participants in proposing synergistic solutions to a scenario they have discussed or one relevant to their particular interests.

7. Apply the ARC system to participants' own culture-based problems.

Intercultural Consulting

Cultural analysis provides an array of consulting tools, and the transparency of the ARC system makes it possible for consultants and clients to collaborate in new ways. Clients learn the system quickly and become active participants in problem solving, allowing consultants to serve primarily as facilitators who guide their clients in recognizing culture-based problems and suggest general solutions. Consultants and clients collaborate to tailor these solutions to specific corporate cultures and structures, with each party contributing what they know best. Advantages of this approach are that:

1. Consultants' offerings are not limited by their knowledge of a particular country, industry, or corporate culture. Using cultural profiles of a client and its international partners pinpoints the cultural differences in their unique relationship, eliminating reliance on country generalizations.

2. Each collaborator transfers only what is necessary to bridge the knowledge gap. Clients apply their knowledge of their industry, corporate culture, and partners, reducing the need to familiarize consultants with these details, and projects move quickly from training to problem solving.

3. Consultants make more appropriate suggestions. They begin by suggesting general culture-based strategies and collaborate with the client in tailoring them to fit the company model.

4. Over time, the client can learn to identify problems and develop solutions on its own, touching base with the consultant only as needed.

Clients may initially worry that being made a "partner" in solving their problems will mean doing more work, but they actually save time normally spent transferring information to the consultant.

I find that taking an "elicitive"[1] approach in training and consulting helps me design structure and content around my clients' goals rather

---

[1] J. P. Lederach, *Preparing for Peace*, (Syracuse University Press, 1995)

than offer a predefined "product." By thinking of my scenarios, examples, slides, and handouts as a basket of resources rather than a single product, I can pick and choose so that the pace, examples, and direction of a presentation are appropriate to the audience. At the same time, I have found that business audiences receive information most readily when it is systematized and packaged, so the approach in this book is already highly "prescriptive," which makes it all the more important to use cultural analysis in a culturally sensitive way.

IV: Background on the ARC System

19

Development of the Framework

The ARC system is the result of my work to make insights from the field of anthropology useful to businesspeople. My early attempts at sharing these insights were a disaster. The implications of rice farming for collectivism in Asia were of no interest to my clients. It was clear that I needed to take them from theory to practice in the shortest time possible, but I wanted to avoid using country stereotypes, lists of dos and don'ts, and other shortcuts that reduce cultural difference to formulas and clichés.

Cultural frameworks seemed a good starting point because they offer quick insight and are easy to grasp. But they're usually used to characterize whole countries—Japan is "high-context" in communication, Nigeria is "sequential" in its approach to time, and so on. These generalizations mask the huge variation among people within a single country, which greatly reduced their usefulness in my work with small groups or individuals. In large numbers, Brazilians are generally more relaxed about deadlines than Germans, but I've worked with hyper-punctual Brazilians and laid-back Germans—the opposite of their countries' profiles.

There were other problems, too. As a consultant, I was often asked to do traditional "Doing Business in Country X" presentations. But these presentations often amounted to a string of unrelated "one-offs." Many people work in multiple cultural environments during their careers, and I wanted to describe each location as part of a universal system. And rather than focusing exclusively on the cultural tendencies of "other" countries, I wanted to start by identifying my clients' own cultural grounding.

Many clients complained that intercultural seminars didn't offer strategies for solving culture-based problems. And as I worked with intercultural teams, I was struck by the benefits of cultural "synergy"—the extraordinary performance that results from integrating cultural tendencies. I wanted to highlight the benefits of synergy and suggest strategies for achieving it.

I created the ARC system to help users decipher culture-based problems for themselves. I developed questions to help people identify their own cultural orientations and identified "tendency indicators" for the orientations of other people and places. To help people react appropriately once they knew which cultural tendencies they were dealing with, I outlined strategies for specific purposes such as negotiations, teamwork, and management. I have spent the past ten years testing and refining these strategies in my work with international executives and business students and discussions with fellow trainers and educators. I find that after mastering the cultural framework, people tend to become more interested in contextual depth. They realize that fine-tuned strategies require an understanding of the historical, political, and social factors that shape others' perceptions, expectations, and behavior.

Relationship to Other Models

The eight cultural dimensions used in this book derive from frameworks developed by researchers in the fields of anthropology and business, modified somewhat and renamed for easier application. The system draws on work by Edward T. Hall,[1] Geert Hofstede,[2] and Trompenaars and Hampden-Turner,[3]

---

[1] E. Hall, *The Silent Language*, (Anchor Books, 1959).

[2] G. Hofstede, *Culture's Consequences: International Differences in Work-Related Values*, Beverly Hills, CA (Sage Publications, 1980).

[3] F. Trompenaars and C. Hampden-Turner, *Riding the Waves of Culture: Understanding Diversity in Global Business*, (McGraw Hill, 1998).

as well as Craig Storti[4] and Richard Lewis.[5] It corresponds most closely to the Trompenaars and Hampden-Turner framework. In case you'd like to consider this system with reference to other frameworks, here's how the cultural tendencies used here correspond to others.

1. Indirect/Direct—derived from Hall's High/Low-Context dimension, simplified and focused primarily on dealing with conflict. Similar to Storti's use of the terms.

2. Neutral/Expressive—comparable to Neutral/Affective in the Trompenaars and Hampden-Turner framework. Overlaps somewhat with Hofstede's Indulgence/Restraint.

3. Achievement/Endowment—comparable to Achievement/Ascription in the Trompenaars and Hampden-Turner framework. Contains elements of Power Distance in Hofstede's paradigm.

4. Rule/Situation—equivalent to Universalism/Particularism in the Trompenaars and Hampden-Turner framework.

5. Network/Process—comparable to Diffuse/Specific in Trompenaars and Hampden-Turner's paradigm, but the system here focuses primarily on partnerships and interpersonal interaction. Overlaps in some respects with Hofstede's Masculine/Feminine features.

6. Independent/Group—equivalent to Individualism/Communitarianism in the Trompenaars and Hampden-Turner framework and Individualism/Collectivism in Hofstede's paradigm.

7. Opportunity/Thoroughness—equivalent to the aspects of Long-Term/Short-Term in Trompenaars and Hampden-Turner's framework as well as Hofstede's, and also high/low Uncertainty Avoidance in Trompenaars and Hampden-Turner, but confined here to corporate strategy and planning (separated from personal time management).

19

---

[4] C. Storti, *Figuring Foreigners Out: A Practical Guide* (Intercultural Press, 1999).
[5] R. Lewis, *When Cultures Collide: Leading Across Cultures* (Nicholas Brealey Publishing, 2006).

8. Schedule/Flow—derived from Hall's Monochronic/Polychronic, similar to Trompenaars and Hampden-Turner's Sequential/Synchronic. Also contains elements of Trompenaars and Hampden-Turner's and Hofstede's Long-Term/Short-Term features relative to organization and time management.

Acknowledgments

Although I am indebted to many, many people for insights into intercultural management, I would like to thank a few in particular. I am grateful to Larry Wolfe, Ray Brimble, and David Platt for their seminal suggestions and consistent encouragement of my work over the years. For their early comments and suggestions, Susan Napier and Steve Coit, Sabine and Charly Wimmer, and Betsy Neidel have my sincere appreciation. Many thanks to Craig Storti for his kind introduction to NB International. I am grateful to my daughter, Claire Bohne, for sharing her marketing expertise and to Sharon Schweitzer for her generous advice. I am indebted to Nicholas Brealey for his guidance and to Nicholas Brealey editor Alison Hankey and production manager Michelle Morgan for their dedication to every aspect of this project. Finally, my deepest gratitude to my husband Michael Kuhn for his creativity, insightful perspectives, and energetic support for all that I do.

Index